Praise for *The Emergence of Islam*

"Gabriel Said Reynolds is one of the most important scholars of Islamic and Quranic studies in our day. In this lucid and accessible resource, he combines his outstanding command of Islamic primary sources with his vast knowledge of Muslim cultures to bring forth a thoughtful, respectful, and critical study of Islam's emergence. For years, I have adopted this book in my Islamic Studies courses, and this new edition is greatly welcomed."
    —Ayman S. Ibrahim, Ph.D., professor of Islamic studies and director of the Jenkins Center
        for the Christian Understanding of Islam, The Southern Baptist Theological Seminary

"This book is a cutting-edge introduction to the foundations and legacy of a major world religion—Islam. It finally offers the public the sophisticated, critical examination of Islam's beginnings long deserved, but only now received. Reynolds masterfully weaves together evidence from late antiquity, biblical studies, and Islamic tradition, with insights from seminal works of modern scholarship, including those of J. Wansbrough and W. M. Watt. The wealth of information is expressed in simple language and complemented with a wealth of images and apparatuses, making this book a must have for all readers interested in *The Emergence of Islam*."
    —Emran El-Badawi, chair of the Department of Modern and Classical Languages, program
        director and associate professor of Middle Eastern studies, University of Houston

"Once again, Gabriel Said Reynolds demonstrates his immense talent as a historian and pedagogue. *The Emergence of Islam* stands out as a fundamental and valuable teaching tool on the origins of Islam that will surely benefit all students and scholars. A real tour de force!"
        —Mehdi Azaiez, professor of Islamology, UCLouvain (Belgium)

"The publication of *The Emergence of Islam* was a landmark event in the study of Islam, and this new edition only reinforces its incomparable status. With a light, compassionate touch, Reynolds presents the contested history of this religion to first-time readers and seasoned scholars alike without cutting corners or avoiding controversial topics. The author's broad sweep ranges from the history of pre-Islamic Arabia to the rise, fall, and now return of the Taliban in Afghanistan. This text is destined to be the best introduction to Islam anywhere in the world. It is genuinely a *tour de force* of historic significance."
        —Anouar Majid, director of the Center for Global Humanities,
            University of New England

"As always, Reynolds makes the landscape of the historical, theological, and intellectual inquiry around Muhammad, the Qur'an, and the emergence of Islam accessible to all. Both a novice learner and a seasoned academic will find new insights in this second edition through new scholarship on pre-Islamic inscriptions that have radically shifted our understanding of the religious practices in Arabia just prior to Muhammad's life.

"Comprehensive and succinct in covering an impressive amount of time and material, Reynolds' approach to critically incorporating traditional Islamic sources honors current scholarship and historical evidence while capturing the integral theological understandings of the nascent Muslim community.

"The layout of this book—including timelines, images, graphs, study questions, profiles of key personalities, descriptions of major concepts, and translations of classical texts—makes this volume an excellent reference tool as well. All around, a welcome addition to my library."
—Ryann Elizabeth Craig, director of student programs and assistant research professor, Georgetown University, Berkley Center for Religion, Peace, and World Affairs.

"Reynolds has distilled vast learning into a carefully and clearly written guide through difficult and complex subjects. This is an outstanding and excellent resource for teacher and student alike."
—Jack Tannous, associate professor of history and Hellenic studies, Princeton University

THE EMERGENCE OF
ISLAM

THE EMERGENCE OF ISLAM

CLASSICAL TRADITIONS IN CONTEMPORARY PERSPECTIVE

SECOND EDITION

GABRIEL SAID REYNOLDS

Fortress Press

Minneapolis

THE EMERGENCE OF ISLAM, 2nd Edition
Classical Traditions in Contemporary Perspective

Cover image: Illuminated folio from the Qur'an, sixteenth century, Iran
Cover design: Kristin Miller (original cover design: Joe Vaughan)
Book design: James Korsmo

Print ISBN: 978-1-5064-7388-8
eBook ISBN: 978-1-5064-7389-5

CONTENTS

Figures

vii

Personalities in Islam

From a Classic Text

Boxes

ILLUSTRATION ACKNOWLEDGMENTS

1.01	Credit: Robert Hoyland.
1.1	Courtesy of Wikimedia Commons.
1.3	Courtesy of The Islamic Bulletin.
1.4	Courtesy of Wikimedia Commons.
2.1	Courtesy of Wikimedia Commons.
2.2	Courtesy of Wikimedia Commons.
3.2	Courtesy of Islamic Wallpapers.
4.1	Cadbury Research Library: Special Collections, University of Birmingham.
4.2a and b	Cadbury Research Library: Special Collections, University of Birmingham.
4.3	© Sam Mugraby (Photos8.com).
4.4	© Vetta Collection / istockphoto.
4.5	Courtesy of Go-Makka.com.
5.1	© The Metropolitan Museum of Art (Art Resource, NY).
6.1	Courtesy of Wikimedia Commons.
7.2	Courtesy of Prof. Erica Hunter, School of Oriental and African Studies, London.
7.3	Courtesy of Saudi-Italian-French archaeological project in Dûmat al-Jandal, G. Charloux (DJ2016a0150)
7.4	Courtesy of Wikimedia Commons.
8.1	Courtesy of Wikimedia Commons.
8.2	Courtesy of Wikimedia Commons.
8.3	Courtesy of Wikimedia Commons.
8.4	Courtesy of Wikimedia Commons.
8.5	Courtesy of Wikimedia Commons.
8.6	Courtesy of quranandscience.com.
8.7	Pew Research Center, July 26, 2017, "U.S. Muslims Concerned About Their Place in Society, but Continue to Believe in the American Dream."

The story of the emergence of Islam, as it is usually told, is rather straightforward. Muhammad was born in Mecca, a pagan city in western Arabia, in 570 CE. At the age of forty, he began to proclaim revelations from the one true God, the God of Abraham, Moses, and Jesus. Because most of the Meccan pagans refused his message, Muhammad traveled to Medina, a city to the north of Mecca, in 622. There he won the fidelity of the Arabs, overcame Jewish tribes who resisted him, and eventually attacked and overcame the forces of the pagan Meccans. When Muhammad died in 632, he had established a small state based on Islam, the religion given to him by God. His successors, the caliphs, launched a great campaign of conquests and carried Islam throughout the Middle East and across North Africa.

The question of how much of this story is historically accurate, however, is less straightforward. Our sources for the study of Islam's emergence are unlike those for the study of Judaism or Christianity, and they present scholars with particular difficulties. The Qur'an is an ancient text, and it certainly contains authentic material from the time of Islamic origins, but it offers almost no explicit biographical information on Muhammad or his companions. Other Islamic sources, such as qur'anic commentaries or biographies of the Prophet, often seem to be based on the Qur'an (And are not records of an independent process of oral transmission). Non-Islamic sources from the time of Islam's emergence are curiously silent. They simply make no mention of a prophet in Mecca.

In light of these complications, scholars today have an important choice to make when they set out to describe Islam's origins. They might choose simply to follow the traditional Islamic biographies of Muhammad, selecting those portions of the biography they consider most reliable and adding their own commentary. This is the approach, for example, of Karen Armstrong in her work *Muhammad: A Prophet of Our Time* (2006). Armstrong emphasizes those elements of the traditional biography that might make the Muslim prophet appealing to a modern Western audience. It is also the approach of Robert Spencer in his work *The Truth About Muhammad* (2006). Spencer, however, emphasizes those elements of the traditional biography that might make him unappealing to a modern Western audience. Scholars might also cast aside the traditional Islamic biographies and present new scenarios for the rise of Islam. This is the approach of *The Hidden Origins of Islam* (2010), a collection of articles in which a number of authors argue that the qur'anic word *muhammad* (which in Arabic means "the praised one") is not the name of a new prophet but an adjective referring to Jesus. The Muhammad of Islamic tradition, in their estimation, never existed.

Francis Peters takes a different approach. In *Muhammad and the Origins of Islam* (1994), Peters first acknowledges how little can be reliably known about Islam's origins: "However long the search has gone on, the 'quest of the historical Muhammad' is still surrounded by enormous difficulties from both the growth and encrustations of centuries of pious regard and the difficulty of the source material" (xii). Yet Peters decides to postpone any discussion of these difficulties. In the body of the book, he proceeds "as if" the traditional story were historically reliable: "This is an issue that must be addressed, but it is highly technical, and rather than put such daunting stuff between the reader and the subject of this book, I have placed [it] in an appendix" (xii). Thus in the body of his book, Peters provides the reader with a thoroughly classical account of Islam's origins, an account that he judges to be fundamentally unreliable.

Approach of This Book

The approach of the present work is different. In part 1, I present the traditional story of Islam's rise, from the birth of Muhammad to the death of his cousin and son-in-law, ʿAli (according to the traditional dates, 570–661 CE); this introduction is divided according to the life of Muhammad in Mecca (570–610 CE; chapter 1), the life of Muhammad in Medina (622–32 CE; chapter 2), and the career of the first four caliphs (632–61 CE, chapter 3). In the course of this presentation, however, I discuss how and why pious Muslim scholars wrote the story of Islam in this manner. Whenever possible, I indicate which elements of the traditional account of Islam's origins are plausible and those that are less so. At the same time, this section of the book is meant to offer readers an appreciation of the Islamic understanding of Muhammad and his pious successors.

In part 2, I provide a critical scholarly perspective on the rise of Islam through a presentation of the Qur'an, our most ancient source for Islam's emergence. I first offer the reader a general presentation of the Qur'an's religious message, and the strategies the Qur'an uses to convince the reader of that message (chapter 4). Then I illustrate the Qur'an's close relationship with biblical literature and biblical traditions (chapter 5). This illustration—which suggests that the Qur'an was preached in a context where Jewish and (especially) Christian traditions were well known—leads to a reconsideration of the traditional biography of Muhammad (chapter 6). Finally, I ask what the Qur'an itself might teach us of the story of Islam's origins (chapter 7). By this point we will have done things in a manner perfectly contrary to the manner in which they are usually done. Whereas most scholars see the Qur'an through the lens of the traditional histories of Islam's emergence, we will see the history of Islam's emergence through the lens of the Qur'an.

The present work also offers the reader insight into contemporary Islamic visions of the Qur'an and Muhammad's life. In part 3 (chapter 8), I illustrate how Islam's interaction with the West has led Muslims to develop new ideas about the Qur'an and the prophet Muhammad today.

Features in This Book

Before turning to the main body of the work, the reader might benefit from some practical remarks about it. For the most part, I have avoided technical Arabic terms. When I do employ such terms, I generally define them at their first occurrence. In addition, readers will find a glossary at the end of this work with technical Arabic terms, English terms used in a specialized manner, and a brief identification of the main historical and religious personalities of early Islam.

In many recent English publications, the God of Islam is named Allah, as though Allah were the personal name of the God of Islam alone (an idea that inspired a 2007 law in Malaysia prohibiting non-Muslims from calling God Allah). In fact, Allah is simply the word "God" in Arabic (for which reason it is used also by Arabic-speaking Christians). Accordingly, in this work, I simply use the English word *God* when referring to the God of Islam.

Biblical citations are from the New Jerusalem Bible. Qur'anic translations are generally those of Arthur Arberry, although I have altered his translation by substituting "Qur'an" for "Koran" (as this latter spelling is rarely used today), and when he uses an especially antiquated word (such as "haply"), I offer a modern equivalent in brackets "[perhaps]." In some cases, however, I present my own translation in order to clarify a point in the underlying Arabic. (Such cases are identified with a parenthetical note.) Instead of using footnotes or endnotes, I present the sources of quotations in abbreviated form in parentheses. The full form of these (and other) sources, and a brief description of them, can be found in the section "Bibliography and Further Reading" at the end of the book.

The present work includes a number of other supplementary features that offer unique insights on Islam's emergence. The opening of the work includes a reference map of the Middle East, a timeline that offers an overview of the traditional chronology of Islam's development, and a chart that presents Muhammad's family background, and his descendants, according to the traditional Islamic account of his life.

More resources are found in the body of the work itself. Interspersed in the text are photographs of pre-Islamic rock inscriptions, Islamic manuscripts and monuments, reproductions of classical objects of Islamic art, and charts/maps meant to illustrate Islamic ideas and traditions. Readers will also discover three types of text boxes: first, the *Emergence of Islam* includes a diverse selection of original Islamic sources, some of which are presented here in English for the first time; second, this work includes instructional text boxes, which offer a quick and simple introduction to basic topics, including the Muslim pilgrimage to Mecca, the Islamic notion of *jinn* (or "genies"), and the Islamic idea of jihad; third, our book contains brief biographies of key Muslim figures in text boxes identified as "Personalities in Islam." Furthermore, at the end of each chapter, study questions are included for individual reflection or group discussion.

At the end of this work (in addition to the section "Bibliography and Further Reading"), readers will find an index of people, places, and subjects, along with a glossary of proper names and technical terms. Entries in this glossary are marked in the body of the text in bold (when they appear for the first time), so that readers can find help on the meaning of a word by flipping to the end of the book.

Preface to the Second Edition/ What's New

Since the publication of the first edition of this book, research has progressed rapidly in a number of areas related to Islam's origins. Most remarkable, perhaps, are the continued discoveries of Arabic inscriptions from the period immediately before the rise of Islam. These inscriptions—which are discussed in the new Introduction to part 1—show that monotheism was widespread among the Arabs at the dawn of Islam, even in the region close to Mecca and Medina. This new edition includes not only a discussion of the importance of these discoveries, but two images [see Figure 1.01 in the introduction and Figure 7.3 in chapter 7] of key, monotheistic, pre-Islamic inscriptions.

Readers will also find in this edition a completely revised chapter 8, on contemporary Islam. This new chapter involves a discussion of the continued growth of Islam in the West and of certain trends, including progressive Islam, among Western Muslims. It includes, moreover, a new analysis of the momentous return to power of the Taliban in 2021. This analysis includes a deep dive into the historical origins of the ideology of the Taliban in Deoband, India, and continues with a discussion of the reasons for their recent triumph in Afghanistan. The new edition also includes revisions throughout, a number of new images and visual features (including a chart of the Taliban's leadership), an updated annotated bibliography, and a revised guide to online resources for the study of Islam in light of recent trends in social media and on the Internet.

Note on Transliteration, Translation, and Abbreviations

The present work uses a simplified transliteration system to refer for the twenty-eight letters of the Arabic alphabet. To indicate a particular Arabic letter, Western scholars generally use the closest equivalent Latin letter (or, in some cases, pairs of letters such as *sh* or *th*) according to English pronunciation. When the same English letter is the closest equivalent to more than one Arabic consonant, scholars often add a dot to the English letter to indicate the emphatic Arabic consonant. Similarly, scholars generally add a macron above *a*, *i*, and *u* to differentiate long Arabic vowels from short Arabic vowels. In the present work, which is not meant to be technical, I include neither dots nor macrons. However, I do include the sign ʿ to indicate the Arabic consonant ʿ*ayn* (which represents a sound close to the bleating of sheep), as in the name ʿAli, and the sign ʾ to indicate the Arabic consonant *hamza* (which represents a sound that takes the place of "tt" in the cockney pronunciation of "bottle" ["boʾel"]), as in the word *Qurʾan*. The combination *ay* represents the diphthong found in the English word *may*, and the combination *aw* represents the diphthong in the English word *doubt*.

Arabic words that have an Anglicized form (such as caliph) or that are now commonly used in English (such as jihad or sharia) are presented as English words and not as transliterations of Arabic words. The reader might find it helpful to know that the Arabic word ʿ*abd*—commonly found in names such as ʿ*Abdallah*—means "servant" (thus ʿ*Abdallah* means "servant of God"). The Arabic word *abu* (or *abi*) means "father" (thus Abu Talib means "the father of Talib"), and the Arabic word *ibn* means "son." Finally, the reader might take note of the following abbreviations:

AH	*anno hegirae* ("in the year of the *hijra*"), a reference to the years of the Islamic calendar
Ar.	Arabic
b.	Ar. *ibn* ("son")
Q	Qurʾan

Acknowledgments

I conducted most of the research for this book, and wrote most of its narrative, during a year of sabbatical leave from the University of Notre Dame, during which time I was in residence in Jerusalem, Beirut, and Brussels. I am accordingly obliged to Notre Dame for the opportunity to take this leave. I am particularly grateful to John Cavadini, former chair of the Department of Theology, and his successor Matt Ashley, both of whom have supported me in my scholarly work and in my vocation as a teacher. At Notre Dame I have benefited time and again from the remarkable work of Cheron Price and Lauren Fox, administrative assistants in the Department of Theology. I have also been greatly aided by DeVan Ard, Nathaniel Johnson, and Joseph Khalil, all of whom have worked as teaching assistants with me. My research leave was made possible by a generous grant from the Louisville Institute, for which I am profoundly grateful. I hope that the present work has at least in part justified the confidence placed in me.

This work is the product of the intellectual mentoring that I have received from colleagues, friends, and scholars. I am particularly indebted to Samir Khalil Samir, who has taught me the importance of clear thought and scholarly precision, although I am hardly his equal in either regard. I have also benefited from many conversations with my friend Mehdi Azaiez, a scholar of great perspicuity and a person of immense kindness. Similarly I am grateful for my friendship with Emran

El-Badawi, likewise a scholar of remarkable insight.

I have learned much (and I am still learning) through the classes that I have taught in the Department of Theology at Notre Dame. My presence as an Islamicist, and scholar of the Qurʾān, in a faculty of Catholic theology has allowed me to see Islam—in the Qurʾan in particular—in a wider perspective. Whereas most Departments of Religion or Near Eastern Studies teach Islam only in the light of Islamic tradition, at Notre Dame I have been challenged to think of the relationship of Islam's origins in the light of Jewish and Christian tradition, and to think of the Qurʾan in the light of biblical literature. At the same time, Notre Dame has often demonstrated, in and out of the classroom, how a Catholic university—a university rightly dedicated to its own tradition—can approach another tradition with a certain appreciation and sympathy that exceeds the approach generally found at secular universities. I discovered something similar at the Institut islamo-chrétien at Université de Saint Joseph in Beirut, where I taught as a visiting professor during the academic year 2011–12.

As this work has moved toward its final stages, I have increasingly relied on the excellent team at Fortress Press, including Ross Miller (Senior Acquisitions Editor) and Marissa Wold (Project Manager). The present work is atypical of introductions to Islam, and yet they have nevertheless been supportive and helpful throughout.

Yet I have received no greater support than that given to me each day by my lovely wife Lourdes. I am grateful with all my heart for the love she has shown me, and for the priceless gift of our children, Luke, Emmanuel, Theresa, René, and Kerline. I would also like to thank our friends, the Kahyas, the Mattas, the Aboukhaleds, the Elias, the Schafers, and the Metcalfes. I am grateful also to my parents and stepparents—Gary, Carole, Lazarus, and Nancy—and to the parents of Lourdes—Elias and Renée. To all of them, and to the Missionaries of Charity in Sad el-Baouchriye (Beirut), who tenderly care for children bereft of parents, I dedicate the present work.

I would like to express my gratitude to Hassan Ahmad, who carefully read through the revised text and offered insights on recent trends in scholarship on Islam. I am also grateful to Timothy Matovina, who served as the chair of Theology at Notre Dame as I was working on the current edition of this book, and to all of my colleagues in the department. I have continued to serve in different capacities with the International Qurʾanic Studies Association and would like to express my gratitude to colleagues there, especially the executive director Hythem Sidky, who have helped sharpen my thinking on Qurʾanic Studies. Many thanks are due as well to Emily King, Bethany Dickerson, and Lisa Eaton for their expertise in the editing and typesetting process.

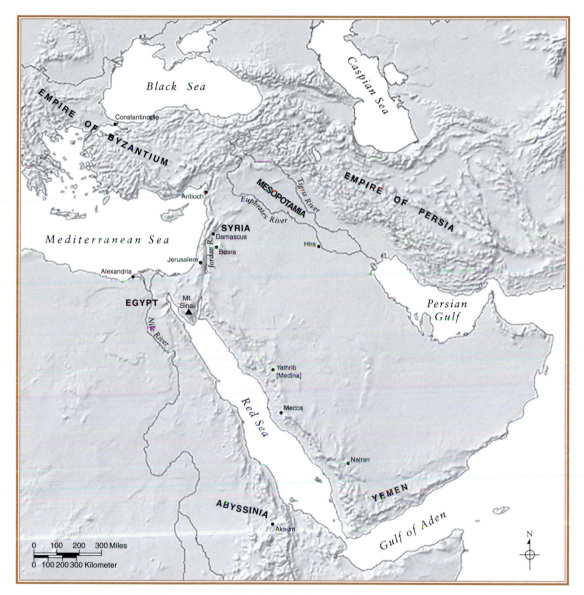

FIGURE 1.00 *A map of the Middle East in the early seventh century.*

The following timeline presents a simplified version of the traditional Islamic chronology of Islam's emergence, although it follows the standard Gregorian calendar, and not the *hijri* calendar used by the medieval Muslim scholars who wrote the early history of Islam. Muslim scholars generally consider Muhammad to be forty years old (by which they mean forty lunar years, or just under thirty-nine standard solar years) at the moment of his call to prophethood. (They may have chosen the number forty for its symbolic value.) The Western scholars who developed this simplified chronology (now widely used) generally followed the biography of Muhammad in Islamic sources, by which his prophetic career lasted twenty-two or twenty-three years. They also placed Muhammad's death date in 632 CE, following Islamic chronicles backward from dates (such as the ascension to the throne of the Umayyad caliph ʿAbd al-Malik in 685 CE) that can be confirmed through non-Islamic sources. Therefore they put Muhammad's call to prophethood at 610 CE and his birth at 570 CE (although, according to solar years that date should be 571 CE). These dates are highly uncertain. (Francis Peters concludes,

"We throw up our hands at the chronology" [*Jesus and Muhammad*, 61].) Islamic sources connect Muhammad's birth to an attack on Mecca by the South Arabian king Abraha (and his elephant), but South Arabian chronicles mention only a campaign that Abraha conducted in central Arabia (they never mention Mecca itself) that took place in 552 CE.

Thus the dates in the following timeline that pertain to the life of Muhammad cannot be considered authoritative. Even the dates for the period of the four "rightly guided" caliphs (that is, from the death of Muhammad to the death of ʿAli) are largely uncertain. For example, in this timeline, the Battle of Yarmuk, the most important battle against the Byzantines in the early Islamic conquests, is put at 636 CE. However, quite a few sources (including the great Muslim historian Ṭabari) put this battle during the reign of the first caliph, Abu Bakr, who according to the simplified chronology below is said to have died in 634 CE. Moreover, the timeline below ignores the question of the historicity of the events listed, a question to which the present work is in part dedicated. Accordingly, the following timeline is best seen as a framework for the traditional account of Islam's origins and not a record of well-known historical events.

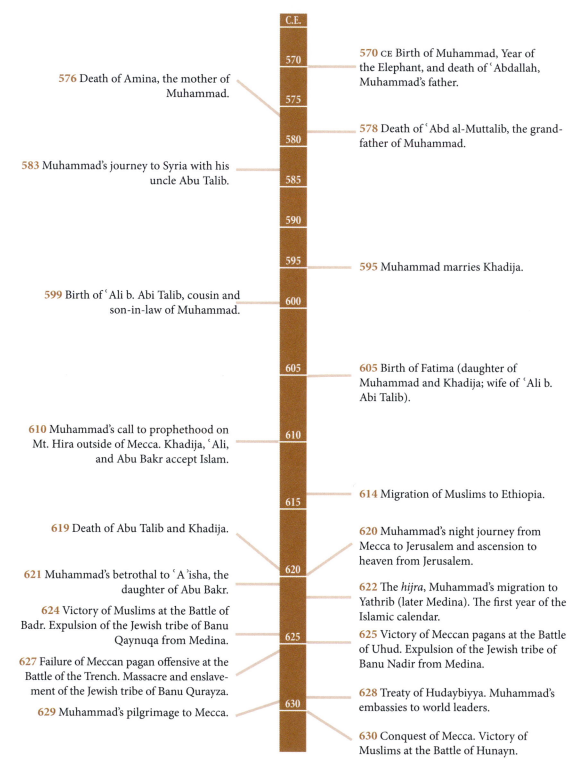

C.E.

570 CE Birth of Muhammad, Year of the Elephant, and death of ʿAbdallah, Muhammad's father.

576 Death of Amina, the mother of Muhammad.

570

575

578 Death of ʿAbd al-Muttalib, the grand-father of Muhammad.

580

583 Muhammad's journey to Syria with his uncle Abu Talib.

585

590

595 Muhammad marries Khadija.

595

599 Birth of ʿAli b. Abi Talib, cousin and son-in-law of Muhammad.

600

605 Birth of Fatima (daughter of Muhammad and Khadija; wife of ʿAli b. Abi Talib).

605

610 Muhammad's call to prophethood on Mt. Hira outside of Mecca. Khadija, ʿAli, and Abu Bakr accept Islam.

610

614 Migration of Muslims to Ethiopia.

615

619 Death of Abu Talib and Khadija.

620 Muhammad's night journey from Mecca to Jerusalem and ascension to heaven from Jerusalem.

620

621 Muhammad's betrothal to ʿAʾisha, the daughter of Abu Bakr.

622 The hijra, Muhammad's migration to Yathrib (later Medina). The first year of the Islamic calendar.

624 Victory of Muslims at the Battle of Badr. Expulsion of the Jewish tribe of Banu Qaynuqa from Medina.

625

625 Victory of Meccan pagans at the Battle of Uhud. Expulsion of the Jewish tribe of Banu Nadir from Medina.

627 Failure of Meccan pagan offensive at the Battle of the Trench. Massacre and enslavement of the Jewish tribe of Banu Qurayza.

628 Treaty of Hudaybiyya. Muhammad's embassies to world leaders.

630

629 Muhammad's pilgrimage to Mecca.

630 Conquest of Mecca. Victory of Muslims at the Battle of Hunayn.

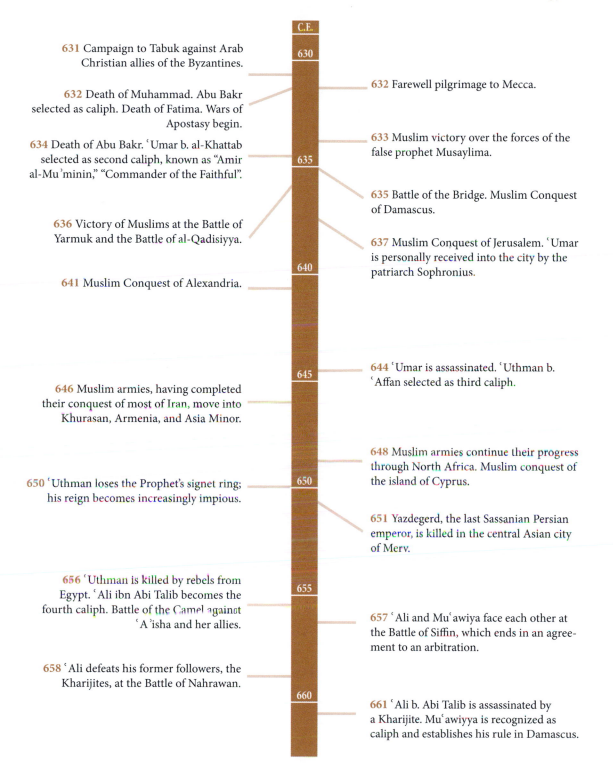

C.E.

630

631 Campaign to Tabuk against Arab Christian allies of the Byzantines.

632 Farewell pilgrimage to Mecca.

632 Death of Muhammad. Abu Bakr selected as caliph. Death of Fatima. Wars of Apostasy begin.

633 Muslim victory over the forces of the false prophet Musaylima.

634 Death of Abu Bakr. ʿUmar b. al-Khattab selected as second caliph, known as "Amir al-Muʾminin," "Commander of the Faithful".

635

635 Battle of the Bridge. Muslim Conquest of Damascus.

636 Victory of Muslims at the Battle of Yarmuk and the Battle of al-Qadisiyya.

637 Muslim Conquest of Jerusalem. ʿUmar is personally received into the city by the patriarch Sophronius.

640

641 Muslim Conquest of Alexandria.

645

644 ʿUmar is assassinated. ʿUthman b. ʿAffan selected as third caliph.

646 Muslim armies, having completed their conquest of most of Iran, move into Khurasan, Armenia, and Asia Minor.

648 Muslim armies continue their progress through North Africa. Muslim conquest of the island of Cyprus.

650

650 ʿUthman loses the Prophet's signet ring; his reign becomes increasingly impious.

651 Yazdegerd, the last Sassanian Persian emperor, is killed in the central Asian city of Merv.

655

656 ʿUthman is killed by rebels from Egypt. ʿAli ibn Abi Talib becomes the fourth caliph. Battle of the Camel against ʿAʾisha and her allies.

657 ʿAli and Muʿawiya face each other at the Battle of Siffin, which ends in an agreement to an arbitration.

658 ʿAli defeats his former followers, the Kharijites, at the Battle of Nahrawan.

660

661 ʿAli b. Abi Talib is assassinated by a Kharijite. Muʿawiyya is recognized as caliph and establishes his rule in Damascus.

The genealogical chart presented here portrays at once the Islamic understanding of Muḥammad as a descendant of Abraham through Ishmael and his relationship—by birth or by marriage—to those figures who play a key role in the traditional account of Islam's emergence. It is a simplified genealogical chart inasmuch as other figures, such as his other wives and children, are not included therein.

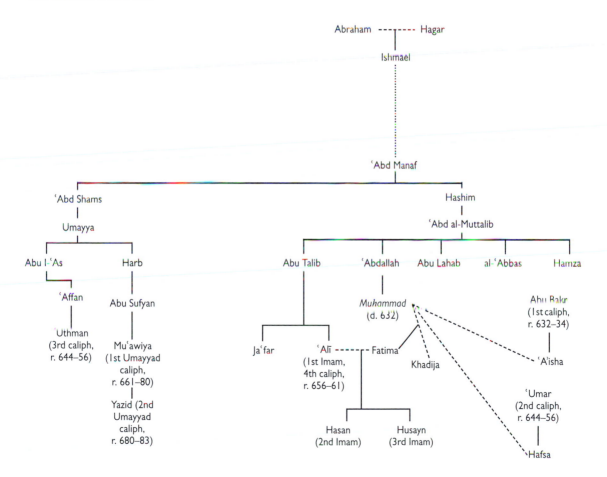

PART I   THE PROPHET MUHAMMAD AND THE RIGHTLY GUIDED CALIPHS

INTRODUCTION TO PART I: HISTORICAL OVERVIEW

Islam today is a global religion with adherents from diverse nations, races, and cultures. The story of its origins, however, takes place among a specific group of people: the Arabs of the late antique Near East. The Arabs at the time lived in an area that stretched from modern-day Yemen in the south to the Taurus Mountains of modern-day Turkey in the north, and from the Mediterranean Sea in the west to the Tigris River in the east. They were in part nomadic, in part settled, and they lived among a number of other peoples in the region. Most of these other peoples spoke a dialect of Aramaic (the language of Christ) known as Syriac, although in large urban centers many spoke Greek. While a significant presence of Jews could be found in Yemen and in cities such as Alexandria and Damascus, the great majority of people in the Near East at the time of Islam's emergence were Christians. Many of the Arabs themselves had become Christians, and some spoke dialects of Aramaic in addition to Arabic.

The notion of Arabs as a unified ethnic group developed only gradually. The Bible generally refers to "Arabs" in the same way it refers to "Ishmaelites." Both terms seem to be labels for nomads: Isaiah (13:20) speaks of Babylon becoming so desolate that not even an "Arab" would pitch his tent there; the author of Genesis has "Ishmaelites" on camels pass by Shechem and purchase Joseph from his brothers (Gen 37:25). The conflation of "Arabs" and "Ishmaelites" in the Bible is not coincidental. We read in Genesis 21 that Ishmael goes out to the wilderness with his mother Hagar. Ishmael, who is prophesied to be the father of "a great nation" (Gen 21:18), settles in the wilderness of Paran (Gen 21:21) and marries an Egyptian.

Jewish and Christian works written after the Bible, but before Islam, often refer to certain groups of Arabic speakers by the name of their tribe. Very often, however, they refer to them as "Hagarenes" or "Ishmaelites." Greek-speaking Byzantine Christian authors tended to use the term "Saracens" (the term that would later become the standard label for Arabs in the Latin West) for Arabic speakers, a term derived from the Greek form of the name of one northern Arabian tribe. Some Christian authors (perhaps beginning with St. Jerome, d. 420) argued that the Arabic speakers themselves used this term in the hope of associating themselves with Sarah (imagined to be connected to the word "Saracen") and thereby to hide their descent from Hagar. Others connected "Saracen" to the Greek word *scenitae*, meaning "tent-dwellers." Both ideas reflect the idea of Arabs as nomads, children of the wilderness.

The Evidence of Pre-Islamic Inscriptions

In recent years our understanding of languages in pre-Islamic Arabia has progressed considerably. The inhabitants of the Arabian Peninsula at this time spoke a variety of languages, most of which are part of the Semitic language family, and they wrote these languages in a variety of scripts. In the southern part of the Arabian Peninsula (around what is now Yemen), Ancient South Arabian (ASA) languages—which form a branch of the Semitic language family distinct from Arabic—were prevalent. In the northern part of the Arabian Peninsula, a variety of Ancient North Arabian (ANA) languages coexisted with Aramaic (and some Greek). These ANA languages (unlike ASA languages) are now largely considered to be part of the Arabic language family, in different dialects or stages of development. Nevertheless both ASA and ANA languages, and their inscriptions, provide valuable information about the religious and historical context in Arabia at the dawn of Islam.

Perhaps the most interesting aspect of these inscriptions is their witness to a dramatic shift from polytheism to monotheism around the fourth and fifth centuries CE. As Ahmad al-Jallad has observed regarding South Arabian inscriptions, "By the fourth century CE, references to the pagan gods disappear almost entirely from the inscriptions, ushering in what scholars have termed the 'monotheistic period'" ("Linguistic Landscape," 122). In South Arabia one notices the rise in worship of God under the name *rhmnn*, meaning "the Merciful" and being closely related to the Qur'anic Arabic term for God *al-rahman*. Beginning in the year 384 CE, monotheistic inscriptions in South Arabia begin to replace polytheistic inscriptions. Some of these inscriptions are so general that it is not clear whether they are written by a Jew, a Christian, or another sort of monotheist. However, in the period up to 525 CE, many inscriptions are distinctly Jewish, as indicated by personal names or references to synagogues or to Jews (*yhd*). In 525, however, the armies of the Christian Kingdom of Axum in Ethiopia invaded South Arabia and spread Christianity there. Intriguingly both the earlier Jewish inscriptions and the Christian inscriptions of the "Ethiopian" period refer to God as "the Merciful" (*rhmnn*). One intriguing South Arabian inscription seems to have an invocation like that at the beginning of almost every chapter of the Qur'an: "In the Name of Allah, Rahman, Rahman lord of the heavens" (Al-Jallad, "Linguistic Landscape," 123).

A similar trend toward monotheism is evident in the inscriptions of North Arabia. These inscriptions are written in dialects that now, thanks to the work of Ahmad al-Jallad, are generally recognized as representing a spectrum of the Arabic language (although there are certainly outliers that might represent independent languages). The move to monotheism appears a bit later than it does in South Arabia, but it occurs definitively before Islam. "By the sixth century," writes al-Jallad, "the pagan gods had completely disappeared from the inscriptions of North Arabia" (Al-Jallad, "Pre-Islamic *Basmala*," 14). Instead these inscriptions refer to one God, usually as *al-ilah*, a form close to the qur'anic name for God: *allah*.

Notably, the few pre-Islamic inscriptions that appear in the Arabic script—which develops out of a form of the Aramaic script (known as Nabataean) and will eventually be used to write the Qur'an—are all monotheistic. There are very few of these inscriptions. Among them are three inscriptions from Syria: an inscription dating 512 CE found in Zebed, an inscription dating 529 CE found in Jabal Says, and an inscription dating 569 CE in the village of Harran. Recently Leila Nehmé has studied an Arabic script, Arabic language Christian inscription from the region of Dumat al-Jandal in northwestern Saudi Arabia (see Figure 7.3 in chapter 7). Meanwhile Ahmad al-Jallad and Hythem Sidky have studied a monotheistic pre-Islamic Arabic inscription to the south, between Mecca and Ta'if (in a pass known as Ri' al-Zallalah). The inscription of Harran—which today is on the lintel of a modern house in the village—is written in Greek and Arabic and marked the space in which it originally appeared as a tomb for a Christian martyr (identified as "the holy John" in the Greek version).

The appearance of Arabic alongside another language in the Harran inscription is not at all an anomaly (the inscription at Zebed is trilingual: Arabic, Greek, and Syriac). Many Arabs in the centuries before the rise of Islam were familiar (to various extents) with Syriac (or another form of Aramaic) and some with Greek. Indeed, certain inscriptions (and certain papyri, especially those found at Petra, in Jordan) are not simply bilingual but are written in a form of Arabic–Aramaic hybrid that speaks to true multilingualism. All of this is interesting for the purpose of the task at hand in the present book because it speaks of a dynamic religious and cultural situation among the Arabs in the fifth, sixth, and early seventh centuries CE. The old gods were

FIGURE 1.01. *An inscription above a doorway in the southern Syrian town of Harran dated to 567. The inscription commemorates a Christian martyr named John and includes both Greek and Arabic. Credit: Robert Hoyland.*

disappearing. Judaism and Christianity were on the rise. Arabic languages were increasingly in contact with Aramaic and Greek. Together these elements present an interesting picture. One can envision a charismatic figure arising among the Arabs who embraced monotheism but insisted on expressing his faith in the Arabic language, and in responding to the claims of Jews and Christians.

For its part, the Qur'an presents itself as a book for the Arabs: "We have sent it down as an Arabic Qur'an; haply ['that perhaps']

you will understand" (Q 12:2). Such verses suggest that the story of Islam's emergence involves not only the appearance of a new religion but also the unification of the Arabic-speaking tribes and the rise of the idea that they all make up one people: they are all Arabs, the descendants of Abraham through Ishmael (as the Jews are his descendants through Isaac).

This connection between Abraham, the Arabs, and Islam is expressed in the genealogy of Muhammad. Although the idea is not explicit in the Qur'an, Muslims make Muhammad a descendant of Abraham through Ishmael; they also relate that Muhammad met Abraham during his ascent to heaven and that the two of them had a nearly identical appearance. Thus Muhammad is presented as a "new Abraham." This presentation presumably offered a way for early Muslims to conceive of and defend their religion in the context of the seventh-century Middle East. With their ethnic identity as Arabs, and their religious identity as descendants of Abraham, Muslims could enter into the religious debates already taking place between Christians and Jews and among various Christian sects.

Yet Muslims did not appear in the Middle East as religious missionaries who sought to make disciples of other nations. They appeared as conquerors who subjected other nations to their rule. Wars justified by religion were nothing new to the Middle East. As Robert Hoyland explains in his masterful work *In God's Path*, between 602 and 628, the Christian Byzantine Empire was locked in a violent conflict with the predominantly Zoroastrian Sasanian Persian Empire. For some time the Persians had the upper hand. In 613, the Sasanians conquered the Byzantine provinces of Syria and Palestine, including the holy city of Jerusalem. They burned many churches and took away with them the relic of the true Cross. The tide of war turned in 622 when the Byzantine emperor Heraclius began a counter-offensive into the Sasanian homelands. By 627, after a series of bloody battles, Heraclius had triumphed. The Persian emperor Khosrow II was killed by his own

subjects and the Sasanians agreed to peace terms. These included the return of the true Cross, which Heraclius piously brought to his capital Constantinople in 629. Both empires, however, were severely weakened by the almost three-decades-long war, and they were not prepared for the new conflict on the horizon.

In the 630s, Arab armies swept through the Near East. The mighty Persian Empire collapsed entirely in the face of their attacks. (The last Persian emperor was killed in 651.) The Byzantine Empire at last withstood the Islamic conquests, but only by establishing a final line of defense in the Taurus Mountains in the early 640s. In the meanwhile, the Byzantines had lost Syria, Palestine (including Jerusalem), and Egypt to the Muslims.

Between the death of Muhammad (traditionally dated to 632) and the transfer of the capital of the Islamic empire from Medina to Damascus in 661, Muslim armies conquered an area that stretched from modern-day Libya in the west to modern-day Afghanistan in the east. Thus Islam emerged as both a religion and a state. This state proclaimed to the world that a new prophet had appeared, a prophet who corrected the errors of Jews and Christians and who instructed his followers on how to establish the law of God, or the sharia, on earth.

The present book begins with the story of this prophet, Muhammad the son of ʿAbdallah, who according to tradition was born in 570 in the western Arabian city of Mecca. In telling this story, I will rely on the oldest

Islamic sources, above all the biography of the Prophet by Ibn Ishaq (d. 767), a native of Medina whose work is largely seen as the most ancient account of Muhammad's life. I will also turn to traditions (Ar. *hadith*) about or by the Prophet preserved by Bukhari (d. 870)—the most famous compiler of such traditions—and to the biography of Muhammad in the monumental history of Abu Ja'far al-Tabari (d. 923), a Persian scholar whose works on the Qur'an and Islamic history represent the fullness of classical Islamic tradition. When I refer in the following chapters to "the traditional biography" of the Prophet, or "the classical Islamic sources," I mean above all the account of Muhammad's life as recorded in these three works.

In speaking of Muhammad, I will also have reason to refer to the Qur'an, a Scripture that, according to the prevailing Islamic belief, existed in heaven even before Muhammad was born. Once God called on Muhammad to be his prophet (in 610), he began to send the angel Gabriel with passages of this heavenly book to Muhammad, and he continued to do so until Muhammad's death (632). Muhammad proclaimed these revelations to his companions, but the collection and codification of the Qur'an was the work of his political successors, or caliphs.

In fact, the Qur'an shows signs of being a much older book than that of Ibn Ishaq, in part because much of Ibn Ishaq's work is a commentary on the Qur'an; that is, it is in large part made up of stories meant to explain otherwise-ambiguous qur'anic passages. Yet the historical value of the Qur'an has often been questioned, since it is a book filled with pious admonitions and not with details on the people, places, and happenings of its historical context.

Thus the question before us—namely, how Islam emerged in its Arab context—is difficult to answer. In the first part of the present work, we will investigate how the first Islamic biographies present Islam's emergence; we will do this by examining how they describe the life of Muhammad and the rule of the first four (or "rightly guided") caliphs. In so doing we will identify reports that seem to be the product of storytellers and not the records of authentic historical events. Indeed, we must remember that Muhammad's biography was first composed by scholars, beginning with Ibn Ishaq, who wrote over one hundred years after the Prophet had died, and who wrote with very particular motives.

The goal of these authors was not limited to producing a faithful account of earlier events. For example, both Sunnis and Shi'ites seem to shape their traditions on the political succession to Muhammad in a way that justifies their religious doctrine. All early Muslim scholars, meanwhile, sought to explain how references and allusions in the Qur'an can be understood in the context of Muhammad's life. They also sought to present his life in a way that responds to the disbelief of Jews and Christians.

These critical observations do not mean that the traditional Islamic biography of the Prophet has no historical value. Certain reports might have an authentic core, even if they have been embellished for various reasons. However, it is difficult to know where to find that authentic core, since we do not have any ancient non-Muslim accounts of the Prophet's life with enough detail to offer grounds for comparison. Thus it is perhaps best to look at the traditional biography of the Prophet as the first record of Islamic self-understanding. From this perspective its value is considerable.

Chapter 1

MUHAMMAD IN MECCA

It is alleged in popular stories (and only God knows the truth) that Amina the daughter of Wahb, the mother of God's apostle, used to say when she was pregnant with God's apostle that a voice said to her, "You are pregnant with the lord of this people and when he is born say, 'I put him in the care of the One from the evil of every envier,' then call him Muhammad." As she was pregnant with him she saw a light come forth from her by which she could see the castles of Busra in Syria.

—*The Life of Muhammad* by Muhammad Ibn Ishaq

Monotheism and Paganism in Muhammad's Arabia

The Prophet Muhammad, according to the traditional Islamic sources, was an orphan. His father, ʿAbdallah, died three months before he was born, and his mother, Amina, died when he was only six. After his mother and grandfather died, Muhammad was adopted by Abu Talib, his paternal uncle. Abu Talib was an important merchant in Mecca, a city of merchants, and when Muhammad was twelve, Abu Talib agreed to take him on a trading journey north to Syria. It was to be a fateful journey.

Muhammad and the Monk

Their route took them near the city of Busra (referred to in the quotation above), by the cave of a Christian hermit named Bahira. Now Bahira had never taken notice of the Meccan caravan before, but on this occasion he noticed a cloud that hovered over the head of the boy Muhammad even as the caravan drove forward. Thus Bahira came down from his cave, stopped the Meccans, and insisted they come eat with him. When the Meccans went up to Bahira's cave, they left the young Muhammad behind with the baggage. Bahira, however, noticed Muhammad's absence and insisted that he be summoned. When Muhammad finally arrived, Bahira examined him closely and found a mark on his back, between his shoulder blades, "the very place described in his book." This, Bahira explained, was the "seal of prophethood." It confirmed to Bahira that the boy was the one predicted by Christ. Before seeing his guests off, Bahira announced to Abu Talib (after warning him that the Jews would plot against Muhammad): "A great future lies before this nephew of yours, so take him home quickly" (Ibn Ishaq, 81).

The account of Muhammad's meeting with the mysterious monk Bahira illustrates three themes in the traditional narrative of Islam's emergence. First, it presents Islam as a religion that completes and corrects Christianity. The figure of the monk is meant to show that a true Christian recognizes Muhammad as a prophet. The Qur'an itself describes the reaction of Christians who hear Muhammad proclaim his revelations: "When they hear what has been sent down to the Messenger, thou seest their eyes overflow with tears because of the truth they

recognize. They say, 'Our Lord, we believe; so do Thou write us down among the witnesses'" (Q 5:83). The reference to a book in Bahira's possession that contained a description of the new prophet (including his birthmark) suggests that Bahira was not reading the Christian Bible but the "true" scriptures of Jesus (which, perhaps, he preserved secretly in his secluded cave). Thus Bahira appears to be a bridge between Jesus and Muhammad. He preserves the Scriptures of the first prophet, Jesus, and he recognizes the appearance of the new prophet, Muhammad.

Second, this account also makes Muhammad the fulfillment, or the consummation, of biblical prophets. It is reminiscent of Samuel's anointing of David as king of Israel (1 Sam 16). When Samuel examines the elder sons of Jesse to find the one whom God has chosen to be king, none pass the test. "Are these all the sons you have?" he asks Jesse. At this Jesse finally brings his youngest son, David (who had been watching not baggage but sheep), and God tells Samuel that David is the chosen one. So, too, this account is reminiscent of Moses leading the Israelites out of Egypt. Yahweh precedes the Israelites in a cloud in Exodus 13, while a cloud hovers over the head of Muhammad in the Bahira story.

The Bahira story is also reminiscent of Jesus's travel as a boy of twelve to Jerusalem with his parents (Luke 2). Jesus's parents find him in the temple, asking questions of the teachers and amazing them with his intelligence. Similarly, Muhammad proves himself unusually wise on religious matters during his meeting with Bahira. When Bahira swears by the pagan goddesses of Mecca—al-Lat and al-ʿUzza—Muhammad rebukes him, saying: "By God nothing is more hateful to me than these two" (Ibn Ishaq, *Life of Muhammad*, 80).

Third, this account evokes the struggle between monotheism and paganism. The Islamic sources make it clear that Bahira himself did not believe in the gods of Mecca; he only swore by them "because he had heard [Muhammad's] people swearing by these gods." Mecca, according to the traditional narrative, was a city awash in idols, a city possessed by the abomination of paganism. Accordingly, the Islamic sources refer to Arab society before the arrival of Islam as the *jahiliyya*: "the realm of ignorance." Muhammad, they relate, was born to be a bearer of light in a city of darkness.

The Pagan City of Mecca and the War of the Elephant

Western scholars generally date the birth of Muhammad to 570 CE (although this date is quite uncertain; it is based only on the assumption that Muhammad was sixty-two at his death, in 632). According to Islamic tradition, the leading figure in Mecca at the time of Muhammad's birth was his paternal grandfather, ʿAbd al-Muttalib, who was known as "'the lord' of the Quraysh" (the principal tribe of Mecca, to which Muhammad belonged).

A descendent of Abraham (through Ishmael), ʿAbd al-Muttalib was a holy man in a city of unholiness. He is closely connected in Islamic traditions with the **Kaʿba**, the square stone shrine in Mecca around which Muslims circle during their pilgrimage.

It was ʿAbd al-Muttalib who, guided by a dream, found the spring next to the Kaʿba

known as Zamzam, originally discovered by Abraham's young son Ishmael when, suffering from thirst in the heat of Arabia, he scratched at the ground with his feet (according to another tradition, the angel Gabriel released the water of Zamzam by digging at this spot with his wing). When Muhammad was born, one tradition reports, ʿAbd al-Muttalib immediately took the child to the Kaʿba to give thanks to God.

This connection with the Kaʿba is also a connection with Abraham himself, who is said to have built the Kaʿba as a shrine for the worship of God (although some traditions insist the Kaʿba was first built by Adam and only restored by Abraham after the great flood). Evidently, the Islamic tradition on Abraham and Mecca departs from the biblical story of Abraham, which never has him travel anywhere near Mecca (a city hundreds of miles south of the biblical land of Canaan).

Most Islamic traditions explain that at a certain point, Abraham asked his second wife, Hagar, and their son, Ishmael (but not Sarah or Isaac), to join him on a journey into the desert that led them to a deserted valley where Abraham built the Kaʿba. Other traditions explain that the Kaʿba was built as a precise replica of a shrine in heaven, around which angels process in prayer. However, in the days of ʿAbd al-Muttalib, the Kaʿba had become a pagan shrine, housing the idols of various Arab tribes (360 idols, according to one count).

By describing the Kaʿba in this way, the Islamic sources suggest that Muhammad did not teach a new religion in Mecca. Instead, he taught people to worship one God, as

FIGURE 1.1. *Muslim Pilgrims around the Kaʿba, Mecca 2007.*

Abraham had done. In other words, monotheism existed in Mecca before the city declined into the darkness of paganism. This idea seems to emerge from a passage in the Qurʾan:

> And when Abraham, and Ishmael with him, raised up the foundations of the House: "Our Lord, receive this from us; Thou art the All-hearing, the All-knowing; and, our Lord, make us submissive [*muslimayni*] to Thee, and of our seed a nation submissive to Thee; and show us our holy rites, and turn towards us; surely Thou turnest, and art All-compassionate. (Q 2:127–28)

Here Abraham and Ishmael ask God to make them "submissive"—in Arabic, *muslimayni*—to God. The followers of Muhammad's religion would later call themselves by this term: Muslims (the ending -*in* makes the word plural in Arabic). Moreover, they would insist that Abraham and Ishmael were not only "submissive" (or *muslims* with a lowercase *m*) but also that they were Muslims (with a capital *M*). Islam, in other words, did not begin with Muhammad. It began long before.

In the qurʾanic passage above, Abraham and Ishmael also pray that God will raise up a nation among their descendants, a nation that will likewise be "submissive" (or *muslim*). In the subsequent verse, the Qur'an has them pray for the appearance of a prophet among them, "Our Lord, do Thou send among them a Messenger, one of them, who shall recite to them Thy signs, and teach them the Book and the Wisdom, and purify them; Thou art the All-mighty, the All-wise" (Q 2:129). To Muslims, Muhammad is this messenger, this new Abraham. The connection between Abraham and Muhammad is seen again in a tradition that Muhammad, after he met Abraham face to face during his ascent

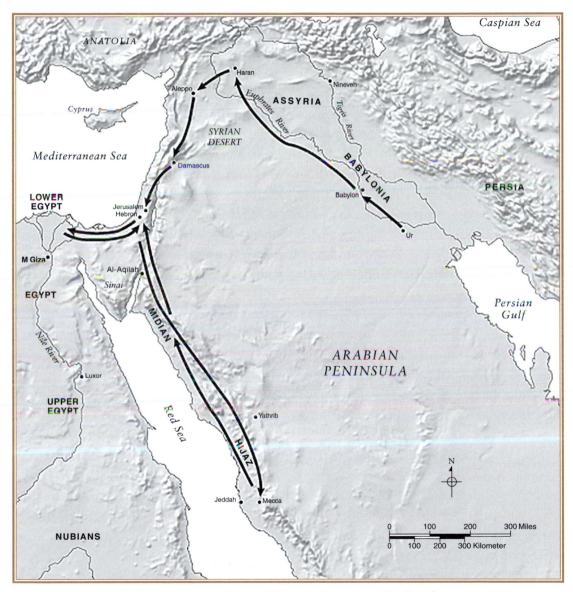

FIGURE 1.2. *A map in a Muslim publication depicting Abraham's route to Mecca.*

to heaven, commented: "Never have I seen a man so much like myself" (Ibn Ishaq, 183).

As for ʿAbd al-Muttalib, in the traditional Islamic narrative, he is an enigmatic figure. He lived and died before Muhammad preached Islam (most accounts have him die when Muhammad was only eight years old), and his close association with the Kaʿba puts him at the city's pagan heart. Nevertheless, he is described as a holy man. ʿAbd al-Muttalib is celebrated in particular for his defense of the Kaʿba during the "War of the Elephant."

The story of this "war" (which in fact does not involve any fighting at all) in the classical Islamic sources centers on the ambitions of Abraha, a Christian ruler from the south of the Arabian Peninsula. Abraha had built a grand cathedral in the city of Sanʿa, and he planned to turn this cathedral into a site of pilgrimage for all of the Arabs—and to make a profit from the pilgrims who would come. The principal obstacle to his plans was the Kaʿba of Mecca and its 360 idols. Many of these idols belonged to individual tribes who made a pilgrimage once a year to Mecca to venerate them. Abraha, according to the story, decided that a good way to convince them to come to Sanʿa instead was to destroy those idols and the building that housed them. Thus Abraha set out to attack Mecca, supplying his troops with an elephant for battle.

A ruler named Abraha is indeed known to us from Christian chronicles and South Arabian inscriptions, but outside of Islamic tradition there is no mention of his attack on Mecca. There are reports in Greek literature of the reign of "Abramos" in Arabia. More tellingly an inscription in Arabia (well to the southeast of Mecca) usually dated to 552 CE describes Abraha's victory over a rival confederation of tribes. This would put the campaign's date well before the traditional date of Muhammad's birth: 570 CE. It is possible that the elephant story was a way of connecting Muhammad's biography to Qurʾan 105: "Hast thou not seen how thy Lord did with the Men of the Elephant? Did He not make their guile to go astray? And He loosed upon them birds in flights, hurling against them stones of baked clay, and He made them like green blades devoured" (Q 105:1–5). Presumably, later Muslim scholars simply attached the well-known name of Abraha to the story they wrote to explain this otherwise opaque passage about the "Men of the Elephant."

In any case, according to this story, ʿAbd al-Muttalib—having heard of Abraha's approach—put the fate of the city in God's hands: "God knows that we do not wish to fight [Abraha] for we have not the power to do so. This is God's sanctuary and the temple of His friend Abraham. . . . If He defends it against [Abraha] it is His temple and His sanctuary; and if he lets [Abraha] have it by God we cannot defend it!" (Ibn Ishaq, 24). Like the Egyptians in the days of Moses, the forces of Abraha were facing not humans but God. The next day, as they prepared for battle, they discovered that their elephant (called Mahmud, a good Islamic name) refused to approach Mecca. Even worse, birds came from the sea and each brought three small stones, which they dropped on the soldiers of Abraha. Everyone hit by these stones was killed. Abraha himself was hit repeatedly and slowly dismembered. By the time he reached Sanʿa, he had nothing but a miserable stump of a body. His heart burst from his chest, and he died. So the year of the War of the Elephant was a year of death. But it was also a year of life, for, according to the traditional story, in that same year Muhammad was born.

Muhammad's Early Life

According to Ibn Ishaq, in the days when Muhammad was born, it was common for city-dwelling Arabs to place their children into the care of Bedouins. Muhammad's mother, Amina, did just that, giving the young boy to a Bedouin woman named Halima. Soon after Halima took Muhammad in, a miracle took place that proved the boy was unlike any other.

Childhood

For some time, Halima had been unable to nurse, but soon after she took in Muhammad, her breasts filled with so much milk that she was able to nurse both Muhammad and her own child. Even the udders of her old she-camel suddenly filled with milk. Halima had once been hesitant to accept Muhammad (a fatherless child), but now she counted herself lucky. "Do you know, Halima, you have taken a blessed creature," exclaimed her husband.

Yet a miracle still more fantastic was to take place during Muhammad's residence with Halima in the desert. Muhammad himself recounts how it took place: "While I was with a [foster] brother of mine behind our tents shepherding the lambs, two men in white raiment came to me with a gold basin full of snow. Then they seized me and opened up my belly, extracted my heart and split it; then

they extracted a black drop from it and threw it away; they washed my heart and my belly with that snow" (Ibn Ishaq, 72). This account seems to symbolize Muhammad's purification in preparation for his call to prophecy, yet that call would not come until many years later.

Marriage and Call to Prophecy

Most accounts of Muhammad's adult life begin with the report that Muhammad worked as a merchant for an older woman named Khadija, known both for her dignity and for her wealth. Many men desired to marry Khadija in order to get to this wealth, but Khadija desired to marry Muhammad, whom she knew to be both reliable and honest (for which he was given the nickname al-Amin, "the Trustworthy").

Even more, Khadija recognized that Muhammad was a holy man. One of Khadija's servants had told her that a monk saw Muhammad sit under a tree where only prophets sit. Khadija's own cousin Waraqa, who is often described as a Christian, explained: "If this is true, Khadija, verily Muhammad is the prophet of this people. I knew that a prophet of this people was to be expected. His time has come" (Ibn Ishaq, 83). Thus Khadija and Muhammad were married. Muhammad would later marry many women, but as long as he was married to Khadija, he remained monogamous. Years later, Muhammad's young wife ʿAʾisha would recall, "I did not feel jealous of any woman as much as I did of Khadija because Allah's Apostle used to mention her very often" (Bukhari, 5:165).

Personalities in Islam 1.1
KHADIJA

According to the traditional biography of the Prophet, Khadija was Muhammad's first wife, the only wife older than him, the only wife to bear him children who lived to adulthood, and the only wife with whom he lived monogamously (that is, Muhammad did not marry other women while Khadija was still alive). Ibn Ishaq describes Khadija as "a merchant woman of dignity and wealth" and adds, "All her people were eager to get possession of her wealth" (Ibn Ishaq, 82). Although Ibn Ishaq does not tell us how Khadija achieved this status (let alone what sort of merchant trade she was involved in), he does credit Khadija for recognizing Muhammad's "truthfulness, trustworthiness, and honorable char-acter." He relates how Khadija hears from another of her employees (named Maysara) that miraculous signs accompany Muhammad (such as angels shading him from the sun). In this way, she recognizes that Muhammad possesses a quality beyond mere virtue and asks to marry him.

Thus Khadija is one of several pious wisdom figures in the biography of the Prophet, figures who insightfully perceive Muhammad's special qualities. Among these is the monk Bahira and Khadija's own cousin Waraqa, who (being learned in the Scriptures) identifies Muhammad as a prophet like Moses.

To Shi'ite Muslims, Khadija is also a figure of particular value as the mother of Fatima. Muhammad's cousin 'Ali—whom Shi'ites recognize as the first Imam, the rightful successor to the Prophet—would marry Fatima. From this marriage would be born Hasan and Husayn (the second and third Imams, grandsons of the Prophet). Shi'ite authors also contrast Khadija, the "woman of dignity," with another wife of the Prophet: 'A'isha, the daughter of Abu Bakr (who, from a Shi'ite perspective, wrongly usurped 'Ali's place as successor to the Prophet).

As for Waraqa, Ibn Ishaq makes him one of four Arabs who broke away from pagan-ism even before Muhammad proclaimed Islam. Islamic tradition names these four figures *hanif*s (or "pure monotheists"), and Muhammad, before his call to prophethood, is sometimes thought to have been influenced by them. He is said to have spent one month of each year praying in a cave on a mountain named Hira, outside Mecca. It was during one of these retreats when Muhammad, who had reached the age of forty, was first visited by the angel Gabriel.

"He came to me," said the apostle of God, "while I was asleep, with a coverlet of brocade whereon was some writing, and said, "Read!" I said, "What shall I read?" He pressed me with it so tightly that I thought it was death; then he let me go and said, "Read!" I said, "What shall I read?" He pressed me with it again so that I thought it was death; then he let me go and said "Read!" I said, "What shall I read?" He pressed me with it the third time so that I thought it was death and said "Read!" I said, "What then shall I read?"—and this I said only to deliver myself from him, lest he should do the same to me again. He said: "Read in the name of thy Lord who created, who created man of blood coagulated. Read! Thy Lord is the most beneficent, who taught by the pen, taught that which they knew not unto men." (Ibn Ishaq, 106)

This final phrase is from Qurʾan 96, verses 1–5, which, according to this account, were the first words God revealed to the Prophet. Over the next twenty-three years, Muhammad continued to receive such revelations from God, brought to him by the angel Gabriel, who would indicate to the Prophet how these revelations, delivered in pieces (such as that cited above), were to be arranged. Muhammad referred to these messages as "The Recitation," or "The Reading"—in Arabic, the *Qurʾan*.

Ibn Ishaq explains that when Muhammad was on his way down from Mount Hira, he heard a voice from above, which declared to him, "Thou art the apostle [that is, the messenger] of God and I am Gabriel" (Ibn Ishaq, 106). When he reached the bottom of the mountain, Muhammad rushed to find Khadija and told her all that he had seen and heard. Khadija declared, "Verily, by Him in whose hand is Khadija's soul, I have hope that thou wilt be the prophet of this people." Thus Khadija believed, becoming the first follower of Muhammad's religion.

When Muhammad told Khadija's cousin Waraqa what had occurred, Waraqa replied, "Surely by Him in whose hand is Waraqa's soul, thou art the prophet of this people." To these words Waraqa added a warning: "Thou wilt be called a liar, and they will use thee despitefully and cast thee out and fight against thee" (Ibn Ishaq, 107). Thus the drama of Muhammad's confrontation with the pagan people of Mecca was set to begin.

Muhammad's Conflict with the Pagans of Mecca

According to the traditional Islamic sources, the Meccans—not unlike the Roman administration of Palestine in the time of Jesus—were hardly zealous in religious matters. The Romans of course had their gods, not least of which was their emperor. After the defeat of the Bar Kochba revolt in 135 CE, they erected a statue of the emperor Hadrian on the site of the Jerusalem temple. But for long stretches of time, the Roman administration allowed Jews to practice their religion. The Romans' principal concern was the preservation of order—and tax revenues.

The Infidelity of the Quraysh

According to Islamic sources, the Quraysh, the ruling tribe of Mecca, had similar concerns. Western scholars generally refer to the Quraysh as pagans, a Latin term (*paganus*, or "civilian," that is, someone who is not in the "army of Christ") that originally referred to non-Christians. Later it became a pejorative label for any polytheists, for which reason Western scholars took to naming pre-Islamic Meccans "pagans." Arabic-speaking Muslim scholars name them "associators" (Ar. *mushrikun*), accusing them of associating gods, or idols, with the one true God. Like Roman pagans, the Meccan pagans of Islamic tradition are imagined to have had multiple gods and diverse religious practices. Worshipers could introduce new gods and new practices, and they were free to choose the gods they would worship and the practices they would follow. At least, this is the story of the Meccan pagans told by the Islamic sources. We have no sources in which the "pagans" speak for themselves.

In other ways, however, the story of the pagans in Mecca is unlike that of the Romans in Jerusalem. In the Jerusalem of Jesus's day, the pagan Romans were ruling over a Jewish city. Yet Mecca in Muhammad's day, as Ibn Ishaq tells us, was both literally and figuratively built around a pagan shrine, the Kaʿba. It was this shrine that gave Mecca its religious prestige. Once a year, tribes from around Arabia came to Mecca for the annual pilgrimage, the Hajj, in order to venerate the idols in the Kaʿba—and to do business. As a result, the Quraysh grew ever richer.

BOX 1.1 ❖ THE HAJJ

Muslims generally consider the Hajj, or pilgrimage to Mecca, to be one of the five pillars of Islam. All able Muslims are expected to perform the Hajj at least once in their lives. The Hajj takes place every year between the seventh and twelfth days of the last month of the Islamic calendar, or Dhu al-Hijja, the "Month of the Hajj." (Since the Islamic calendar is based on a lunar year, and not a solar year, the dates of the Hajj on the standard Gregorian calendar move back approximately eleven days each year.) Before entering Mecca, the male pilgrim puts on a simple white cloak, leaving his head uncovered (a woman is simply to remain modestly veiled); during the period of the pilgrimage, he must refrain from certain acts (from shaving to sexual activity) understood to break this state of purity. The rituals of the Hajj include (1) proceeding seven times around the Kaʿba and kissing, if possible, the black stone embedded in it; (2) processing seven times between two rocky mounds, in imitation of Hagar, who did so as she searched for water (when she was left behind in Mecca by Abraham); (3) spending an afternoon standing near a small mountain known as ʿArafat, about fifteen miles east of Mecca; (4) casting stones at a wall (originally three pillars, joined together in 2004), which symbolizes Satan, in commemoration of Abraham's confrontation with the devil; and (5) slaughtering an animal (usually a sheep), in imitation of Abraham, who was given an animal by God to sacrifice in the place of his son whom he was prepared to kill (according to the majority view of Muslims, not Isaac but Ishmael).

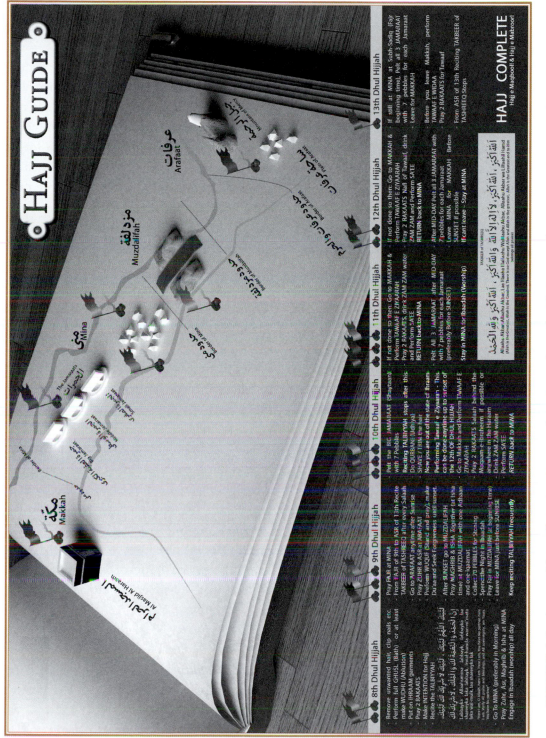

FIGURE 1.3. *A pamphlet with instructions on how to perform the Hajj correctly, meant to be carried by pilgrims.*

The Scottish scholar William Montgomery Watt argues that in the days of Muhammad, Mecca had become a wealthy city. The city's wealth, he maintains, was in part due to the presence of the Kaʿba. Watt reports that the area around the Kaʿba was considered a sanctuary, an inviolable refuge in which business could be conducted without fear of harassment. Watt argues additionally that the Quraysh benefited economically from the strategic location of their city, since Mecca "stood at the cross-roads of routes from the Yemen to Syria and from Abyssinia to Iraq." The Quraysh, by his telling, dominated "most of the trade from the Yemen to Syria—an important route by which the West got Indian luxury goods as well as South Arabian frankincense" (*Muhammad at Mecca*, 3). Watt adds that the privileged economic situation of the Quraysh had led them to become a crafty and money-hungry people, "skilful in the manipulation of credit," and "shrewd in their speculations" (*Muhammad at Mecca*, 3). This is quite an impressive description of Mecca's trade empire. But is it accurate?

In fact, there is no record at all of this Meccan trade in non-Islamic sources, and Mecca is hardly the easiest land route between Yemen and Syria. (In order to get to Mecca from the coastline of the Red Sea, an arduous inland detour is necessary.) Indeed, it seems that the idea of Mecca as a trading center, and the Quraysh as a tribe of greedy merchants, is an idea developed by Islamic tradition to explain certain qurʾanic passages (notably Q 106, a sura titled "Quraysh"). This idea, or myth, was then used by Western scholars

such as Watt who were eager to find social and cultural factors to explain the emergence of Islam.

Maxime Rodinson went further. He argued that the caravan trade had enriched the nomadic Bedouins, who began to settle in cities, notably Mecca. Their riches, and the comforts of settled life, soon led them to forget their old tribal values. A moral crisis ensued, as some began searching for new, more universal values: "The poor, the young and the honest were suffering from upstart arrogance. There was a vague feeling that the old tribal principles, which might have been invoked to prevent it, were somehow out of date" (Rodinson, *Muhammad*, 36). To Rodinson, this vague feeling lies behind the rise of Islam in Mecca.

But if there was so much trade going on in Mecca before Islam, it is amazing that the Islamic sources have essentially *nothing* to say about Meccan trade after the city became Islamic. Watt speculates that Islamic rules against usury "stopped the old lucrative speculations in high finance" (*Muhammad at Medina*, 76), but one wonders why trade continued in other Islamic cities. Indeed, as Francis Peters correctly notes, the only problem with the idea of Mecca as a major trading center is that "it happens not to be true" (*Jesus and Muhammad*, 59.)

For their part, the Islamic sources attribute the rise of Islam not to any "vague feeling" but to God. Nevertheless, they still emphasize the Meccans' involvement in trade. The idea of the Quraysh as a tribe of greedy traders presumably lies behind the report that on several occasions they sought to pay Muhammad to keep quiet. Muhammad, however, would not betray his cause, declaring at one point: "If they put the sun in my right hand and the moon in my left on the condition that I abandoned this course, until God has made it victorious, or I perish therein, I would not abandon it" (Ibn Ishaq, 119).

In most accounts of the Quraysh's opposition to Muhammad, however, the issue is not Meccan trade but Meccan pride. Jerusalem, after all, was a foreign city to the Romans stationed there, but the pagans of Mecca were in their native city. Muhammad was one of their own, and he was insulting the religion of their fathers.

Accordingly, when Muhammad began preaching Islam, a group of the Quraysh complained to his uncle, Abu Talib, declaring: "Your nephew has cursed our gods, insulted our religion, mocked our way of life and accused our forefathers of error!" (Ibn Ishaq, 119). On a second occasion, they came to Abu Talib and complained, "By God, we cannot endure that our fathers should be reviled" (Ibn Ishaq, 119). For its part, the Qur'an condemns the unbelievers' attachment to the religion of their fathers: "And when it is said to them, 'Follow what God has sent down,' they say, 'No; but we will follow such things as we found our fathers doing.' What? And if their fathers had no understanding of anything, and if they were not guided?" (Q 2:170).

The standoff continued for some time. Most of the Quraysh refused to accept Islam, and Muhammad continued to malign their religion. Eventually, the Quraysh sought to attack him. On one occasion, they threatened him and seized his robe in front of the Ka'ba, but Muhammad's friend Abu Bakr intervened and saved him. On another occasion, Muhammad's fiercest opponent, Abu Jahl, approached the Prophet with a stone in order to attack him, but he was confronted with a vision of a terrible camel. "He made as though he would eat me," Abu Jahl later explained (Ibn Ishaq, 135).

The Quraysh also began to persecute Muhammad's growing number of followers. According to one report, 'Umar, who would later become a Muslim (and the second caliph), beat one of his slave girls who had become a Muslim until he could hit her no more. "I have only stopped beating you because I am tired," he said. "May God treat you in the same way," she replied.

Eventually, Muhammad became so distraught at the persecution of his followers that he decided to send some of them to the Christian kingdom of Ethiopia across the Red Sea, where they were welcomed and given protection. Most traditions put this event in the fifth or sixth year of Muhammad's ministry (ca. 614–15 CE).

The Quraysh, Islamic tradition tells us, responded by sending two men of their own to the Ethiopian king, in order to deprive Muhammad's followers of this refuge. They lavished gifts upon the Ethiopians and asked the king to hand over the Muslims to them. The king, however, insisted on hearing about the Muslims' new religion first. In response, one of the Muslims (a son of Abu Talib named Ja'far) explained Islam briefly and then read a passage from the Qur'an. The Christian king (who cried until his beard was wet) stood up and proclaimed: "Of a truth, this and what Jesus brought have come from the same niche. You two may go, for by God, I will never give them up to them and they shall not be betrayed" (Ibn Ishaq, 152). Although nothing is said of this incident in Ethiopian tradition, Islamic tradition recounts that the Muslims remained peacefully in Ethiopia and that the king himself became a Muslim before he died.

The Satanic Verses

Nevertheless, Muhammad's conflict with the pagans in Mecca continued. When the Quraysh perceived Muhammad's power growing, they signed a pact to boycott the two clans with the largest numbers of Muslims. Muhammad cursed the man who wrote the pact, and his fingers miraculously withered, but the Quraysh enforced the boycott (which included abstaining from business and marriages) nevertheless.

They also began to confront Muhammad publicly. On one occasion, a member of the pagan Quraysh took out an old bone, crushed it, and blew it in pieces before Muhammad's face in order to ridicule the idea (preached by Muhammad) of the resurrection of the body. The pagan declared: "Do you allege that God can revivify this after it has decayed?" Muhammad replied, "Yes I do say that. God will raise it and you, after you have become like this. Then God will send you to Hell" (Ibn Ishaq, 165).

It was this state of affairs, so the classical Islamic sources tell us, that led to the proclamation of the satanic verses. Muhammad had grown increasingly depressed by the hard-heartedness of the Quraysh—his own people—and he meditated often on how he might convince them to accept Islam. He was in this state of longing when God revealed the first part of chapter 53 in the Qur'an, up to the verses (19–20) that mention the pagan goddesses of the Meccans: "Have you considered El-Lat and El-'Uzza, * and Manat the third, the other?"

However, Satan, too, was meditating, and this was the moment he chose to act, whispering to the Prophet a false revelation: "These are the exalted cranes, whose intercession is approved." The Quraysh heard the Prophet praise their goddesses and bowed down in prostration with the Muslims. But the angel Gabriel intervened, declaring to the Prophet, "What have you done, Muhammad?" (Ibn Ishaq, 166). Muhammad realized his mistake and repented. He retracted the verses that had come from Satan, and God gave him new verses in its place.

A Heavenly and an Earthly Journey

Indeed, if Satan was prowling about looking for ways to seduce Muhammad, God was constantly finding ways to support him. This support frequently took the form of miracles. When a man named Rukana, famed among the Quraysh for his strength, expressed his doubt in Muhammad's claims, the Prophet challenged him to a wrestling match (Ibn Ishaq, 178). Muhammad promptly threw him to the ground. Rukana was amazed, and

Muhammad added, "I can show you something more wonderful than that if you wish." (Ibn Ishaq, 178). At this the Prophet called out to a tree, which traveled across the earth and planted itself before him.

The Prophet's Journey to Heaven

Toward the end of the Prophet's time in Mecca, the Prophet himself would miraculously travel to Jerusalem on a fabulous creature and, once there, ascend into heaven. Ibn Ishaq quotes a number of different traditions on Muhammad's night journey and ascension. According to one of them, the Prophet was sleeping next to the Kaʿba one night when the angel Gabriel stirred him with his foot three times. Muhammad stood up and saw "a white animal, half mule, half donkey, with wings on its sides" (Ibn Ishaq, 182). Muhammad mounted this animal, named Buraq, and flew to Jerusalem (some versions have him stop first at Mt. Sinai and in Bethlehem) on its back, with Gabriel accompanying. Today the "Western Wall" in Jerusalem is accordingly known to Muslims as the "Wall of Buraq." In Jerusalem, Muhammad met Abraham, Moses, Jesus ("a reddish man with many freckles on his face as though he had just come from a bath"; 184), and other prophets. He led them in prayer and then returned to Mecca. However, a second tradition, attributed to the Prophet's beloved wife ʿAʾisha, relates that the Prophet indeed traveled to Jerusalem, but only in sprit.

According to still other accounts, the Prophet's business that night did not end in Jerusalem. One tradition relates that while Muhammad was in Jerusalem, a ladder was brought to him. He climbed up it with the angel Gabriel until he reached the entrance of heaven. At the entrance of heaven, he saw a man who would not smile. This, Gabriel explained, is Malik, the keeper of hell. Muhammad had Gabriel ask Malik to open the cover to hell. Muhammad recounts what happened when Malik did so: "The flames blazed high into the air until I thought that they would consume everything. So I asked Gabriel to order him to send them back to their place which he did" (Ibn Ishaq, 185).

Thereafter Muhammad began to climb up through the various levels of heaven. On the first level, he saw Adam, who was reviewing souls, his offspring all, passing by him. According to a tradition in Bukhari, the Prophet saw Adam looking right and laughing and looking left and weeping. Muhammad asked Gabriel to explain why Adam was acting this way, and the angel replied: "Those on his right are the people of Paradise and those on his left are the people of Hell and when he looks towards his right he laughs and when he looks towards his left he weeps" (Bukhari, 1:345).

On the second level, Muhammad met Jesus and John the son of Zechariah (John the Baptist of Christian tradition). On the third level, he met Joseph, and on the fourth a Prophet named Idris. On the fifth level, he met Aaron, and on the sixth level Moses ("a dark man with a hooked nose"). Finally, he arrived at the seventh heaven, where he met Abraham.

FIGURE. 1.4. *A sixteenth century Islamic painting of the Prophet Muhammad on the heavenly mount Buraq, guided by Gabriel and escorted by angels on his ascent to heaven.*

According to one version of this story, Muhammad also met God himself in the seventh heaven, who imposed on him the requirement of fifty prayers a day. On Muhammad's way down from the seventh heaven, however, Moses stopped him and, after learning how many prayers he had been commanded to perform, explained: "Prayer is a weighty matter and your people are weak, so go back to your Lord and ask him to reduce the number for you and your community" (Ibn Ishaq, 186). Muhammad went back to God, and God removed ten prayers, but Moses insisted that forty was still too many. Again and again, Muhammad went between God and Moses, until the number of prayers had reached five. Moses urged him to ask for a further reduction, but Muhammad explained that he was too embarrassed to go back again. He later explained to his followers that whoever prays the five prayers "in faith and trust will have the reward of fifty prayers" (Ibn Ishaq, 187).

The Prophet's Journey to Medina

Back in Mecca, the Prophet began to look for allies in his struggle against the pagan Quraysh, and he would soon find them in a city to the north named Yathrib. Watt reports that Yathrib—usually described as a settlement built around the cultivation of date palms—suffered from overpopulation. This overpopulation had led the city into "a malaise as serious as that of Mecca" (*Muhammad at Mecca*, 142). Watt's interpretation finds little clear support in the Islamic sources.

For their part, the Islamic sources tell us that the problem in the Yathrib was a long, and at times bloody, conflict between the two principal Arab clans in the settlement. Muhammad was to provide the solution. Members of both clans had heard of his preaching in Mecca. Some of them, on both sides, converted to Islam and looked to Muhammad to resolve their conflict.

Thus the traditional sources relate that (in what would be the year 621) twelve Arabs of Yathrib (presumably a symbolic number, like the twelve apostles of Jesus) met with Muhammad during an annual trading fair at a site outside of Mecca named Aqaba. There they pledged their loyalty to the Prophet (a pledge sometimes known as "pledge of the women" since it did not involve a promise to fight). In the following year, seventy-two Arabs of Yathrib met with Muhammad at Aqaba, swearing now to protect him, even in battle: "By Him Who sent you with the truth we will protect you as we protect our women. We give our allegiance and we are men of war possessing arms which have been passed on from father to son" (Ibn Ishaq, 203).

Thus, Muhammad made up his mind to leave Mecca and to pursue his destiny in Yathrib, soon to be known as the "City of the Prophet" (Ar. *madinat al-nabi*), or simply, Medina. Those Muslims who moved to Medina with the Prophet would be known in Islamic tradition as *muhajirun* ("the migrants"); those Medinans who joined Muhammad's religion would be known as the **ansar** ("the helpers"). The Islamic sources have precious little to say about the resolution of the earlier conflict between the two clans in the settlement—they imply that all of the Arabs were almost immediately unified under the banner of Islam.

Islamic tradition insists that Muhammad had his followers leave for Medina before him, and that the pagan Quraysh let them go freely. Watt suggests that the Quraysh were happy to see the troublesome Muslims leave (although one wonders why the Quraysh once attempted to impede the Muslims' emigration to Ethiopia). Muhammad was one of the last to make the journey, which he arranged to do with his friend Abu Bakr. The only Muslims they would leave behind were Abu Bakr's family and Muhammad's cousin ʿAli, the son of Abu Talib.

Before Muhammad left on his emigration (Ar. *hijra*), he became aware of a Quraysh plot to kill him. They planned—not unlike the assassins of Julius Caesar—to have one man from each clan stab him in his sleep, believing that thereby they would all be safe from vengeance (since Muhammad's followers would not be able to seek revenge from all of the clans). But the angel Gabriel warned the Prophet of their plot. Muhammad thus had ʿAli lay down in his bed on the night of the attack, while he escaped to the desert. According to Tabarī (6:144), when the Quraysh found ʿAli they were furious but eventually let him go unharmed.

Meanwhile, Muhammad, accompanied by Abu Bakr, is said to have departed to a cave south of Mecca (in the opposite direction from Medina), on a mountain named Thawr. There they remained for three days. However, Ibn Ishaq's description of their stay in the cave hardly inspires confidence in its authenticity. He tells us that Abu Bakr instructed his son to come up to the cave every night to relay news from Mecca, and his daughter to come up to the cave with food. If these visits would not have been enough to give away their hideout, presumably Abu Bakr's instructions to a servant to bring his entire flock to the cave at night would have done the job. But the traditional narrative explains that the pagan Quraysh were confounded in their attempts to find Muhammad. Thus the Prophet and

Abu Bakr proceeded to Medina, and ʿAli joined them three days later.

As the young Muslim community settled into a new city, a second dramatic development was about to take place. Just before the *hijra*, Muhammad received a revelation from God permitting him to unsheathe his sword. God told him: "Fight [the unbelievers] until there is no more disorder and the religion is God's alone" (Q 2:193a, my translation). The conflict between Muhammad and Quraysh was soon to be a bloody one.

Muhammad in Mecca and Historical Research

How much of this story told above—based primarily on the traditional biography of Ibn Ishaq—can be considered historically reliable? This is a difficult question to address, and one we will return to in part 2 of this work. For now, we should note that we know of these events only from Islamic sources such as Ibn Ishaq. No pagan, Jewish, or Christian authors who lived at the same time as Muhammad mention them (or him) at all. This does not mean, of course, that the story is entirely legendary. Indeed, if there are no non-Islamic sources that confirm this story, there are also none that contradict it, and much of the account of Muhammad in Mecca could very well have taken place as Ibn Ishaq describes it.

Yet in order to arrive at a closer estimation of the reliability of the traditional story, we must appreciate the nature of the Islamic sources. All of these sources (other than the Qurʾan)

date well after the emergence of Islam. Some of the accounts they relate include fantastic supernatural anecdotes, such as the account of a tree obediently coming forward at the Prophet's call. Other accounts seem simply impractical—as when Muhammad and Abu Bakr successfully escape notice in a cave even though various people and animals visited them regularly.

Finally, the Islamic sources often include contradictory versions of the same account. As we saw, Ibn Ishaq describes Muhammad's physical night journey to Jerusalem but then quotes a tradition in which ʿAʾisha insists that he journeyed only in spirit. In a further tradition (found in Bukhari), we find that the night journey skips Jerusalem entirely. Here it is combined with the story of the washing of Muhammad's heart, and Muhammad travels directly from Mecca to heaven, skipping Jerusalem: "While I was at Mecca the roof of my house was opened and Gabriel descended, opened my chest, and washed it with zam-zam water. Then he brought a golden tray full of wisdom and faith and having poured its contents into my chest, he closed it. Then he took my hand and ascended with me to the nearest heaven" (Bukhari, 1:345).

In brief, it is difficult to know how much the traditional narrative of Muhammad in Mecca tells us about the Muhammad of history. But it does teach us two important lessons about the Muhammad in whom Muslims believe: First, Muhammad did not found a new religion but rather preached anew the very religion that Abraham, Moses, and Jesus preached before him; second, Muhammad and his followers, not unlike the Israelites in Egypt, suffered abuse and persecution in Mecca. Their state of affairs, however, was soon to change dramatically.

STUDY QUESTIONS

1 Describe the traditional Islamic portrayal of pre-Islamic Mecca. What role does this portrayal have in the biography of the prophet Muhammad?

2 Who were Bahira and Waraqa? What function do they have in the biography of the Prophet?

3 What is the symbolic importance of the story of Muhammad's night journey and ascent to heaven?

4 What are the principal differences between the two stories of emigration (the first to Ethiopia; the second to Yathrib/Medina)?

Chapter 2

MUHAMMAD IN MEDINA

When it was the day of Badr, and the Messenger of God looked at the polytheists and their number, and then looked at his companions, who were something over three hundred, he turned toward [Mecca] and began to pray, saying, "O God, fulfill what you have promised me. O God, if this band of Muslims perishes, you will not be worshipped on the earth." He continued to say this until his cloak fell off. Abu Bakr picked it up and put it back on him, then grasped him from behind and said, "O Prophet of God, whom I value more than my father and mother, this is enough of calling upon your Lord. He will assuredly fulfill what he has promised you." Then God revealed, "When ye sought help of your Lord and he answered you (saying): I will help you with a thousand of the angels, rank on rank."

— *The History of al-Tabari* 7:54

The Fight for Islam

The Prophet's migration from Mecca to Medina held such great significance to later Muslims that they chose it to mark the beginning of the Islamic calendar. Thus Islamic years are abbreviated AH, from the Latin *anno hegirae*, "in the year of the *hijra*." (One Islamic year corresponds to twelve cycles of the moon, not the revolution of the earth around the sun, and so it is shorter than the standard Gregorian year.) This choice suggests that the key moment in Islam's emergence was not the birth (570 CE) or the death (632 CE) of the Prophet, or the year in which he was called by God (610 CE), but rather his arrival in Medina (622 CE), where Islamic rules would first be established and Islamic law enforced.

In fact, the move to Medina is a watershed in the traditional biography of Muhammad. From this point on, Tabari changes the organization of his history. He now groups his reports Islamic year by Islamic year. Moreover, Ibn Ishaq and Tabari (and most other biographers) now focus their attention above all on the Prophet's battles against and raids on the unbelievers. A third early historian, al-Waqidi, names his biography of Muhammad simply "The Book of Raids [*maghazi*]."

For all of these biographers, the Prophet's call in Medina for an Islamic holy war (or jihad) is not a problem to explain away but a pious act to celebrate. We see this conviction in a *hadith* preserved by Bukhari:

> A man came to Allah's Apostle and said, "Instruct me as to such a deed as equals Jihad [in reward]." He replied, "I do not find such a deed." Then he added, "Can you, while the Muslim fighter is in the battle-field, enter your mosque to perform prayers without cease and fast and never break your fast?" The man said, "But who can do that?" (Bukhari, 4:44)

Today, however, jihad is a controversial topic. Anti-Islamic polemicists, following a long tradition of Western caricatures, often present Muhammad as an immoral, intolerant, and merciless bandit who converted people to Islam by the sword. Robert Spencer titles one of his recent books to this effect: *The Truth about Muhammad: Founder of the World's Most Intolerant Religion*. For their part, some apologists, deliberately ignoring the most ancient Islamic traditions, present Muhammad as a peace activist. Muhammad Abdel Haleem, for instance, writes that Muhammad fought all of his raids in self-defense, even if Ibn Ishaq reports that the Prophet "went forth raiding" (281) almost immediately after his arrival in Medina (only to be frustrated when he could not find any Quraysh to attack). A recent book by Juan Cole refers to Muhammad as "The Prophet of Peace."

Later in this work, I will discuss further the question of the Prophet's moral standing on matters such as war. For now, we simply note that for the authors of the classical sources the Prophet's moral standing is not a problem. The Prophet's feats in war are miraculous signs of divine blessing, similar to his other miraculous signs, such as the tree that came forth to meet Muhammad. The point of stories in which Muhammad outsmarts, outmaneuvers, and triumphs over superior forces in battle is neither that war is good or bad, nor that Muhammad always acted in self-defense or with aggression. Rather, the point is that only a prophet could do such a thing. We might compare the attitude about war in the classical Islamic sources to the flag of Saudi Arabia today, which presents the words "There is no god but God and Muhammad is His messenger" written above an unsheathed sword. The sword is a sign of Muhammad's victories in battle, and those victories are a sign that he is the messenger of God.

FROM A CLASSIC TEXT ❖ 2.1

Hadith on the Virtues of the Prophet

Bukhari named his collection of hadith (that is, reports or statements attributed to Muhammad) "The Valid" (Ar. sahih) because of his conviction that the hadith it contains relate the very words or deeds of the Prophet himself, perfectly preserved by a process of oral transmission. Yet the relevance of the hadith he includes to the context of the medieval Islamic world suggests that may date from a period well after the life of the Prophet.

The hadith in Bukhari's book "Virtures and Merits of the Prophet and His Companions" give to Muhammad those qualities that medieval Muslim scholars considered proper for all Muslims, or miracles meant to prove that Muhammad was a prophet. Other hadith seem to respond to the curiosity of Muslims, for whom drawings or paintings of Muhammad were forbidden, to visualize Muhammad's appearance. Later mystical (or Ṣufi) works make Muhammad a mystic who experienced a certain unity with God and who taught his followers to value above all the hidden mysteries of the faith. Thus in Islamic tradition the figure of Muhammad appears above all through the lens of the faith of later Muslims.

The Example of the Prophet

(*on Muhammad's fidelity to the Islamic law*)

Narrated ʿAʾisha:

The people of Quraish worried about the lady from Bani Makhzum who had committed theft. They asked, "Who will intercede for her with Allah's Apostle?" Some said, "No one dared to do so except Usama bin Zaid the beloved one to Allah's Apostle." When Usama spoke about that to Allah's Apostle, Allah's Apostle said (to him), "Do you try to intercede for somebody in a case connected with Allah's Prescribed Punishments?" Then he got up and delivered a sermon saying, "What destroyed the nations preceding you, was that if a noble amongst them stole, they would forgive him, and if a poor person amongst them stole, they would inflict Allah's Legal punishment on him. By Allah, if Fatima, the daughter of Muhammad stole, I would cut off her hand." (Bukhari, 4:681)

Narrated ʿAʾisha:

Whenever Allah's Apostle was given the choice of one of two matters, he would choose the easier of the two, as long as it was not sinful to do so, but if it was sinful to do so, he would not approach it. Allah's Apostle never took revenge (over anybody) for his own sake but (he did) only when Allah's Legal Bindings were outraged in which case he would take revenge for Allah's Sake. (Bukhari, 4:760)

(on Muhammad's acceptance of different readings of the Qur'an)

Narrated Ibn Mas'ud:

I heard a person reciting a (Quranic) Verse in a certain way, and I had heard the Prophet reciting the same Verse in a different way. So I took him to the Prophet and informed him of that but I noticed the sign of disapproval on his face, and then he said, "Both of you are correct, so don't differ, for the nations before you differed, so they were destroyed." (Bukhari 4:682)

(On good manners)

Narrated Abu Huraira:

The Prophet never criticized any food (presented him), but he would eat it if he liked it; otherwise, he would leave it (without expressing his dislike). (Bukhari, 4:764)

The Miracles of the Prophet

(The Multiplication of Loaves)

Narrated Anas bin Malik:

Abu Talha said to Um Sulaim, "I have noticed feebleness in the voice of Allah's Apostle which I think, is caused by hunger. Have you got any food?" She said, "Yes." She brought out some loaves of barley and took out a veil belonging to her, and wrapped the bread in part of it and put it under my arm and wrapped part of the veil round me and sent me to Allah's Apostle. I went carrying it and found Allah's Apostle in the Mosque sitting with some people. When I stood there, Allah's Apostle asked, "Has Abu Talha sent you?" I said, "Yes." He asked, "With some food?" I said, "Yes." Allah's Apostle then said to the men around him, "Get up!" He set out (accompanied by them) and I went ahead of them till I reached Abu Talha and told him (of the Prophet's visit). Abu Talha said, "O Um Sulaim! Allah's Apostle is coming with the people and we have no food to feed them." She said, "Allah and His Apostle know better." So Abu Talha went out to receive Allah's Apostle. Allah's Apostle came along with Abu Talha. Allah's Apostle said, "O Um Sulaim! Bring whatever you have." She brought the bread which Allah's Apostle ordered to be broken into pieces. Um Sulaim poured on them some butter from an oilskin. Then Allah's Apostle recited what Allah wished him to recite, and then said, "Let ten persons come (to share the meal)." Ten persons were admitted, ate their fill and went out. Then he again said, "Let another ten do the same." They were admitted, ate their fill and went out. Then he again said, "Let another ten persons (do the same.)" They were admitted, ate their fill and went out. Then he said, "Let another ten persons come." In short, all of them ate their fill, and they were seventy or eighty men. (Bukhari, 4:778)

(*Spraying water from his fingertips*)

Narrated ʿAbdallah:

We used to consider miracles as Allah's Blessings, but you people consider them to be a warning. Once we were with Allah's Apostle on a journey, and we ran short of water. He said, "Bring the water remaining with you." The people brought a utensil containing a little water. He placed his hand in it and said, "Come to the blessed water, and the Blessing is from Allah." I saw the water flowing from among the fingers of Allah's Apostle, and no doubt, we heard the meal glorifying Allah, when it was being eaten (by him). (Bukhari, 4:779)

(*Mastery over the rain*)

Narrated Anas:

Once during the lifetime of Allah's Apostle, the people of Medina suffered from drought. So while the Prophet was delivering a sermon on a Friday a man got up saying, "O Allah's Apostle! The horses and sheep have perished. Will you invoke Allah to bless us with rain?" The Prophet lifted both his hands and invoked. The sky at that time was as clear as glass. Suddenly a wind blew, raising clouds that gathered together, and it started raining heavily. We came out (of the Mosque) wading through the flowing water till we reached our homes. It went on raining till the next Friday, when the same man or some other man stood up and said, "O Allah's Apostle! The houses have collapsed; please invoke Allah to withhold the rain." On that the Prophet smiled and said, "O Allah, (let it rain) around us and not on us." I then looked at the clouds to see them separating forming a sort of a crown round Medina. (Bukhari, 4:782)

(*A crying tree-trunk*)

Narrated Ibn ʿUmar:

The Prophet used to deliver his sermons while standing beside a trunk of a datepalm. When he had the pulpit made, he used it instead. The trunk started crying and the Prophet went to it, rubbing his hand over it (to stop its crying). (Bukhari, 4:783)

(*Giving the power of memory to a companion known for reporting hadith*)

Narrated Abu Huraira:

I said, "O Allah's Apostle! I hear many narrations from you but I forget them." He said, "Spread your covering sheet." I spread my sheet and he moved both his hands as if scooping something and emptied them in the sheet and said, "Wrap it." I wrapped it round my body, and since then I have never forgotten a single Hadith. (Bukhari, 4:84)

The Appearance of the Prophet

Narrated Rabia bin Abi Abdur-Rahman:

I heard Anas bin Malik describing the Prophet saying, "He was of medium height amongst the people, neither tall nor short; he had a rosy color, neither absolutely white nor deep brown; his hair was neither completely curly nor quite lank. Divine Inspiration was revealed to him when he was forty years old. He stayed ten years in Mecca receiving the Divine Inspiration, and stayed in Medina for ten more years. When he expired, he had scarcely twenty white hairs in his head and beard." Rabi'a said, "I saw some of his hairs and it was red. When I asked about that, I was told that it turned red because of scent." (Bukhari, 4:747)

Narrated Al-Bara:

Allah's Apostle was the handsomest of all the people, and had the best appearance. He was neither very tall nor short. (Bukhari, 4:749)

Narrated Anas:

I have never touched silk or Dibaj (i.e., thick silk) softer than the palm of the Prophet nor have I smelt a perfume nicer than the sweat of the Prophet (Bukhari, 4:761)

The Mysticism of the Prophet

We said, "Prophet of God, whenever we see you, our hearts grow soft and we become like the people of the Hereafter. When we leave your company, this world becomes attractive to us and we embrace women and children." The Prophet said, "If you were to remain at all times in the condition in which you were when you were with me, the angels would shake your hands with their very own, and visit you in your houses" (Ibn Hanbal [d. 855], *Musnad*, trans. T. Khalidi, *Images of Muhammad*, 164–65)

"The Prophet was asked about the best kind of jihad. He replied, "It is a just word in the presence of an unjust ruler." (al-Qushayri [d. 1072], *Epistle on Sufism*, trans. T. Khalidi, *Images of Muhammad*, 166)

The Respectfulness of the Prophet

(*On respecting the dead of other religions*)

Narrated ʿAbdur Rahman bin Abi Laila:

Sahl bin Hunaif and Qais bin Sad were sitting in the city of Al-Qadisiya. A funeral procession passed in front of them and they stood up. They were told that funeral procession was of one of the inhabitants of the land, i.e., of a non-believer, under the protection of Muslims. They said, "A funeral procession passed in front of the Prophet and he stood up. When he was told that it was the coffin of a Jew, he said, "Is it not a living being (soul)?" (Bukhari, 2:399)

FIGURE 2.1. *The Prophet's mosque in Medina.*

The Great Battle of Badr

Thus Ibn Ishaq describes with pride, and not with embarrassment or consternation, the manner in which the small band of Muslims in Medina began attacking the Quraysh. After a number of raids that ended, for the most part, without bloodshed, Muhammad decided (about twenty months after his emigration from Mecca) to ambush a caravan of the Quraysh at Badr, a site near Medina. Abu Sufyan, one of Muhammad's fiercest opponents in Mecca, was leading the caravan, which was returning from Damascus on its way to Mecca. Initially it seemed that Muhammad's plot would end in disaster. A woman in Mecca had a vision and divulged his plans, and a man named Damdam rushed to Mecca after learning of the ambush and did the same. Although the chronology seems improbable, Ibn Ishaq tells us that the Meccans found the time to organize a large force—led by an impious man named Abu Jahl—that met up with Abu Sufyan's caravan before Muhammad could launch his ambush.

The Muslims, however, were not discouraged. One of them, referring to the Israelites who refused to fight with Moses when they heard reports of a people of giants living in the promised land (Num 13), exclaimed, "We will not say as the children of Israel said to Moses, 'You and your Lord go and fight and we will stay at home" (see Q 5:24), but you and your Lord go and fight, and we will fight with you" (Ibn Ishaq, 293–94). What is more, God was with them: he sent a rain that miraculously hindered the progress of the Quraysh but not that of the Muslims.

Before the battle, Muhammad had his forces block up the wells in reach of the Quraysh and secure their own water in a cistern. Soon a series of individual contests took place—not unlike that between Achilles and Hector before the walls of Troy. Finally, the fighting began. Ibn Ishaq reports: "The apostle took a handful of small pebbles and said, turning towards Quraysh, 'Foul be those faces!' Then he threw the pebbles at them and ordered his companions to charge. The foe was routed" (Ibn Ishaq, 303).

Ibn Ishaq explains that the Muslims received the help of angels. He quotes a veteran of the battle of Badr who told his companions, "If I were in Badr today and had my sight I could show you the glen from which the angels emerged." Another Muslim warrior remembers, "I was pursuing a polytheist at Badr to smite him, when his head fell off before I could get at him with my sword" (Ibn Ishaq, 303). Muhammad himself considered the defeat of the polytheists a divine act. When he inspected the severed head of Abu Jahl, the leader of the forces that had come from Mecca, he gave praise to God.

Muhammad's praise on this occasion might be compared to that of Moses, who in the book of Exodus leads the Israelites in a song of praise to Yahweh after the demise of the Egyptians in the Sea, shouting, "Horse and rider He has thrown into the sea!" In Exodus Yahweh triumphs over the Egyptians who had enslaved his people and provoked his wrath with their disdain for Him. In the biography of Muhammad, the God of Islam triumphs at Badr over those who had defied him with their unbelief. Badr is thus a story that expresses the sentiment of the Muslim slogan: *Allahu akbar*, "God is *greater*" (not "God is the greatest," as it is often translated).

The story of Badr, in other words, is shaped as a lesson on the power and might of a God who humiliates those who challenge him. The importance of this lesson to Ibn Ishaq is evident from the unusual attention he pays to this account. He describes the birth of Muhammad in less than a page, Muhammad's call to prophecy on Mount Ḥiraʾ in a page and a half; to the description of the Battle of Badr Ibn Ishaq dedicates twenty-five pages. To this he adds twelve pages of lists of the Muslims who fought at Badr, the polytheists who were killed there, and the polytheists who were taken captive there, and twenty-one pages of poetry about the battle.

Badr and Muhammad

The story of Badr, nevertheless, is still very much about Muhammad. The Qurʾan insists that there is no separating devotion to God and devotion to Muhammad: "Say: 'Obey God, and the Messenger.' But if they turn their backs, God loves not the unbelievers" (Q 3:32). The Islamic profession of faith, moreover, involves more than monotheism. It also involves the belief that Muhammad is the Prophet of God. And to Muslims, Muhammad is not just any prophet. He is the last prophet and the greatest prophet. No person ever has, or ever will, match Muhammad's virtue. To Muslims, then, the Battle of Badr is also a story of Muhammad's greatness.

Although Muslims do not consider Muhammad divine, their veneration of him can hardly be overestimated. When the Wahhabi movement spread in the Arabian Peninsula in the late eighteenth century, they insisted on destroying the tomb-shrines of Muslim mystics and other holy figures. They did not, however, touch the tomb of Muhammad, which remains a site of veneration in Medina (although it is kept out of view). Similarly, over the centuries, most Muslim leaders (although not the Taliban) have come to permit figural representations of people in books (which many early Muslim jurists thought of as a sort of idolatry). Almost none, however, will allow Muhammad to be represented, whether in an image, statue or even on film. In the 1976 film *The Message*, the narrative of which centers on the story of Muhammad's life, Muhammad himself is neither seen nor heard.

To this end, it might be added that insults of God may pass without notice in the Islamic world, but insults of Muhammad inevitably lead to public outrage, and sometimes to bloodshed. In part, this eagerness to defend Muhammad might be inspired by the reports in his biography that suggest that the Prophet did not take insults lightly. Ibn Ishaq tells the story of Uqba, a man who had maligned the Prophet in Mecca before being taken prisoner at the Battle of Badr. Although Muhammad spared other Meccan prisoners that day, he ordered Uqba to be killed, even after Uqba protested, "But who will look after my children, O Muhammad?" (Ibn Ishaq, 308).

Muhammad's Relationships in Medina

If battles are at the center of the traditional biography of the Prophet, his marriages still have a significant place in them as well. Ibn Ishaq reports that after Khadija died, but before Muhammad left Mecca, he married an older woman named Sawda and was betrothed to ʿAʾisha, the young daughter of Abu Bakr. ʿAʾisha, however, was so young at the time of the betrothal, Ibn Ishaq explains, that their marriage was only consummated after the Prophet's arrival in Medina.

The Mothers of the Believers

Sunni tradition gives ʿAʾisha a special position among the Prophet's wives (although the same is not true, as we will see, in Shiʿite tradition). In a tradition cited by Tabari, she boasts of nine virtues that distinguish her from the Prophet's other wives.

> The angel brought down my likeness; the Messenger of God married me when I was seven; my marriage was consummated when I was nine; he married me when I was a virgin, no other man having shared me with him; inspiration came to him when he and I were in a single blanket; I was one of the dearest people to him; a verse of the Qurʾan was revealed concerning me when the community was almost destroyed; I saw Gabriel when none of his other wives saw him; and he was taken [that is, died] in his house when there was nobody with him but the angel and myself. (Tabari, 7:7)

'A'isha's tone of boasting in this tradition suggests that she, or (if this tradition is a later forgery) the author of the tradition, considered her young age at the time of her marriage to the Prophet to be a virtue. Evidently this tradition shows no concern for modern ideas regarding a minimum age for marriage. Many modern Muslims, of course, are concerned for such things. Accordingly, Salih Al-Wardadi, author of the 1997 work *Difa' 'an al-rasul did al-fuqaha' wa-l-muhaddithun* ("the defense of the Messenger from jurisprudents and theologians"), rejects the tradition of 'A'isha's young age. Al-Wardadi, after noting the contradictions between various reports on the Prophet's marriage to 'A'isha (including a report that has her married to a man named Jubayr *before* Muhammad), argues that these reports are false, that they were invented in order to distinguish 'A'isha from the Prophet's other wives, and from the older Khadija in particular.

Personalities in Islam 2.1
'A'ISHA

In Ibn Ishaq's biography of the Prophet, Muhammad spends the final moments of his life close to his young wife 'A'isha. She softens a stick for him to chew on and, when Muhammad informs her that the moment of his death has arrived, she proclaims, "You were given the choice and you have chosen, by Him Who sent you with the truth!" (Ibn Ishaq, 682). This scene illustrates the principal role of 'A'isha in the biography of the Prophet: She is Muhammad's intimate companion, who knows the private details of his life. Accordingly, many of the *hadith* that purport to preserve something of the Prophet's personal habits are told on her authority: "Narrated 'A'isha: Whenever Allah's Apostle took a bath of Janaba [ritual washing after sexual relations], he washed his hands first" (Bukhari, 1:262); "Narrated 'A'isha: The Prophet said, "Fever is from the heat of the (Hell) Fire, so cool it with water" (Bukhari, 4:485); "Narrated 'A'isha: I used to perfume Allah's Apostle with the best scent available till I saw the shine of the scent on his head and beard" (Bukhari, 7:806).

The traditional biography of the Prophet seems to emphasize the intimacy between Muhammad and 'A'isha. Ibn Ishaq does not shy away from describing Muhammad's passionate love for 'A'isha or the degree of influence that she had over him; indeed, he seems to emphasize both. 'A'isha's influential personality also appears in the accounts of her conduct after the Prophet's death. She actively supports her father, Abu Bakr, when he is named caliph, condemning the partisans of 'Ali for their hesitation to acknowledge his authority. Moreover, when 'Ali is finally elected, (the fourth) caliph, 'A'isha, organizes a force to oppose him and only relents when she is defeated at the "Battle of the Camel" (so-named because 'A'isha watched the battle from her perch on a camel's back).

Similarly, classical Muslim authors are not worried by Muhammad's polygamy. Although modern authors often explain away the Prophet's polygamy by arguing that he married for political or social reasons, the authors of the classical Islamic sources never see it as a problem. In these works, the authors consider the wives of Muhammad—known in Islamic tradition as the "mothers of the believers"—to be honored and blessed by their union with him. And if Muhammad married more than the four wives allowed to other Muslims, he did so because God himself granted him this privilege. Indeed, the sources describe how God intervened in his marital life on more than one occasion.

One day while in Medina, his biographers relate, Muhammad went to visit his adopted son Zayd. When Muhammad arrived at Zayd's house, however, he happened to see Zayd's wife Zaynab without a veil, and he was smitten by her beauty. Zayd soon learned what had happened and immediately offered to divorce Zaynab so that Muhammad could marry her. The Prophet hesitated, but God granted him permission to do so in a revelation: "So when Zayd had accomplished what he would of her, then We gave her in marriage to thee" (Q 33:37).

This was not the only time that God intervened in the Prophet's marital life. According to the traditional narrative, toward the end of his life a ruler in Alexandria gave Muhammad a Christian Egyptian girl named Mariyya as a gift. The sources disagree on whether the Prophet married Mariyya or she remained his concubine, but many of them report that he was so attracted to her that he lay with her in bed on a night when he was supposed to be with his wife Hafsa (daughter of ʿUmar), and that he did so in Hafsa's bed to boot. When Hafsa found the two together, she became so angry that the Prophet, in order to calm her, swore he would never touch Mariyya again. God, however, revealed Qurʾan 33:51: "Thou mayest put off whom thou wilt of them, and whom thou wilt thou mayest take to thee." Hearing of this new revelation, ʿAʾisha proclaimed, "I feel that your Lord hastens in fulfilling your wishes and desires" (Bukhari, 6:311).

Most traditional sources report that Muhammad had thirteen wives in all, although those sources that count Mariyya and a Jewish woman from Medina named Rayhana as wives (and not concubines) may raise that number to fifteen. Some of his wives, including Hafsa, the daughter of ʿUmar, had become widows when their husbands were killed while fighting Meccans. The Prophet's decision to marry them, therefore, is appropriately presented as an act of compassion and as a manner of honoring their former husbands, martyrs in the struggle for Islam.

Muhammad and the Jews

In Medina, the struggle for Islam was no longer exclusively a question of confronting pagans. According to Ibn Ishaq, the city of Medina was dominated by three Jewish tribes, and when Muhammad arrived he sought their allegiance. He even established a sort of treaty with the Jews—known today as the "Constitution of Medina"—a treaty that required each community to help the other. This document, Ibn Ishaq relates, began as follows.

> In the name of God the Compassionate, the Merciful. This is a document from Muhammad the prophet between the believers and Muslims of Quraysh and Yathrib [i.e., Medina], and those who followed them and joined them and labored with them. They are one community to the exclusion of all men. (Ibn Ishaq, 231–32)

Some Western scholars argue that during this early period in Medina, Muhammad shaped even his religious teaching in order to win the support of the Jews. They find proof for this idea in the traditional report that while in Medina Muhammad instructed the Muslims to follow the Jewish Yom Kippur fast and to pray toward Jerusalem, the Jewish direction of prayer.

BOX 2.1 ❖ DAILY PRAYERS

According to the doctrine of Sunnis and Shiʿites alike, all Muslims are obliged to perform five prayers a day. Indeed, according to one school of Sunni jurisprudence (the Hanbali school), failure to do so is enough to make one an unbeliever. The doctrine of five daily prayers, however, is based not on the Qurʾan but on the hadith. The Qurʾan itself refers only to three times of prayer (Q 24:58 mentions prayer at dawn and at night; Q 2:238 and 17:78 refer to a "middle prayer"). For this reason, some members of the contemporary "Qurʾanist" movement (according to whom Islam should be based on the Qurʾan alone) recognize only three daily prayers, and Shiʿites generally permit the five daily prayers to be combined so as to be completed during only three sessions.

According to Islamic belief, God imposed these prayers on humanity. The angel Gabriel taught Muhammad every word, and every movement, of each prayer. Muhammad's followers imitated his manner of praying, and Muslims today are to do the same. Muslims may add personal invocations before or after their obligatory prayers, but the obligatory prayers are to be performed according to the standard Islamic formula. Thus all Muslims pray in Arabic (whatever their native language and whether or not they understand Arabic), since God, through the angel Gabriel, taught Muhammad his prayers in Arabic. Nevertheless, there are a fair number of details surrounding the daily prayers (from the proper position of the hands, to the number of prostrations, to the manner of performing the obligatory washing beforehand), which are the subject of disagreement between Muslim scholars.

Muslims generally agree, however, that when praying, the believer must be oriented toward the Islamic **qibla**, or proper direction, namely the Kaʿba in Mecca. For this reason, all mosques include a small niche (known as a *mihrab*) to indicate the direction of Mecca. Today Muslims may also use mobile devices with GPS to locate the *qibla* from any place in the world.

However, Muhammad's friendly relationship with the Jews did not last long. Several months before the Battle of Badr, according to the traditional sources, God commanded Muhammad to change the direction of prayer, or *qibla*, to Mecca, or, more specifically, to the Kaʿba. At the time when God revealed this command, Muhammad was in the midst of his prayer prostrations, and facing Jerusalem, to the north. He stood up, turned around, and made his next prostration toward the south. (Today a mosque in Medina known as "The Mosque of Two Qiblas" commemorates this event.) Around this same time—another tradition reports—God also revealed Qurʾan 2:185, which instituted a fast for the Arab month of Ramadan.

BOX 2.2 ❖ RAMADAN FAST

Muslims generally consider the Ramadan fast, like the Meccan pilgrimage, to be one of the five pillars of Islam (the other three being the profession of faith, prayer, and almsgiving). Ramadan is the only month mentioned in the Qurʾan by name. The second sura declares that the "Qurʾan" was sent down in the month of Ramadan; it adds: "And whosoever of you is present, let him fast the month" (Q 2:185). Two verses later, the Qurʾan announces to its audience, "It is permissible to go into your wives during the night of the fast" and adds, "so eat and drink until you can distinguish a white thread from a black thread" (that is, by virtue of the morning light; Q 2:187).

Later Muslim scholars established precise instructions for the Ramadan fast. Muslims, according to most of these scholars, are to fast from eating, drinking, smoking, and engaging in sexual relations during daylight hours (although certain people, such as those who are traveling or women in menstruation, are exempt). At night, all of these activities are permissible, and in the Islamic world the nights of Ramadan often have a festal atmosphere. In a number of hadith, the Prophet promises heavenly benefits to those who fast well during Ramadan. The angels, according to one tradition, implore God to forgive all of the sins of those who are fasting until the moment they break their fast in the evening.

To many Western scholars, the new direction of prayer and the new fast are signs that Muhammad, frustrated in his attempt to win the allegiance of the Jews, had decided to give Islam an Arab character. William Montgomery Watt explains Muhammad's decision accordingly.

> So long as Muhammad claimed to be receiving revelations identical in essence with the revelation in the hands of the Jews, they were in a strong position, and could either support Muhammad by acknowledging the similarity or hinder his cause by drawing attention to differences. It was mostly the latter that they chose to do, and consequently they threatened to undermine the intellectual foundations of his political and religious position. (Watt, *Muhammad at Medina*, 204)

For his part, Maxime Rodinson argues that when Muhammad turned away from the Jews, he decided to shape his preaching around the notion that the Arabs were heirs of Abraham's monotheistic legacy.

> From then on, from an ideological point of view, the situation was reversed. It was no longer Muhammad, the untutored son of a barbarous and idolatrous people without scriptures or Law, who was entering into the community of the keepers of the revelation of Moses. It was the Jews, the faithless children of those to whom that revelation had been addressed, who were called upon to confess the truth of the messages which Allah sent to a descendant of their common ancestor. (Rodinson, 187)

However, Ibn Ishaq puts the change in the Islamic *qibla*, and the institution of the Ramadan fast, before Muhammad's first conflict with the Jews (a sequence of events which would not seem to confirm the ideas of Watt and Rodinson).

Muhammad, Ibn Ishaq explains, first confronted the Jews some time after the Battle of Badr, when he accused one of the three Jewish tribes of Medina, Banu Qaynuqa, of treachery against him:

> The apostle assembled [Banu Qaynuqa] in their market and addressed them as follows: "O Jews, beware lest God bring upon you the vengeance that He brought upon Quraysh and become Muslims. You know that I am a prophet who has been sent—you will find that in your scriptures and God's covenant with you." They replied, "O Muhammad, you seem to think that we are your people. Do not deceive yourself because you encountered a people with no knowledge of war and got the better of them; for by God if we fight you, you will find that we are real men!" (Ibn Ishaq, 363)

Fighting did indeed soon break out between the Muslims and Banu Qaynuqa, but it was the Muslims who proved to be the "real men." Banu Qaynuqa surrendered, and the Prophet expelled them from the city.

A similar fate awaited a second Jewish tribe, Banu Nadir. According to Ibn Ishaq, one of the Jews of this tribe plotted to kill Muhammad at some point after the Battle of Uhud, the second major confrontation between the Meccans and the Quraysh (about which I will comment below). He climbed up on top of a house while the Prophet was sitting below and prepared to throw a rock on him, but "news came to [Muhammad] from heaven . . . so he got up and he went back to Medina" (Ibn Ishaq, 437). Muhammad then called for a raid against Banu Nadir and had their palm trees (on which they counted for the harvest of dates) cut down and burned. The Jews surrendered to the Prophet, who sent them, like the Banu Qaynuqa, into exile.

A more ominous fate was in store for a third Jewish tribe, the Banu Qurayza. The traditional sources report that Banu Qurayza offered to cooperate with the Quraysh against the Muslims in a third battle, the Battle of the Trench (AH 5/627 CE). The planned cooperation fell through (in part because Banu Qurayza refused to fight on the Sabbath), and the offensive of the Quraysh failed. However, the angel Gabriel informed Muhammad of the Jews' evil intentions, and the Prophet attacked them. Besieged, the Banu Qurayza submitted themselves, as had the other two Jewish tribes, to Muhammad's mercy. On this occasion, however, little mercy was forthcoming. He ordered their men beheaded and their women and children enslaved. Then he divided the property of the Banu Qurayza among the Muslims, after first taking possession of one-fifth of it himself, his regular share of booty.

Muhammad and the Christians

Thus the traditional sources insist that the Prophet's relationship with Jews was marked by confrontation and, ultimately, bloodshed. The Prophet's relationship with Christians, however, is described in different terms. Ibn Ishaq relates that soon after the Prophet arrived in Medina, before the Battle of Badr, a deputation of sixty Christians came to visit him from the Yemeni city of Najran.

It is hard to imagine that Muhammad—when he had so few followers—would have attracted this sort of a deputation, and from so far away (it would have taken a caravan no less than thirty days to reach Medina from Najran). Nevertheless, Ibn Ishaq recounts in detailed fashion how one day the Christians of Najran entered Medina wearing sumptuous robes while Muhammad was at afternoon prayer. He greeted them, and when the time came for the Christians to pray, the Prophet allowed them to do so in his mosque.

Ibn Ishaq then informs the reader that the Christians in the delegation from Najran were divided over their teaching on Christ. He reports that one group among them declared that Christ was "God," because "he used to raise the dead, and heal the sick, and declare the unseen, and make clay birds and then breathe into them so that they flew away [Q 3:49; 5:110]"; a second group declared that he was "Son of God" because "he had no known father; and he spoke in the cradle [Q 3:46; 19:30–33]"; a third group declared that he was the "third of three" (cf. Q 5:73) because God says, "We have done" instead of "I have done" (Ibn Ishaq, 271).

While the division of Christians into three groups reflects the division of the Eastern church in the Middle Ages into Melkites (or Chalcedonians), Miaphysites, and Nestorians (or East Syrians), the manner in which Ibn Ishaq defines the three groups of the delegation of Najran does not. He seems to have imagined how three Christian groups might have been divided on the basis of the Qur'an. The miracles of Jesus with which he associates the first group come from the Qur'an; the idea that Christians would argue that Christ is "Son of God" on the basis of the Virgin Birth is implied by the Qur'an, and the description of God as "the third of three" (Q 5:73) is an accusation made by the Qur'an against unbelievers. Moreover, the very idea that the Christians were divided among themselves may be taken from the Qur'an, in which God announces, "We have stirred up among [the Christians] enmity and hatred, till the Day of Resurrection" (Q 5:14).

Otherwise, the story of the deputation of Christians seems to have been written to explain why a large section of the Qur'an's third sura (titled "The Family of Imran") is dedicated to Christians. To this end, Ibn Ishaq relates:

> The apostle said [to the deputation of Christians], "Submit yourselves." They said, "We have submitted." He said: "You have not submitted, so submit." They said, "Nay, but we submitted before you." He said, "You lie. Your assertion that God has a son, your worship of the cross, and your eating pork hold you back from submission." They said, "But who is his father, Muhammad?" The apostle was silent and did not answer them. So God sent down concerning their words and their incoherence the beginning of the Sura of the Family of Imran. (Ibn Ishaq, 272)

Ibn Ishaq proceeds to quote much of this sura, including verse 59, which compares Jesus to Adam. He has Muhammad explain to the Christians that the creation of Jesus without a father is "no more wonderful" than the creation of Adam with neither a father nor a mother. Finally, Muhammad challenges the Christians to a sort of ordeal in which God's curse would come upon the party that lied. Before the ordeal takes place however, the Christian deputation gives up, backing down from the challenge and turning around to begin the long journey back to Najran.

The story of the ordeal (which seems peculiar, since nowhere else in the Prophet's biography do we read of such a practice) is meant to explain the verses that follow, in sura 3. In verse 61, the Qur'an declares, "And whoso disputes with thee concerning him, after the knowledge that has come to thee, say: 'Come now, let us call our sons and your sons, our wives and your wives, ourselves and your selves, then let us humbly pray and so lay God's curse upon the ones who lie.'" Two verses later, the Qur'an explains, "And if they turn their backs, assuredly God knows the workers of corruption."

In any case, this story illustrates an important difference in the way the classical sources portray Muhammad's relations with the Jews and the Christians. The Jews are the personal opponents of Muhammad. As they turned against Moses in the Old Testament, and Jesus in the New Testament, they now turn against Muhammad. On the one hand, this portrayal of the Jews as a stubborn and vindictive people reflects the Qur'an's description of them as the killers of prophets (Q 4:155), a people whose hearts God has hardened (Q 5:13), and a people who, along with the polytheists, are the most severe in their enmity to Muslims (Q 5:82).

The Christians, on the other hand, have gone astray in their beliefs, not in their deeds. Indeed, they may have friendly relations with the believers (see Q 5:82)—as did the king of Ethiopia and the deputation from Najran—but their teaching on Christ is an offense against God.

The Triumph of Islam

In any case, the central drama of the traditional biography of Muhammad is neither his relationship with the Jews nor his relationship with the Christians but rather his confrontation with the pagans. Only three months after the Battle of Badr, the classical sources relate, the Quraysh, seeking revenge, organized a force of some three thousand men—several times that at Badr—and marched to Medina. They circled around to the north side of Medina and took up a position at the foot of a mountain named Uhud. When Muhammad prepared for battle, some of his followers insisted that it would be wiser to stay within the city, but he explained, "It is not fitting that a prophet who has put on his armor should lay it aside until he has fought" (Ibn Ishaq, 372).

Muhammad's Ultimate Victory over the Pagans

The Muslims set out in the evening and surreptitiously found their way around the Quraysh. The next morning, they were on the slopes of the mountain itself, a strategically advantageous position. In the battle that ensued, however, the Meccan cavalry outflanked the Muslims when some of the Muslim archers left their position on the high ground. The Muslims were forced into retreat, during which the prophet himself was struck in the face. As he washed away the blood from his wound, Muhammad exclaimed, "The wrath of God is fierce against him who bloodied the face of His prophet" (Ibn Ishaq, 382).

Among the slain at the Battle of Uhud was the Prophet's paternal uncle Hamza. At Badr, Hamza had killed the brother and the father of Hind, wife of the Meccan leader Abu Sufyan. Now Hind, in an act of vengeance, found the dead body of Hamza on the battlefield, carved out his liver, and ate it.

However, the Meccans did not continue their pursuit of the Muslims and did not attempt to sack Medina. Thus Muhammad's position there was in no way weakened; in fact, his position there was strengthened once he exiled the Jewish tribe Banu Nadir.

Realizing their mistake, the Meccans decided to return to Medina two years later (AH 5, or 627 CE) to lay siege to the city itself. This time they gathered a confederacy of ten thousand men, while the Muslims could only muster three thousand. The Muslims foiled the Quraysh, however, when a Persian convert to Islam named Salman proposed the idea of building a trench around the city. The sources relate that the Meccans—even though their force was made up primarily of infantry— were completely confounded by this trench and, after twenty nights, gave up trying to cross it.

Watt, who reasonably doubts that a trench could have caused this much trouble, proposes that the Meccans also suffered because of unusually cold weather or because their hopes for help from the last Jewish tribe, Banu Qurayza, came to naught (Watt, *Muhammad at Medina*, 39).

Ibn Ishaq relates that after the failure of the Meccan siege, often referred to as the Battle of the Trench, Muhammad began to launch an increasing number of raids on pagan Arab tribes. The Muslim forces were almost always victorious in these raids, and the vanquished tribes generally accepted Muhammad's authority over them. Other tribes, having heard of Muhammad's growing power, came to Medina of their own will to swear their allegiance to the Prophet. But Muhammad was not yet ready to attack Mecca itself. Instead, he decided to visit it.

The Return to Mecca

According to Ibn Ishaq, in the year after the Battle of the Trench (AH 6/628 CE), Muhammad decided to perform the lesser pilgrimage, or Umra, and went out toward Mecca with a large group of followers, "with no intention of making war" (Ibn Ishaq, 499). The Quraysh, however, came forth from Mecca to block his way. Meanwhile, Muhammad's camel knelt down at a place named Hudaybiyya and would move no more. Muhammad explained, "The One who restrained the elephant from Mecca [when Abraha attacked] is keeping it back" (Ibn Ishaq, 501). Guided by this divine sign, he met with the Quraysh and came to terms. He agreed to turn back to Medina and to keep a ten-year truce, the Quraysh having assured him that he could perform the minor pilgrimage the following year.

Otherwise, the Prophet remained as ambitious as ever. Later that same year, Tabari reports, Muhammad sent out letters to a number of leaders, including the ruler of Alexandria, named al-Muqawqis; the ruler of the Arab Ghassanid tribe, allies of the Byzantines; the Byzantine emperor himself, Heraclius (r. 610–41); the ruler of the Arab tribe Banu Hanifa; the Persian emperor Khosrau (that is, Khosrau II, r. 590–628); and the Ethiopian king (Tabari, 8:98). The Prophet invited these leaders to accept Islam for their own good. Ibn Ishaq compares the sending out of these letters to Jesus sending out his apostles to different peoples throughout the world (Ibn Ishaq, 653).

FROM A CLASSIC TEXT ❖ 2.2

Muhammad's Letters to the Emperors of Byzantium and Persia

Most critical scholars question the tradition by which Muhammad sent out letters to world leaders—including the Byzantine emperor Heraclius (r. 610–641) and the Persian emperor Khosrau (i.e., Khosrau II, r. 590–628)—with invitations to accept Islam. This episode is never mentioned in Byzantine or Persian (or any other non-Islamic) sources. If indeed it was a tradition developed by medieval Muslim scholars, it is still valuable for what it shows of their religious vision. The idea that Muhammad wrote letters to the rulers of the Eastern Roman and Persian Empires seems to be a way of affirming that Islam is a religion meant for the entire world, not only the Arabs. The idea that he did so when he ruled over nothing but a small corner of western Arabia seems to be a way of offering a sign, or proof, of his prophethood (for it suggests that Muhammad knew even then that his followers would overwhelm the Byzantines and the Persians alike).

The account of the letter to Heraclius quoted below comes from the hadith collection of Bukhari (which includes a more detailed account of this letter than Ibn Ishaq's biography) and the account of the letter to Khosrau from Ibn Ishaq. The contrast between the two accounts is telling. Heraclius is presented as a tragic figure, a ruler who recognized (like other righteous Christians in Muhammad's biography) the truth of Islam but who was prevented by his followers from forsaking Christianity. Khosrau, however, is a figure of arrogance. He refuses to recognize the truth of Islam (whereas one of his followers does so) and, not surprisingly, he is soon killed. The relatively positive portrayal of Heraclius may be a way of explaining his victory over the Persians in the war that preceded the Islamic conquests and the relatively successful resistance of the Byzantines in their later confrontation with Islam. Whereas the Persian Empire was annihilated by the Muslim forces, Heraclius managed to establish a line of defense in southern Anatolia that would hold for centuries. It may also show a preference for Christians over Zoroastrians.

Muhammad's Letter to Heraclius

(Abu Sufyan, Muhammad's erstwhile opponent in Mecca, is made to recount a conversation he had with Heraclius during a trip to Syria [before his conversion to Islam]. After posing a number of questions, Heraclius concludes:)

"If what you have said is true, [this prophet] will very soon occupy this place underneath my feet and I knew it (from the scriptures) that he was going to appear but I did not know that he would be from you, and if I could reach him definitely, I would go immediately to meet him and if I were with him, I would certainly wash his feet." Heraclius then asked for the letter addressed by Allah's Apostle, which was delivered by Dihya to the Governor of Busra, who forwarded it to Heraclius to read. The contents of the letter were as follows:

"In the name of Allah the Beneficent, the Merciful (This letter is) from Muhammad the slave of Allah and His Apostle to Heraclius the ruler of Byzantine. Peace be upon him, who follows the right path. Furthermore I invite you to Islam, and if you become a Muslim you will be safe, and Allah will double your reward, and if you reject this invitation of Islam you will be committing a sin by misguiding your Arisiyin [heretics]. (And I recite to you Allah's Statement: 'O people of the scripture! Come to a word common to you and us that we worship none but Allah and that we associate nothing in worship with Him, and that none of us shall take others as Lords beside Allah. Then, if they turn away, say: Bear witness that we are Muslims (those who have surrendered to Allah).'" (Q 3:64).

Abu Sufyan then added, "When Heraclius had finished his speech and had read the letter, there was a great hue and cry in the Royal Court. So we were turned out of the court. I told my companions that the question of [the Prophet Muhammad] has become so prominent that even the King of [the Byzantines] is afraid of him. Then I started to become sure that he (the Prophet) would be the conqueror in the near future till I embraced Islam (i.e., Allah guided me to it)." (Bukhari 1:6)

Muhammad's Letter to Khosrau
(Ibn Ishaq's report of Khosrau's rejection of Muhammad's invitation to accept Islam is followed by a narrative set in Persian-occupied Yemen. Muhammad's prophethood is thereby evident by his miraculous knowledge of the assassination of Khosrau [killed by his son after the Battle of Nineveh in 627]).

'Abdallah *b. Hudhafa brought the apostle's letter to Khosrau and when he had read it he tore it up. When the apostle heard that he had torn his letter up he said, "His kingdom will be torn in pieces."*

Then Khosrau wrote to Badhan, who was governor of Yemen, "Send two stout fellows to this man in the Hijaz and tell them to bring him to me." So Badhan sent his steward Babawayh who was a skilled scribe with a Persian called Kharkhasrah to carry a letter to the apostle, ordering him to go with them to Khosrau. He told Babawayh to go to this man's country and speak to him and then come back and report. . . .

The two men came to the apostle and Babawayh told him that the king of kings Khosrau had written to the governor Badhan ordering him to send men to bring him to him and that they had been sent to take him away. If he obeyed, Badhan would write to the king of kings on his behalf and keep him from him; but if he refused to come he knew what sort of man he was: he would destroy his people and lay waste to his country. They had come in to the apostle's presence with shaven beards and long moustaches, so that he could not bear to look at them. He advanced on them and said, "Who ordered you to do this?" To which they replied, "Our Lord" meaning Khosrau. The apostle answered, "But my Lord has ordered me to let my beard grow long and to cut my moustache." Then he told them to come back in the morning.

News came from heaven to the apostle to the effect that God had given Shirawayh power over his father Khosrau and he had killed him on a certain night of a certain month at a certain hour. Thereupon he summoned them and told them. They said: "Do you know what you are saying? We can take revenge on you. What is easier? Shall we write this as from you and tell the king of it?" He said, "Yes, tell him that from me and tell him that my religion and my sovereignty will reach limits which the kingdom of Khosrau never attained. Say to him, 'If you submit I will give you what you already hold and appoint you king over your people in Yemen.'" Then he gave Kharkhasrah a girdle containing gold and silver which one of the kings had given him.

They left him and came to Badhan and reported. He exclaimed, "This is not the speech of a king. In my opinion he is a prophet as he says. We will see what happens. If what he said is true then he is a prophet who has been sent by God; if it is not, we must consider the matter further." Hardly had he finished speaking when there came a letter from Shirawayh saying that he had killed Khosrau because he had angered the Persians by killing their nobles and keeping them on the frontiers. He must see that his men pledged their obedience to the new king. He must see the man about whom Khosrau had written, but not provoke him to war until further instructions came.

When Badhan received this letter he said, "Without doubt this man is an apostle," and he became a Muslim, as did the Persians with him in Yemen. (Ibn Ishaq, 658–59)

There are no records in Byzantine or Persian documents of a letter from a prophet in Arabia (although a museum in Istanbul claims to have a copy of the letter that Muhammad sent to Heraclius). It would be easy to understand why later Muslims would create the tradition of Muhammad's letters: it would have been a useful way of asserting that Islam is a religion for the entire world and not for the Arabs alone.

Ibn Ishaq insists that Muhammad's concern after the truce at Hudaybiyya was to establish his dominance in the immediate region. After waiting two months, Ibn Ishaq reports, Muhammad conquered Khaybar, a Jewish settlement where the exiled Banu Nadir had taken refuge, and divided up its spoils.

The following year (AH 7/629 CE), Muhammad indeed carried out the minor

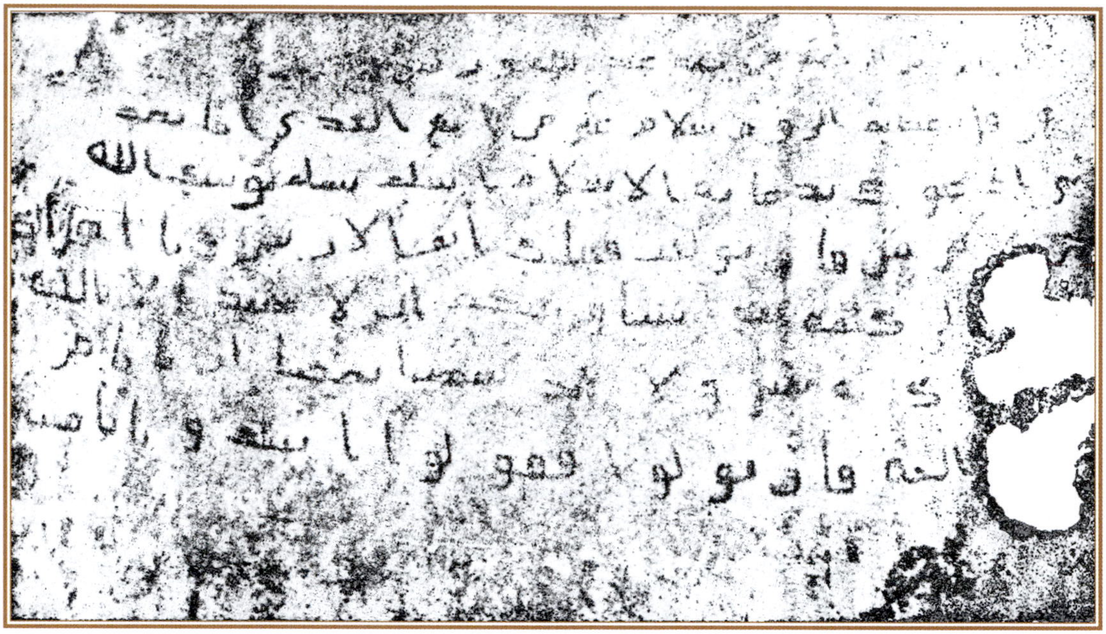

FIGURE 2.2. *Purported manuscript of a letter from Muhammad to the Byzantine emperor Heraclius.*

pilgrimage as stipulated in his agreement with the Quraysh. The ten-year truce, however, did not last. When the Quraysh aided one of their allies, the Banu Bakr tribe, in an attack against an ally of Muhammad, the Khuzaʿa tribe, the Prophet determined that the truce was broken and began preparations for an attack on Mecca.

Abu Sufyan, Muhammad's old nemesis, recognized the imminent danger and went to Medina to beg for a new truce. In Medina, he stayed in the house of his own daughter, Umm Habiba, who had become Muhammad's wife. When she refused to let her father sit on the Prophet's carpet, Abu Sufyan exclaimed, "My dear daughter . . . I hardly know if you think that the carpet is too good for me or that I am too good for the carpet!" Umm Habiba explained, "It is the apostle's carpet and you are an unclean polytheist" (Ibn Ishaq, 543). Muhammad refused to speak with him, and when Abu Sufyan asked for the help of ʿUmar, the latter replied, "Should I intercede for you with the apostle! If I had only an ant I would fight you with it" (Ibn Ishaq, 543).

Thus Abu Sufyan, Ibn Ishaq explains, returned to Mecca in shame. When Muhammad marched with his forces and camped outside of Mecca the following year (AH 8/630 CE), Abu Sufyan went out to the Muslims' camp, on the back of a mule, to beg for mercy. Upon seeing Abu Sufyan, 'Umar shouted out, "Let me take off his head!" (Ibn Ishaq, 547), but Muhammad agreed to spare his life along with all those in Mecca who took refuge in his house, or in the Ka'ba, or who locked themselves in their own houses.

With the submission of Abu Sufyan, there was little fight left in the Meccans, and Muhammad entered his native city with almost no resistance at all. Muhammad honored the amnesty he had agreed to with Abu Sufyan, although Muhammad sought vengeance on a few individuals. Ibn Ishaq relates,

> The apostle had instructed his commanders when they entered Mecca only to fight those who resisted them, except a small number who were to be killed even if they were found beneath the curtains of the Ka'ba. Among them was 'Abdallah b. Sa'd. . . . The reason he ordered him to be killed was that he had been a Muslim and used to write down revelation; then he apostatized and returned to Quraysh and fled to 'Uthman b. 'Affan [later the third caliph]. . . . The latter hid him until he brought him to the apostle after the situation in Mecca was tranquil, and asked that he might be granted immunity. They allege that the apostle remained silent for a long time till finally he said yes. When 'Uthman had left he said to his companions who were sitting around him, "I kept silent so that one of you might get up and strike off his head!" One of the [Medinans] said, "Then why didn't you give me a sign, O apostle of God?"

He answered that a prophet does not kill by pointing. (Ibn Ishaq, 550)

The Muslims killed several other Meccans—most of whom were accused of mocking Muhammad—but otherwise the conquest of the city took place quickly and peacefully. As for Abu Sufyan, he became a Muslim and took up arms alongside Muhammad. In one of their raids, on the city of Ta'if, Abu Sufyan lost an eye. Years after the death of Muhammad, while fighting the Byzantines at the Battle of Yarmouk, he lost the other.

Muhammad's triumph over the Meccans was now complete. Watt comments: "He had harried them and provoked them; then he had wooed them and frightened them in turn; and now practically all of them, even the greatest, had submitted to him" (Watt, *Muhammad at Medina*, 70).

On the same day of the conquest, Ibn Ishaq reports, Muhammad entered into the Ka'ba. According to one tradition, Muhammad pointed a stick at the idols housed inside and "they collapsed on their backs one after the other." A second tradition relates that Muhammad ordered all of the pictures in the Ka'ba erased, except for certain pictures of Jesus and Mary that the Quraysh had placed there (Ibn Ishaq, 552). Other traditions, whose authors were perhaps uncomfortable with this concession to Christianity, relate simply that he ordered all pictures to be erased. Thus the Ka'ba, which Abraham had dedicated to the worship of the one God, was returned to its original state of purity.

BOX 2.3 ❖ REPRESENTATIONS OF MUHAMMAD

Whereas at different times certain Christian movements or denominations have condemned the veneration of holy images (a position known as iconoclasm), Muslims have—to varying degrees—opposed the representation of any humans or animals in general and the representation of the Prophet Muhammad in particular. This position is often justified with reference to those qurʾanic passages (e.g., Q 37:83–99) in which Abraham opposes the idol worship of his people (and his own father), and with reference to the story of Muhammad cleaning out the Kaʿba of idols (a story that might be based on the Abraham material in the Qurʾan). For their part, Sunni jurisprudents were particularly influenced by a series of *hadith* in which Muhammad explains that angels will not enter a house with pictures ("I heard Allah's Apostle saying, 'Angels [of Mercy] do not enter a house wherein there is a dog or a picture of a living creature'"; Bukhari, 4:448). These *hadith* are generally not found in Shiʿite collections, and Shiʿites historically (especially in the Iranian world) were in fact less strictly opposed to figural representation—even of the Prophet Muhammad. Indeed Muhammad is depicted in the Iranian Shiʿite image of the night journey above (fig. 1.4). Today there is a great diversity of opinions among Shiʿites and Sunnis on images. Pious Sunni Muslims may still refuse to have pictures hanging on the walls of their home, but very few would refuse to have photos or books with pictures in them. Sunnis and Shiʿites alike, however, are generally opposed today to the representation of the Prophet Muhammad. This opposition was evident in the violent response to malevolent cartoons of the Prophet published in a Danish newspaper in 2005 and a French newspaper in 2015.

The Final Years of the Last Prophet

Soon after the conquest of Mecca, a tribe known as the Hawazin—old rivals of the Quraysh—gathered their forces to confront Muhammad. The Prophet rode out to meet them, Ibn Ishaq reports, with twelve thousand men. Yet as they were riding through a canyon, the Muslims fell into an ambush and were soon in disarray. The Prophet called out to them, "Where are you going men, I am God's apostle! I am Muhammad the son of ʿAbdallah!" (Ibn Ishaq, 569). Only the best men of Islam rallied to him, one hundred men in all. Nevertheless, they turned to face their enemy together, and God sent down angels to fight with them, as He had at Badr, and they soon routed the Hawazin. According to Ibn Ishaq, the Hawazin had brought all of their women, children, and livestock with them to the battle; now the entire lot fell into Muslim hands. They took special care to distribute this booty to newly converted Muslims (or to offer it as an incentive for pagans to convert), a practice referred to as *ta'lif al-qulub*, "the firming-up of hearts."

A month later, the Muslims unsuccessfully laid siege to Ta'if, an important city in the high grounds near Mecca. But the resistance of the city (which would later surrender to Muslim forces anyway) was only a minor annoyance to the Prophet, who now set his sights further afield. Ibn Ishaq reports that Muhammad (who had no intention of settling in his native city of Mecca) soon returned to Medina and ordered his followers to prepare for a raid on the Byzantines. If Muhammad had once sent out a letter inviting the Byzantine emperor to convert to Islam, he was now ready to send out an army to attack him.

According to Ibn Ishaq, Muhammad's followers were not eager for this new raid. One man requested to be excused from the campaign on the grounds that he would lose his self-control if he saw Byzantine women. Others refused to go on the grounds that they could not bear the long journey in fearsome heat (Ibn Ishaq, 602–3). In fact, both of these reports seem to be ways of explaining qur'anic verses (Q 9:49: "Among them is the one who says, 'Give me leave and do not tempt me'" [my translation]; and Q 9:81: "They said, 'Go not forth in the heat.' Say: 'Gehenna's fire is hotter,' did they but understand").

In any case, Ibn Ishaq explains that the raid never took place. When Muhammad arrived at a site named Tabuk near the northern point of the Red Sea, he made a treaty with the Christian governor of Ayla (modern day Eilat, or Aqaba) and soon began the long trip back to Medina.

The following year (AH 10/631–32 CE) is remembered in Islamic sources as the year of deputations, as the Prophet received a large number of deputations from Arab tribes eager to become Muslims and thereby win his favor. By the end of the year, however, the Prophet sensed that his death was near, and he set out for Mecca to perform the major pilgrimage, or *hajj*. The Islamic sources remember this event as the "farewell pilgrimage," the occasion on which Muhammad taught his followers the proper rites of the pilgrimage, rites the angel Gabriel himself had given him. During this time, the Prophet also delivered a public address in which he finalized a number of religious laws and Islamic principles. According to Ibn Ishaq, Muhammad began the address with the words, "O men, listen to my words. I do not know whether I shall ever meet you in this place again after this year." He concluded with the words: "Know that every Muslim is a Muslim's brother, and that they are brethren. It is only lawful to take from a brother what he gives you willingly, so wrong not yourselves. O God, have I not told you!?" (Ibn Ishaq, 651).

But if the Prophet sensed that his death was near, he had lost none of his military ambitions. In the final months of his life, Ibn Ishaq reports, Muhammad sent out an increasing number of raids, including attacks against Byzantine territory in the north and Persian-controlled Yemen to the south. This, the Islamic sources told us, signaled to his successors that the Islamic conquests were meant to continue.

The Prophet himself had grown ill and took to staying in the house of his beloved wife 'A'isha. In these final days, he would ask to have water poured over him and to have his head bound in a cloth, in order to relieve the pain of his illness. When Muhammad's illness became so severe that he was unable to lead the prayer, he asked Abu Bakr to pray in his place. To Sunni Muslims this report, by which Abu Bakr physically took the place of the Prophet, is a proof that Muhammad wished Abu Bakr to take his place as leader of the Islamic community after his death.

According to a tradition that Ibn Ishaq reports on the authority of ʿAʾisha, the circumstances of the Prophet's death were as follows:

> The apostle came back to me from the mosque that day and lay in my bosom. A man of Abu Bakr's family came in to me with a toothpick in his hand and the apostle looked at it in such a way that I knew he wanted it, and when I asked him if he wanted me to give it him he said Yes; so I took it and chewed it for him to soften it and gave it to him. He rubbed his teeth with it more energetically than I had ever seen him rub before; then he laid it down. I found him heavy in my bosom and as I looked into his face, lo his eyes were fixed and he was saying, "Nay, the most exalted companion is of paradise." I said, "You were given the choice and you have chosen, by Him Who sent you with the truth!" And so the apostle was taken. (Ibn Ishaq, 682)

Tabari reports that Muhammad died in the month of First Rabiʿ, the third Islamic month, of the eleventh Islamic year, on a Monday (Tabari 9:183). He adds, "The oath of allegiance was given to Abu Bakr on Monday, the very day on which the Prophet died" (Tabari 9:183). This oath of allegiance, which led to Abu Bakr's rise as the first caliph, assured stability for the Islamic community for the time being. The same oath of allegiance, however, sowed the seeds of the greatest division in that community, a division that has lasted to our days.

STUDY QUESTIONS

1   Why do you think later Muslims chose the Prophet's migration to Medina as the starting point of the Islamic calendar?

2   What is the importance of the Battle of Badr to Islamic self-understanding?

3   What role does Muhammad's conflict with the Jews have in his larger biography?

4   What is the importance of Muhammad's military successes to classical Muslim authors such as Ibn Ishaq?

Chapter 3

THE BIRTH OF AN EMPIRE

When the apostle was dead ʿUmar got up and said, "Some of the disaffected will allege that the apostle is dead, but by God he is not dead: he has gone to his Lord as Moses . . . went and was hidden from his people for forty days, returning to them after it was said that he had died. By God, the apostle will return as Moses returned and will cut off the hands and feet of men who allege that the apostle is dead." When Abu Bakr heard what was happening he came to the door of the mosque as ʿUmar was speaking to the people. He paid no attention but went in to ʿAʾishaʾs house to the apostle, who was lying covered by a mantle of Yamani cloth. He went and uncovered his face and kissed him, saying, "You are dearer than my father and mother. You have tasted the death which God had decreed: a second death will never overtake you." Then he replaced the mantle on the apostle's face and went out. ʿUmar was still speaking and he said, "Gently, ʿUmar, be quiet." But ʿUmar refused and went on talking, and when Abu Bakr saw that he would not be silent he went forward to the people who, when they heard his words, came to him and left ʿUmar. Giving thanks and praise to God he said: "O men, if anyone worships Muhammad, Muhammad is dead: if anyone worships God, God is alive, immortal."

—*The Life of Muhammad* by Muhammad Ibn Ishaq

The First Caliph and the First Imam

The Prophet was dead and no new prophet was to be born. In the Bible (2 Kgs 2), the prophet Elisha takes up the mantle of the prophet Elijah, but no one—according to Islamic belief—could take up Muhammad's mantle. The Qur'an describes Muhammad as the "seal of the prophets" (33:40). This phrase, according to Islamic tradition, means that Muhammad was the last prophet. God will not speak to humans again before the Day of Resurrection.

Nevertheless, as Ibn Ishaq and other classical Sunni sources tell it, with the death of Muhammad the Muslim community still needed a political successor, a caliph—a leader to ensure that the religion of God would not disappear with the disappearance of God's prophet. That leader was to be Abu Bakr.

The Election of Abu Bakr

The citation above, in which Abu Bakr is a picture of calm and prudence at a time of tragedy, encapsulates his role in the story of Islam's emergence. Abu Bakr, the faithful friend of Muhammad who once had remained hidden with the Prophet in a cave for three days during the *hijra*, was now to be the one who kept the community faithful to the Prophet's religion.

But according to the classical sources, the process by which Abu Bakr became the first caliph was anything but smooth. Soon after the Prophet's death, Ibn Ishaq and Tabari report, the Muslims of Medina (known as the *ansar*, or "helpers") gathered together to discuss the future of their community. Among them was a man named Sa'd b. 'Ubada, one of the original twelve Medinans who had pledged allegiance to Muhammad even before the *hijra*. Sa'd, who had grown so sick that he could no longer speak in a loud voice, had the following statement read on his behalf.

> Company of the *ansar*! You have precedence in religion and merit in Islam that no [other] tribe of the Arabs can claim. Muhammad remained ten-odd years in his tribe, calling them to worship the Merciful and to cast off idols and graven images, but only a few men of his tribe believed in Him. . . . Then God bestowed upon you faith in Him and in His Apostle, and protection for him and his companions and strength for him and his faith, and battle [*jihad*] for his enemies. . . . [So] keep [control of] this matter to yourselves, to the exclusion of others, for it is yours and yours alone. (Tabari 10:2)

When the statement was read, most of the *ansar* shouted their approval and demanded that a caliph be chosen from among their ranks. Others, however, were worried about how the Meccans (known as the *muhajirun*) would react. They accordingly proposed a compromise, namely that one leader be chosen for the *muhajirun* and another for themselves. Sa'd moaned, "This is the beginning of weakness" (Tabari, 10:3).

When 'Umar and Abu Bakr heard that the *ansar* had gathered, they were not pleased. They rushed to join the meeting—which was being held in a portico belonging to a Medinan clan named Banu Sa'ida—and refused to turn back when two of the *ansar* tried to stop them. Entering into the portico, Abu Bakr addressed the gathering.

> Oh company of the *ansar*, your superiority in religion and great precedence in Islam are undeniable. May God be satisfied with you as helpers [*ansar*] for His religion and His Apostle. He made his *hijra* to you, and the majority of his wives and his companions are among you; so after the first *muhajirun*—there is no one among us who is in your station. We are the leaders, and you the helpers. (Tabari, 10:5)

Thereafter one of the *ansar*'s own, Bashir b. Sa'd, stood up and declared, "In truth Muhammad was from Quraysh, and his people are more entitled to [hold] (authority) and more suitable" (Tabari, 10:7). At this Abu Bakr proposed that 'Umar or Abu 'Ubayda (another leader of the *muhajirun*) be designated as the Prophet's successor. Both 'Umar and Abu 'Ubayda, however, insisted that Abu Bakr was more deserving. They swore their allegiance to him, followed by Bashir and a number of *ansar*, and soon

most of the city of Medina had done so. Sa'd, however, refused, and confusion ensued. 'Umar lost his cool and stepped on his head (Sa'd, apparently, had been knocked down by this point), shouting, "Kill him; may God slay him!" Sa'd, apparently, was up to the fight: he grabbed 'Umar's beard and grunted, "By God, if you remove a single hair from [my head] you'll return with no front teeth in your mouth" (Tabari, 10:9).

But Sa'd was not the only one who did not swear allegiance to Abu Bakr. Tabari reports that during the meeting at the portico of Bani Sa'ida, 'Ali was busy preparing the Prophet's body for burial, in the Prophet's own house. He did not, according to Tabari, cease his burial arrangements in order to swear loyalty to Abu Bakr. Indeed, he refused to do so as long as his beloved wife Fatima, the daughter of the Prophet, was alive. (By some accounts, 'Ali held back from acknowledging Abu Bakr because Abu Bakr refused to allow Fatima to inherit her father's property.) When Fatima died six months later, 'Ali summoned Abu Bakr and explained: "It is neither the denial of your good qualities nor the rivalry of good, which God has given you, that prevented us from giving you the oath of allegiance, but the fact that we considered that we have a right in this authority which you have monopolized" (Tabari, 9:197). That same day, after the noon prayers, 'Ali publicly swore allegiance to Abu Bakr, whom the people now universally acclaimed as the first caliph.

Personalities in Islam 3.1
ABU BAKR

Ibn Ishaq has the Prophet comment, "I have never invited anyone to accept Islam but he has shown signs of reluctance, suspicion, and hesitation, except Abu Bakr. When I told him of it he did not hold back or hesitate" (Ibn Ishaq, 116). This quotation captures the essence of Abu Bakr's character in the traditional biography of the Prophet. Therein Abu Bakr is the first free, adult male to accept Islam. After his conversion, he never wavers from his Islamic faith or from his devotion to Muhammad. For this constancy, Islamic tradition offers him the nickname al-Siddiq, "The Faithful One." This faithfulness is exhibited in the story of Muhammad's flight (*hijra*) to Medina, the moment of Muhammad's greatest vulnerability. He has sent most of his followers before him, and his Meccan enemies have collectively vowed to end his life. It is Abu Bakr, and Abu Bakr alone, who travels with him on this fateful journey, three days of which they spend hiding in the darkness of a cave.

When Muhammad dies ten years later, Abu Bakr (according to the standard account) insists that a successor be chosen from among the Prophet's Meccan tribe. He proposes that either ʿUmar or Abu Ubayda, two of his Meccan friends, be appointed caliph. Yet when both ʿUmar and Abu Ubayda insist that Abu Bakr alone has the merit to be caliph, he does not refuse the position. To Sunnis, it is precisely Abu Bakr's merit that is the point. The biography of the Prophet does not have Muhammad designate, or appoint, Abu Bakr as his successor. It does, however, have Muhammad demonstrate trust in him. When the Prophet, struck by illness toward the end of his life, is unable to lead the public prayer in Medina, he asks Abu Bakr to do so in his place. This ceremonial act, in which Abu Bakr stands in the place of Muhammad while he is still alive, is seen by many Sunni scholars as proof that he was the right choice to lead the Islamic community after the Prophet's death.

Once chosen to be the first caliph, Abu Bakr proves to be an aggressive leader. When certain Arab tribes insist that they be free of his authority (since they had only pledged allegiance to Muhammad), Abu Bakr goes to war to compel them to accept it. His victorious campaigns against them are remembered as the "Wars of Apostasy."

From the perspective of Shiʿites, however, ʿAli remained opposed to Abu Bakr privately. Seeing that the impious plot of Abu Bakr and ʿUmar to gain power (which transpired while ʿAli was piously attending to the Prophet's burial) had been successful, he knew that opposition to them now would lead to a civil war. Thus for the sake of the Islamic community, he did not protest Abu Bakr's rule. However, he refused to fight with the Islamic armies under Abu Bakr and his two successors (ʿUmar and ʿUthman). Instead, ʿAli lived a quiet life of prayer and farming, a signal of his inner opposition.

According to these sources, ʿAli was opposed to Abu Bakr's rule because Muhammad had personally designated him to lead the Islamic community. According to a tradition cited in Shiʿite (and some Sunni) sources, the Prophet, while returning from his final pilgrimage, stopped at a pond named Khumm. There he raised ʿAli's hand and declared, "Whoever considers me his master, ʿAli is his master." The eleventh century Shiʿite scholar al-Shaykh al-Mufid explains, "This is clear [evidence] of the nomination of him for the Imamate and for succession to his position" (Shaykh al-Mufid, 3).

The term "Imamate" generally means "leadership." To Shiʿites, however, this term carries a second meaning. According to Shiʿite doctrine, it was not God's will to have a political successor, a caliph, chosen by the Islamic community after the death of the Prophet. Instead, God willed that a line of twelve descendants of Muhammad, or Imams, be his representatives on earth until the Day of Resurrection. Thus Muhammad was the last Prophet and ʿAli the first Imam. Abu Bakr, for his part, was an usurper.

Western scholars generally follow instead the Sunni version of these events as recounted by scholars such as Ibn Ishaq and Tabari. Accordingly, they are left to wonder how Muhammad, an astute politician committed to the unity and expansion of his community, failed to appoint a successor. One explanation, famously presented by a French scholar named Paul Casanova, is that Muhammad believed that the end of the world would come before the end of his life.

A Western scholar with Shiʿite sympathies, Wilfred Madelung, poses a second question to those who follow the Sunni sources. If those gathered (except for Saʿd) at the portico of Banu Saʿida agreed that it was fitting to choose a successor from the Prophet's own people—the Quraysh—would it not have been still more fitting for them to choose a successor—ʿAli—from the Prophet's own family? ʿAli himself asks a similar question in a beloved Shiʿite work known as the *Peak of Eloquence*: "How strange? Could the caliphate be through the [Prophet's] companionship but not through [his] companionship and [his] kinship?" (*Peak of Eloquence*, 609).

Abu Bakr and the Wars of Apostasy

In any case, Sunni and Shiʿite sources agree that Abu Bakr became the first caliph, for better or for worse. They also agree that he went to war almost immediately. According to the traditional narrative, when Muhammad died a number of tribes in the central Arabian region known as Najd refused to pay taxes to the new caliph. Other tribes, in Bahrain in eastern Arabia, and in Oman and Yemen in southern Arabia, demanded complete political independence. None of these tribes, according to the traditional narrative, rejected Islam. We might imagine that they simply saw no need to follow a man—Abu Bakr—who claimed to be Muhammad's successor after his death, when Muhammad never appointed a successor during his life. Or, like the *ansar*, they might have wanted a ruler from among their own people.

Yet the classical sources report that Abu Bakr was also faced with four groups of rebels led by "false" prophets. Among these was a religious leader named Musaylima (inevitably referred to in Islamic sources as Musaylima "the Liar"), who had gathered a large following in the central-Arabian region of Yamama. During Muhammad's lifetime, Musaylima, according to Ibn Ishaq, sent a letter to Muhammad with two heralds, proposing that he and Muhammad share power. When Muhammad read the letter, he shouted, "By God, were it not that heralds are not to be killed I would behead the pair of you!" (Ibn Ishaq, 649). Another of the rebel leaders was Sajah, a "false" prophetess, who gained a following among the tribes of northeastern Arabia and ultimately joined forces with Musaylima against Abu Bakr.

The story of Musaylima, whether or not it is historically reliable, offers a number of insights on Islamic beliefs. Ibn Ishaq reports that Musaylima was a monotheist (although he preferred to call God "Al-Rahman" ["The Merciful"] instead of "Allah"), that he believed in the final judgment, and that he instructed his followers to pray daily and to fast regularly. In other words, his teachings were not fundamentally unlike those of Muhammad. Thus this story demonstrates that allegiance to Muhammad, and no one else, is a *sine qua non* of Islamic identity. Earlier prophets, of course, might be acknowledged, but only when it is understood that they were all proto-Muslims who prepared the way for Muhammad. And anyone such as Musaylima who lived during or after the time of Muhammad, and claimed to be a prophet, was a liar.

BOX 3.1 ❖ MUHAMMAD'S PROPHETHOOD

Despite the traditional Islamic teaching on the finality of Muhammad's prophethood, a number of religious movements have been founded in recent centuries by those who claimed to have completed his teaching. Sikhism, first taught by Guru Nanak (d. 1539) in what is now the Pakistani Punjab, emerged in the late fifteenth century. Although Guru Nanak came from a Hindu family, he is said to have traveled to Mecca, and his teaching is indeed often presented as a correction of Islamic doctrine. The Baha'i faith is shaped by the doctrine that Baha'ullah (d. 1892), who was born an Iranian Shi'ite Muslim, is the final prophet, sent by God to unify all religions—including Islam—in one universal teaching. Because of their belief in Baha'ullah's prophethood, Baha'i's have suffered frequent persecution in the Islamic world, notably in Baha'ullah's native Iran, where, since the 1979 Islamic revolution, the government has orchestrated a sustained campaign to encourage or compel the conversion of Baha'i's to Islam. The Ahmadiyya may be the most famous of these communities. Founded by Mirza Ghulam Ahmad (d.1908), the Ahmadiyya see themselves as a messianic Muslim revival movement. Most Ahmadiyya live in either the West or in Pakistan. The latter designated them non-Muslims in 1979, marking the beginning of a history of persecution. A still more recent post-Muhammadan Muslim prophet is Rashad Khalifa, an American of Egyptian background who taught that he was given an inspiration to reveal the full meaning of the Qur'an (the religious movement that follows his teaching today is known as "The Submitters"). Khalifa was murdered inside a mosque in Tucson, Arizona, in 1990.

Accordingly, the Islamic sources describe those who followed Musaylima as apostates and Abu Bakr's war against them as the Wars of Apostasy. Although the Qurʾan does not recommend any punishment for apostates (insisting only that God will punish them in the afterlife), in a well-known *hadith* the Prophet declares that their punishment should be death (Bukhari, 9:27). The story of Abu Bakr's campaign against the Arabian rebels exemplifies this teaching: the rebels were either to return to Islam or be killed.

The Wars of Apostasy, however, involved more than apostasy. Abu Bakr, according to Tabari, was as determined to fight against those who refused to pay taxes as he was to fight against false prophets. When several tribes informed Abu Bakr that they would continue to pray the Islamic prayers but would cease paying the alms tax, he declared: "If they refuse me even [a leather strap], I shall fight them for it" (Tabari, 10:45).

The account of the Wars of Apostasy thus proved useful to later Islamic rulers, who used it as a justification to enforce tax collection. It was also useful to religious leaders who sought to warn people against any religious deviancy. The warning would have appeared especially effective at the end of the story, when all four false prophets are killed.

According to Tabari, Abu Bakr personally led the Muslim armies in campaigns against those rebels located closest to Medina, and he did so mercilessly: "Abu Bakr swore that he would certainly make slaughter among the polytheists [in vengeance for] every killing [of

a Muslim]" (Tabari, 10:49). To those who submitted, however, Abu Bakr showed leniency and thereby won their favor.

He also sent various forces against those rebels in more distant regions. Among these was Khalid b. al-Walid, who had once led the cavalry of the pagan Quraysh against the Muslims at the Battle of Uhud. Khalid, who had since become a Muslim, was now one of the community's greatest generals. Abu Bakr sent him out to fight against the rebels in Najd, and then against Musaylima's forces in Yamama. Khalid devastated the forces of the false prophet—Tabari remarks that ten thousand of Musaylima's men were killed in a spot known thereafter as the Garden of Death. Musaylima himself was killed, he adds, while suffering from demonic possession and unable to defend himself.

When Muslim forces had subdued all the rebels, Abu Bakr turned his vision further afield. He sent out forces to attack the Persian Empire in Iraq and the Byzantine Empire in Syria before his death in August 634. The Islamic conquests had begun.

The Early Islamic Conquests

Retelling the story of these conquests is no easy task. There is no question, of course, that the Islamic conquests took place. Skeptical scholars might reasonably doubt much of the biography of Muhammad, but there is no doubting that Arab armies swept through the Middle East in the middle decades of the seventh century. Nevertheless, our understanding of these conquests is far from perfect.

For example, Islamic sources provide over a dozen different versions of the conquest of Syria (which in a classical sense consists of modern day Jordan, Israel/Palestine, Lebanon, and Syria), versions that differ even on basic matters of chronology. For example, Tabari puts the great battle between the Muslims and the Byzantines—the Battle of Yarmuk—before the death of Abu Bakr in August 634. Most other sources, however, date Yarmuk to the caliphate of ʿUmar, in the year 636. Meanwhile, non-Islamic sources present very few details on the conquests, and they describe the conquerors in a way that hardly agrees with the Islamic account. In fact, and as Robert Hoyland points out, this earlier period of Islamic history is poorly attested generally: "Whatever the reason, writers who lived at the same time as the first four caliphs—Abu Bakr (632–34), ʿUmar (634–44), ʿUthman (644–56) and ʿAli (656–60)—recorded next to nothing about them, and their names do not appear on coins, inscriptions, or documents." (*In God's Path*, 98; a possible exception to this might be an inscription found in northwest Arabia written by a man named Zuhayr, who mentions a certain ʿUmar, possibly the caliph, and mentions his death in 24 AH) Thus the reader should be aware that any description of the Islamic conquests is speculative. We are still swimming in very murky historical waters.

The Conquest of Syria

The standard reconstruction of the conquests is that of Fred Donner, who concludes that they began when Abu Bakr sent his general Khalid to the desert region west of the Euphrates sometime in 634/635. While Khalid subdued the nomadic Arab tribes there and towns with large Arab populations such as al-Hira, other Muslim forces launched an offensive against the Arab allies of the Byzantines in Syria. According to Tabari, many of these Arab allies willingly deserted the Byzantines to join the Muslims. On one occasion, when the Muslim armies approached a larger force of Arabs, the latter simply abandoned their camp. "Nearly all those who had gathered against [the Muslims] entered Islam," Tabari comments (Tabari, 11:77). Thus the Muslims soon came to dominate the open countryside of Syria.

When Khalid marched across the barren Arabian desert to meet up with the Muslim generals in Syria, they began to attack the towns. The first town they took was Bostra, a significant Byzantine settlement (with a largely Arab population) in what is now southern Syria. Bostra withstood a siege for some time before submitting to the Muslims. The Christians there agreed to acknowledge Islamic authority and to pay a tax, or *jizya*, demanded of non-Muslims. In return, the Muslims spared their lives and property.

The account of Bostra's submission helps explain the success of the Islamic conquests in Syria. While the population of fighting-age men in Byzantine Syria certainly far outnumbered the invading Muslim armies (one source reports that there were no more than twenty thousand Muslim fighters in Syria), very few of those fighting-age men in fact fought. Moreover, many of them were religiously Christians but ethnically Arabs. To them, Arab Muslim rule may have been no more objectionable than the rule of Greek-speaking Christians.

In addition, although most of the population of Syria (Arab or otherwise) was Christian, most Christians there belonged to the Jacobite or West Syrian church, which differed from the Melkite, or Chalcedonian, church of the Byzantine Empire. Thus on religious grounds they might have felt no great hesitation about submitting to the Muslim forces. For their part, the Muslim forces seem to have been primarily interested in establishing their political authority and collecting taxes in the conquered cities. The revenues from these taxes, meanwhile, allowed them to recruit more and more fighting men into their forces. And so the conquests continued.

Meanwhile, it is important to remember that the Byzantine Empire was reeling from a long series of traumas. Robert Hoyland explains:

> "The weakness of the Byzantine and Persian empires certainly played a part in their swift defeat. The continual outbreaks of war between these two powers since 502, and in particular the almighty clash of 603–28, was a huge drain on their finances and manpower. Recruitment of troops was also adversely affected by the recurrent bouts of plague that troubled the whole region from ca. 550. Plague spreads fast in areas of high population density, where contagion works its deadly spell, but in open areas, where human occupation is sparse, it quickly loses its power." (*In God's Path*, 93–94)

In August 635, Damascus fell—like Bostra before it—when the city capitulated after a long siege. Soon a number of smaller cities in Syria also fell, and the Byzantine emperor Heraclius (r. 610–41) was forced to act. He sent a great force (although probably not the one hundred thousand men that Islamic sources report) to Damascus. The Muslims retreated to the south, first to the Golan Heights and then to the banks of the River Yarmuk, a river that feeds into the Jordan River from the northeast, in modern-day Jordan. There the armies met, and the Muslims routed the Byzantines. Those who were not killed by the sword fell to their death into a ravine while fleeing the battlefield. A measly remnant retreated to the north.

Now one Syrian city after another fell into Muslim hands in rapid succession, including Jerusalem, Caesarea, Tyre, Sidon, Beirut, Aleppo, and Antioch. Finally, the Byzantine forces regrouped and made a stand at the Taurus Mountains, in the south of modern-day Turkey, and there the Byzantine/Islamic border would stand for centuries.

The Conquest of Iraq

In Iraq, the conquests transpired differently. The Sassanian Empire was in the midst of intense political turmoil, in part caused by their decisive defeat at the hands of Byzantines at the Battle of Nineveh in 627

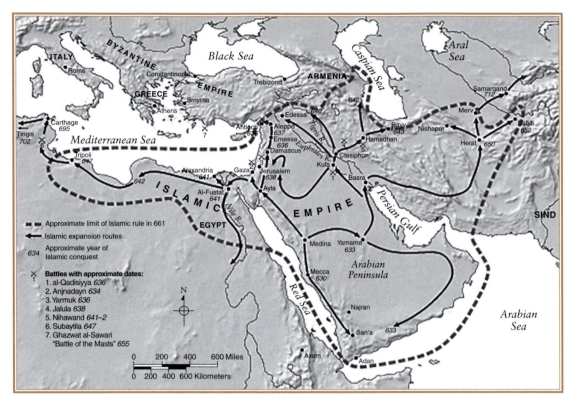

FIGURE. 3.1. *The Early Islamic Conquests.*

and the ensuing overthrow of the emperor Khosrau II. Khosrau's son, Kavadh, was enthroned in his place, but he soon died, and then in great rapidity a series of rulers fell victim to political conspiracies. Despite this instability, however, a Sassanian force managed to defeat the invading Muslim armies when the two sides first met in Iraq, in a conflict known as the Battle of the Bridge. However, the Sassanian ruler (repeating the mistake of the Quraysh at Uhud) failed to pursue the Muslim armies, as he was compelled to return to the capital city, Ctesiphon, to deal with a new uprising.

Meanwhile, the new caliph, ʿUmar, responded to news of the defeat quickly, sending a larger force to attack Iraq. By the time they entered Sassanian territory, a new Persian emperor, Yazdegird III, had taken the throne. Yazdegird, it seemed, had finally ended the chaos raging in the royal house, and he prepared a massive force to meet the Islamic threat. The two sides met at the edges of the Iraqi desert, near the city of Qadisiyya, probably in 636. (Tabari reports that veterans from the Battle of Yarmuk arrived just in time to support the Muslims at Qadisiyya.) The Persians far outnumbered the Muslims, but they were defeated anyway and fell into an unorganized retreat.

The Muslims (unlike the Persians after the Battle of the Bridge) pursued their enemies and decimated them: "They killed them in every village, in every thicket, and on every river bank, and then returned in time for the noon prayer" (Tabari, 12:127–28). Meanwhile, the youngest members of the Muslim army were sent out to inspect the battlefield: "They gave water to the Muslims in whom there was a breath of life and killed the polytheists in whom there was a breath of life" (Tabari, 12:127).

The next year, Muslim forces reached Ctesiphon itself, which fell after a two-month siege. The emperor and his followers now fled in desperation to the northeast, but the Muslim forces pursued them relentlessly, month after month, year after year. Finally, Yazdegerd, the last emperor of the Sassanian Persian Empire, was seized and killed in far-off Merv—modern-day Turkmenistan—in 651. The Persian Empire had collapsed, and a new Islamic empire had risen in its place.

How, we might ask, did the Islamic conquests succeed so terrifically, when the Muslims had fewer fighting men and, presumably, more-primitive weapons than their enemies? In answering this question, Donner notes that historical circumstances favored the Muslims. The Byzantines ruled over ethnically or religiously disaffected subjects. The Sassanians were weakened by political feuds. Both were exhausted from long mutual warfare. He argues, however, that the key factor was Islam:

> The Muslims succeeded, then, primarily because they were able to organize an effective conquest movement, and in this context the impact of the new religion of Islam, which provided the ideological underpinnings for this remarkable breakthrough in social organization, can be more fully appreciated. In this sense, the conquests were truly an *Islamic* movement. (Donner, 269)

One might observe that his analysis smacks of the thought of a Muslim historian of many centuries earlier, Ibn Khaldun (d. 1406), who attributed the rise of civilizations to a "group feeling of solidarity" (ʿ*asabiyya*).

In Praise of the Holy War

Thus at its emergence, Islam was at once a religion and a movement of extraordinary military conquests. Accordingly, it is no surprise to find chapters on the merits of fighting the jihad in the classical collections of the Prophet's *hadith*.

BOX 3.2 ❖ JIHAD

Today the word *jihad* is commonly used in English and is (almost) inevitably associated with the Islamic holy war. In the Qur'an, jihad (and the verb *jahada, "to strive,"* to which it is related) indeed seems to be used in this way. The Qur'an frequently praises those who *jahada* "in the path of God" (e.g., Q 2:218; 8:74; 9:20) and those who *jahada* "with their money and their selves" (e.g., Q 8:72; 9:88; 49:15). These references match the Qur'an's commands elsewhere to "fight" (*qatala*) "in the path of God" (e.g. Q 2:190, 244, 246). The *hadith* collections of Bukhari and Muslims both include books on jihad that are exclusively concerned with when and how Muslims are to pursue holy war. By the eleventh century, however, a tradition appeared in some Islamic sources according to which Muhammad, upon returning from a battle, said to his companions, "You have come from the lesser *jihad* to the greater *jihad*." When his companions asked him what this greater jihad could be, he answered, "The striving of a servant against his lust." This idea of a "greater jihad" is emphasized by Muslim mystics, who elevate the spiritual life above worldly matters, and by Muslims today in order to advance peaceful Islamic teaching.

Presumably, these *hadith* were written with the purpose of convincing believers to join the campaigns of Muslim armies. To this end, they have Muhammad describe the battlefield martyr as the noblest Muslim of all.

> The example of a *mujahid* [the jihad warrior] in Allah's Cause—and Allah knows better who really strives in His Cause—is like a person who fasts and prays continuously. Allah guarantees that He will admit the *mujahid* in His Cause into Paradise if he is killed, otherwise He will return him to his home safely with rewards and war booty. (Bukhari, 4:46)
>
> The Prophet said, "Last night two men came to me (in a dream) and made me ascend a tree and then admitted me into a better and superior house, better of which I have never seen. One of them said, 'This house is the house of martyrs.'" (Bukhari, 4:49)
>
> The Prophet said, "Nobody who dies and finds good from Allah (in the Hereafter) would wish to come back to this world even if he were given the whole world and whatever is in it, except the martyr who, on seeing the superiority of martyrdom, would like to come back to the world and get killed again (in Allah's Cause)." (Bukhari, 4:53)

It is far from certain that Muhammad really said any of these things. The *hadith* come from collections written down only in the ninth century and have many legendary, tendentious, or anachronistic features. But whether or not they are forgeries, these *hadith* reflect the belief that the best Muslims will join the fight against non-Muslims. These Muslims fight for Islam, for the honor of its Prophet, and for the glory of his community.

We see this same attitude in later Muslim scholars' division of the world into two domains: the "Sphere of Islam" (*Dar al-Islam*) and the "Sphere of War" (*Dar al-Harb*). Indeed, if Christians sent out missionaries to strange lands to convert unbelievers, Muslims conquered strange lands and then encouraged the conversion of their subjects: "During Muhammad's lifetime, and for very long thereafter, conversion to Islam followed upon conquest; it never *preceded* it" (Peters, *Jesus and Muhammad*, 168).

The Lives of 'Umar, 'Uthman, and 'Ali

According to most Western scholars, the greatest personality behind the early Islamic conquests was 'Umar, who was chosen as caliph in 634 upon Abu Bakr's death. This choice, according to most sources, was met with little if any objection, even though Abu Bakr never publically declared 'Umar to be his successor. 'Umar, however, had shown himself to be Abu Bakr's right-hand man during the controversies that followed the Prophet's death. 'Umar is also remembered as an assertive, even fearsome, man. One tradition relates to this effect how 'Umar visited Muhammad's house one day and a group of women sitting with the Prophet retreated in fear behind a curtain. Muhammad remarked, "If the devil himself were to meet you on the street he would dodge into a side alley!" (See Andrae, *Muhammad: The Man and His Faith*, 130). One imagines that few would have dared to oppose 'Umar when he became caliph.

'Umar: The Commander of the Faithful

In the classical sources, 'Umar is the first caliph to be called *amir al-mu'minin*, "Commander of the Faithful," a title that may reflect his devotion to the holy war. 'Umar is also said to have been devoted to the strict enforcement of Islamic law. 'Umar, it is said, even beat his his own son, whom he caught drinking alcohol. Yet 'Umar is also said to have lived modestly and to have demanded that all Muslims be treated with compassion and respect.

Tabari reports that when 'Umar named a new governor, he would stipulate that the governor "not ride an expensive horse, or eat white bread, or wear any fine cloth, or prevent the people's needs [from being satisfied]" (Tabari, 14:113). 'Umar was a man, according to the traditional sources, who cooked food for the hungry with his own hands and distributed money to the poor with his own hands. Yet he was also a man who carried a whip in his hands to punish anyone who acted haughtily or irreligiously.

After a ten-year reign, however, 'Umar was murdered. According to Tabari, he was killed by a Christian (or, according to other sources, Zoroastrian) slave named Abu Lu'lu'a, who was upset by a tax imposed by the caliph (although some Western scholars theorize that he might have been killed by an assassin sent by 'Ali). Abu Lu'lu'a met 'Umar as the latter entered a mosque to pray and stabbed him six times.

'Umar knew that his wounds were fatal, Tabari reports, but he refused to appoint a successor. Instead he appointed a council, or *shura*, of the Prophet's companions to make this decision (an act some Muslim reformists cite today as a precedent for democracy). The classical sources disagree on the exact makeup of this council, but they agree that both 'Ali and 'Uthman were part of it, and that the two were in an open rivalry. Eventually 'Uthman prevailed, and 'Ali left the council with the parting words: "[God's] decree will come in its time!" (Tabari 14:153).

'Uthman and the Prophet's Ring

'Uthman would reign as caliph for twelve years. According to most traditions, he did so piously—as 'Umar had before him—for the first six years. But otherwise, he held little in common with his predecessor. The people admired 'Umar for his zealous defense of Islam and his leadership in warfare. 'Uthman, however, had not fought at Badr and was often considered to be indolent: "The lack of energy and initiative ascribed to 'Uthman had become clear right from the start of his career, and must have been a real defect of character" ("'Uthman," *Encyclopaedia of Islam*, 10:946b). But 'Uthman had family connections going for him; he was a member of the powerful Umayyad clan—which included Muhammad's former nemesis Abu Sufyan—and he had married two of the Prophet's daughters (Ruqayya and Umm Kulthum).

After six years, however, the accusations against 'Uthman became more severe. Now he was accused not only of indolence but also of impiety. A number of traditions report that 'Uthman's impiety began when he lost the ring that Muhammad once wore, and which had been passed down to Abu Bakr and 'Umar. Tabari explains,

> 'Uthman b. Affan ruled and wore [the ring] for six years. He dug a well in Medina to supply water for the Muslims. He was sitting on the edge of the well and began fiddling with the ring and twisting it around his finger. The ring slipped off and fell into the well. They searched for it and [even] drained the well of its water, but without success. ['Uthman] established a magnificent reward for anyone who could bring it [to him] and became deeply depressed. (Tabari, 15:63)

'Uthman's loss of the Prophet's ring—which was never found—foreshadowed his infidelity to the Prophet's commands. Complaints soon arose that 'Uthman appointed his own relatives as provincial governors regardless of their religious merits and that he put aside war booty for his own family, depriving in part the Muslim fighters who had risked their lives to win it.

'Uthman is also credited with compiling the standard version of the Qur'an during the last half of his reign. According to the standard account, he did so to address conflicts among his soldiers over how the Qur'an was to be pronounced (one of his generals, Hudhyafa, is said to have implored him, "Save this nation before they differ about the Book as Jews and Christians did before them!"). Yet in compiling an official version of the Qur'an, 'Uthman had all competing versions burned, an act that infuriated certain elder companions of the Prophet. Among them was Ibn Mas'ud, who brawled with the men whom 'Uthman had sent to seize his version of the Qur'an. On this occasion, Ibn Mas'ud is said to have shouted that he was already a Muslim when, Zayd, the Qur'an scribe of 'Uthman, was still in the loins of an unbeliever.

Thus opposition to 'Uthman spread. Finally, in the year 656, a large contingent of protestors arrived in Medina from Egypt with a list of demands. 'Uthman, the sources tell us, agreed to them all, but as the protestors made their way back to Egypt, they intercepted a messenger of the caliph who was carrying orders for the execution of their leaders. Immediately they returned to Medina and laid siege to the caliph's palace. 'Uthman claimed that the orders were forged, but he could no longer pacify the rebels. They broke into the caliph's residence and stabbed him to death. At the moment when he was attacked, 'Uthman—the caliph accused of impiety—was piously reading the Qur'an, and his blood poured out onto the holy text.

'Ali and the Prophet's Family

From the perspective of Sunni Muslims, the murders of 'Umar and 'Uthman were tragic. The killing of 'Uthman was especially so, for it was not the act of a disgruntled infidel but rather the act of pious Muslims; moreover, it ushered in a period of internal dissension—known as the *fitna*—that would not be resolved for generations. From the perspective of Shi'ite Muslims, on the other hand, a greater tragedy had already taken place when 'Ali was not made the ruler after Muhammad's death. Now, with the death of 'Uthman, 'Ali finally had his chance.

After the death of 'Uthman, Tabari reports, the (Meccan) clan that had supported him—the Umayyads—fell into disarray, unsure how to react to the assassination of their relative. The (Medinan) *ansar* thus seized the opportunity to elect their own man. While 'Ali was not one of them—he was of course a Meccan from the family of the Prophet—he was also not an Umayyad and he had been no ally of Abu Bakr, 'Umar, and 'Uthman. This was enough to win the support of the *ansar*.

Ultimately, most of the Meccans also agreed to support 'Ali, but not all of them did so willingly. Talha, an elder companion of Muhammad, is reported to have said: "I gave allegiance with a sword over my head" (Tabari, 16:9). A second elder companion, Zubayr, is reported to have said something similar: "I gave allegiance with a sword at my neck," he declared (Tabari, 16:15). But if these men declared their support for 'Ali only reluctantly, it was a woman who refused to do so at all.

'A'isha, the beloved wife of the Prophet and the daughter of Abu Bakr, was no friend of 'Uthman. According to Tabari, when 'Uthman's murder was imminent, she did not hang around Medina to support him but rather left for Mecca under the pretense of a pilgrimage. Only after 'Uthman's murder did she begin

Personalities in Islam 3.2
ʿALI

If Abu Bakr is remembered as the first free, adult male to accept Islam, ʿAli is remembered as the first male, of any age, to accept Islam. In the biography of the Prophet as told by Ibn Ishaq, ʿAli is only a boy of ten at the time he accepts Islam, and thus his acceptance is considered less valuable than that of a full-grown man. Still, Shiʿite Muslims are quick to point out that ʿAli had certain merits that Abu Bakr lacked. He is a cousin of Muhammad himself. What is more, Muhammad took ʿAli into his own house after the death of ʿAli's father, Abu Talib (who had raised Muhammad as his own son). Thus ʿAli is from the same family, and from the same house, as Muhammad. It is perhaps appropriate, then, that ʿAli takes the place of the prophet—sleeping in his bed—when Muhammad flees for Medina with Abu Bakr. The importance of this act for Shiʿites should not be underestimated. It is ʿAli, and not Abu Bakr, who is in the more dangerous position. He has taken the place of the Prophet, knowing of the conspiracy against him, and is willing to die for his sake.

The intimacy of the relationship between Muhammad and ʿAli is suggested by a *hadith* reporting that ʿAli's favorite nickname was "Father of the Dust" (*Abu l-Turab*). The name hardly appears flattering, but ʿAli cherishes it because it was given to him by Muhammad when the Prophet found him sleeping on the dirt floor near the wall of a mosque. In another hadith the Prophet folds a cloak around ʿAli, Fatima (Muhammad's daughter and ʿAli's wife), Hasan, and Husayn (the two sons of ʿAli and Fatima) and prays for their purification. This prayer, to Shiʿites, suggests that the line of ʿAli and Fatima ("The People of the House [of the Prophet]," *ahl al-bayt*) is favored by God, and that the twelve Imams (the first of whom was ʿAli himself) were protected from sin and error.

Islamic tradition also makes much of ʿAli's prowess and courage in war, and piety in religion. ʿAli is victorious in individual combat before the larger battle at Badr, slaying his opponent Walid b. ʿUtba. Later he receives a sword with two points at the end, named "Dhu l-Fiqar" (the notion of two points might be imagined from the term *fiqar*, "bifurcated"), with which he fights at Uhud, and which is an iconic symbol to Shiʿite (and other) Muslims today. In one tradition, Muhammad gives ʿAli this sword from the booty seized after the Battle of Badr. In another tradition, an angel brings this sword down to ʿAli from heaven.

the trip back to Medina. On the way, how-ever, she learned of ʿAli's election. ʿAʾisha and ʿAli already had a bitter relationship when the Prophet was still alive, and the bitterness between them had only intensified when ʿAli hesitated to accept the election of her father, Abu Bakr, as the first caliph. If ʿAʾisha had been secretly pleased at ʿUthman's murder, she was now openly furious that ʿAli had been chosen to replace him. She immediately turned around, retraced her steps to Mecca, and began to organize resistance to the new caliph.

Talha and Zubayr soon joined her in Mecca. The three of them rallied a small group of followers and set out across the desert toward Iraq, where they hoped to gar-ner further support. ʿAli, however, had no intention of letting them proceed peacefully. Egypt was in turmoil, and Syria was con-trolled by an Umayyad named Muʿawiya, one of ʿUthman's governors and the son of Abu Sufyan; If ʿAli lost Iraq, he would have no significant power base left. Thus he inter-cepted their party and attacked them. In the conflict that ensued, known as the Battle of the Camel, ʿAli's forces killed Talha and Zubayr and routed their followers. For his part, ʿAli was magnanimous in victory; he mourned their death and treated ʿAʾisha with honor.

But ʿAʾisha's resistance was not the end of his troubles. Muʿawiya remained stubbornly opposed to ʿAli's election. How, Muʿawiya complained, could ʿAli be elected caliph when he had failed to punish those responsible for the murder of (Muʿawiya's relative) ʿUthman? Could ʿAli himself have been involved some-how with this insidious act? ʿAli, for his part, was not prepared to back down (as doing so presumably would have been a fatal show of weakness).

In fact, the brewing conflict involved more than a proper investigation of ʿUthman's killing. In part, it was a conflict between the Medinan supporters of ʿAli and the Meccan Umayyad clan (a strange echo of the Prophet's own struggles with the Meccans when they were led by Muʿawiya's father, Abu Sufyan). It was also a conflict between Iraq, from which ʿAli drew most of his support, and Syria. And of course, according to later Islamic sources, this was a conflict between those who recog-nized ʿAli as the first Imam, the Shiʿites, and those who did not.

Whatever the reasons for their rivalry, the forces of ʿAli and Muʿawiya finally met in 657 on a battlefield near the Syrian plain of Siffin, on the banks of the Euphrates. There they fought for three days. When, on the third day, the tide finally began to turn against Muʿawiya, his followers attached leaves of the Qurʾan to their lances and shouted, "The law of God shall decide between us!" ʿAli, distressed by the killing of Muslims on both sides, agreed to submit to an arbitra-tion. In doing so, however, ʿAli estranged his most fervent supporters. Insisting that ʿAli's election was an act of God, which could not be left to human arbitration, a large contingent of them (by some counts twelve thousand men) left the battlefield. They consequently became known as the Kharijites ("Those who depart").

According to Tabari, the arbitration eventually took place some months later in the Arabian Peninsula, but the arbiters were themselves divided. In the end, nothing changed, but ʿAli had lost much of his prestige. Moreover, he was now faced with the additional opposition of the Kharijites, whom he was forced to confront in Iraq, at a site named Nahrawan, the following year. The

battle ended in a slaughter of the Kharijites, but it was a pyrrhic victory, for ʿAli had slaughtered his former followers. In fact, this battle would lead to ʿAli's demise.

One of the Kharijites who had survived the battle of Nahrawan, by the name of Ibn Muljam, sought out ʿAli at the entrance to the Great Mosque in the Iraqi city of Kufa two years later, in early 661. Seeking revenge for the martyrs of Nahrawan, Ibn Muljam attacked the caliph with a poisoned sword. Two days later, ʿAli—the cousin of the Prophet and his son-in-law, who had once laid down in the Prophet's bed when Muhammad fled to Medina—now lay dead.

FIGURE 3.2. *A pious Shiʿite rendering of the shrine containing ʿAli's tomb (in Najaf, Iraq).*

FROM A CLASSIC TEXT ❖ 3.1

The Assassination of ʿAli, "Commander of the Faithful"

Al-Shaykh al-Mufid (d. 1022) presents ʿAli as a figure whose life imitated that of the Prophet Muhammad himself. He compares ʿAli's struggles during the caliphates of Abu Bakr, ʿUmar, and ʿUthman to Muhammad's struggles in Mecca. He compares ʿAli's struggles during his own caliphate—when he was confronted with rebels led by ʿAʾisha and Muʿawiya—to Muhammad's struggles in Medina (where he was confronted with pagan enemies and duplicitous Muslims). Finally al-Shaykh al-Mufid has ʿAli die, just like Muhammad (see Bukhari 4:736), at the age of sixty-three.

The Imamate [period during which he was God's chosen leader] of the "Commander of the Faithful" [ʿAli]—peace be on him—was for thirty years after the Prophet—may God bless him and his family. For twenty-four years and six months of these he was prevented from administering the laws (of the office) (and had to) exercise precautionary dissimulation and withdrawal. For five years and six months of these, he was troubled by wars against the hypocrites, those who broke their pledges, the unjust and those who deviated (from the religion) and he was plagued by the seditions of those who had gone astray. In the same way the Apostle of God, may God bless him and his family, had been prevented from (administering) the laws (of his office) through fear and through being spied upon, and through being a fugitive and through being exiled, so that he had no power to fight the unbelievers and no means of defending the believers. Then he emigrated and for ten years after the emigration he remained making war on the unbelievers and being troubled by the hypocrites until the time that God—may His name be exalted—took him unto Himself and made him dwell in the gardens of Paradise.

The death of the Commander of the Faithful—peace be on him—occurred before dawn of Friday, the twenty-first of the month of Ramadan, in the year 40 A.H. He was a victim of the sword. Ibn Muljam al-Muradi—may God curse him—killed him at the mosque of Kufa, which he had come out to in order to wake the people for the dawn prayer on the night of the nineteenth of the month of Ramadan. He had been lying in wait for him from the beginning of the night. When he [ʿAli] passed by him while the latter was hiding his design by feigning sleep amid a group of people who were asleep, he [Ibn Muljam] sprang out and struck him on the top of his head with his sword which was poisoned. He lingered through the day of the nineteenth and the night and day of the twentieth and the first third of the night of the twenty-first. Then he—peace be on him—died a martyr and met his Lord, Most High, as one who has been wronged. He—peace be on him—knew of that before its time and he told the people of it before its time. His two sons, al-Hasan and al-Husayn—peace be on them—performed (the tasks) of washing him and shrouding him according to his bequest. Then they carried him to al-Ghari at

Najaf in Kufa and they buried him there. They removed the traces of the place of his burial according to his bequest which was made about that to hath of them by him, because of what he—peace be on him—knew about the regime of the Umayyads (which would come) after him, and their hostile attitude towards him. (For he knew) the evil action and abuse to which they would be led by their wicked intentions if they had been able to know that (place). His grave—peace be on him—remained hidden until al-Sadiq Jafar b. Muhammad, peace be on them, pointed it out during the Abbasid regime. For he visited it when he came to visit Abu Ja'far (al-Mansur) while the latter was in al-Hira. Then the Shi'a knew of it and they began from that time to make visitation to his (grave), peace be on him and on his pure offspring.

On the day of his death he was 63 years of age. (al-Shaykh al-Mufid, trans. Howard, 5–6)

Mu'awiya acted immediately. He moved his forces into Iraq and compelled 'Ali's eldest son, Hasan, to acknowledge him as the caliph. Thereafter he succeeded in winning almost universal acknowledgment of his rule. But Mu'awiya never moved to Medina—the city of the Prophet—where the caliphs before him had ruled. Instead, he remained in Damascus, a city by now familiar to him. A new era of Islam, the Umayyad dynasty, had begun. The fourth rightly guided caliph, or the first Imam, was dead. Ruling in his place was the son of Abu Sufyan.

STUDY QUESTIONS

1   By what logic do Sunni Muslims defend the selection of Abu Bakr as the first caliph?

2   By what logic do Shi'ite Muslims argue that 'Ali should have been the leader of the Islamic community after Muhammad?

3   What does the account of the Wars of Apostasy reflect of the Muslim understanding of Islam?

4   What is the Muslim understanding of the early Islamic conquests?

CONCLUSION TO PART ONE

In his work *Muhammad at Medina* (published in 1956), William Montgomery Watt introduces his examination of Muhammad's moral character in the following way: "We may ask, 'Was Muhammad a good man according to the standards of the Arabia of his day?' or we may ask, 'Was he a good man according to the standards of, say, the best people in Europe about the year 1950?'" (327). Watt concludes that Muhammad was an excellent man for his time but that he cannot be considered a moral exemplar for all times, as Muslims would have him be.

With this matter (as with others), Watt proves to be careful in his analysis of the Islamic sources but careless of the larger problem of the sources themselves. Watt sorts through the reports found in Ibn Ishaq and other classical sources, removing whatever seems to him superstitious, irrational, impractical, anachronistic, or politically convenient. Thus he rejects some of the reports that would make Muhammad's character suffer (by the standards of a good European in 1950) but retains others, such as his appetite for women or the massacre of the Banu Qurayza.

In today's context, those who would demonize Muhammad use a similar strategy; they ignore the reports that make him sincere and tenderhearted. Those who would defend Muhammad also use the same strategy, rejecting or explaining away less pleasant reports. All of these approaches, however, miss the basic problem of Muhammad's biography.

In the first two chapters of this work, we saw how the most ancient biographers of the Prophet show no particular interest in the moral questions that concern modern observers, such as women's rights or just warfare. Instead, they are concerned above all with (1) the presentation of Muhammad in a way that proves he was a prophet like the prophets of the Bible; and (2) the explanation of qur'anic passages with stories about Muhammad. All of the traditions they relate about the Prophet, whether they make him look good or bad according to the standards of 1950—or any other year—are shaped by these two concerns. Thus there is no way to say that reports on Muhammad's involvement in raids, polygamy, or concubinage are more or less authentic than reports on his concern for justice and compassion, or, for that matter, on his fondness for toothpicks.

When it comes to the lives of the first caliphs, the Islamic sources again appear to be shaped by particular concerns. From a Shi'ite perspective, the rule of Abu Bakr, 'Umar, and 'Uthman was an age of unrighteousness; the family of the Prophet was oppressed by its enemies, and unholy men were falsifying Islam. Indeed, some earlier Shi'ite scholars go so far as to say that 'Uthman falsified the Qur'an itself, erasing verses that referred to 'Ali and the other Imams (an opinion rarely expressed today).

Yet the light of (true, Shi'ite) Islam was not completely extinguished by this treachery. While 'Ali's son Hasan never became caliph, he was nonetheless the second Imam (his brother Husayn became the third Imam after

him). All twelve Imams, even if they could no longer act as political leaders as God intended, continued to act as the source of wisdom on religious and spiritual matters. To Shi'ites, the twelve Imams are not only infallible leaders, they are also the very center of existence (Ar. qutb, "pole," or axis mundi), around which all of creation revolves.

But the Sunni rulers who followed Mu'awiya continued to oppose the Imams. Most Shi'ite scholars insist that the first eleven Imams were all murdered by their Sunni enemies. For this reason, God cast a state of invisibility on the twelfth Imam, Muhammad al-Mahdi, soon after he was born (c. 869). Today this "Hidden" Imam is still alive and present in this world, waiting for the moment when God will cast visibility upon him again. At that moment, he will rise up with the sword and take revenge against the Sunnis. He will finally establish the law of Islam, or sharia, in its true form, and he will prepare the way for the final era of humanity. Thus Shi'ites wait still today for this era, this golden age, to arrive.

From the Sunni perspective, however, the period of the rightly guided caliphs—when Muslims were vanquishing their enemies and holy men were meticulously enacting the law of God—was that golden age. Sunnis insist that the proper role of these caliphs—Abu Bakr, 'Umar, 'Uthman, and 'Ali—was to guard the sharia and to lead the Islamic community (God's community!) in its military campaigns. They were not "divinely chosen" leaders. They were simply pious Muslims. No one after Muhammad

FROM A CLASSIC TEXT ❖ CONCL. 1.1

The Peak of Eloquence

The 241 sermons attributed to ʿAli b. Abi Talib, collected by al-Radi (d. 1015) in work known as the Peak of Eloquence, are considered by many Shiʿites to have a spiritual value second only to the Qurʾan itself. A number of these sermons present the Shiʿite narrative of the struggles for leadership of the Islamic community after the death of Muhammad. Others, such as sermon 197, offer wisdom for the spiritual life. While not denying the importance of Islamic law and outward religious practice, such sermons ask Muslims to turn their gaze inward and to examine the state of their soul.

Sermon 197

Allah's Attribute of Omniscience

Allah knows the cries of the beast in the forest, the sins of people in seclusion, the movements of the fishes in the deep seas and the rising of the water by tempestuous winds. I stand witness that Muhammad is the choice of Allah, the conveyor of His revelation and the messenger of His mercy.

Advantages of Fear of Allah

Now then, I advise you to fear Allah, Who created you for the first time; towards Him is your return, with Him lies the success of your aims, at Him terminate (all) your desires, towards Him runs your path of right and He is the aim of your fears (for seeking protection). Certainly, fear of Allah is the medicine for your hearts, sight for the blindness of your spirits, the cure for the ailments of your bodies, the rectifier of the evils of your breasts, the purifier of the pollution of your minds, the light of the darkness of your eyes, the consolation for the fear of your heart and the brightness from the gloom of your ignorance.

Therefore, make obedience to Allah the way of your life and not only your outside covering, make it your inner habit instead of only outer routine, subtle enough to enter your ribs (up to the heart), the guide for all your affairs, the watering place for your getting down (on the Day of Judgment), the interceder for the achievement of your aims, asylum for the day of your fear, the lamp of the interior of your graves, company for your long loneliness, and deliverance from the troubles of your abodes. Certainly obedience to Allah is a protection against encircling calamities, expected dangers and the flames of burning fires. (*Nahjul Balagha*, 407) was divinely chosen. God had given humanity sharia, and sharia offers humanity all the guidance it needs.

Thus pious Sunnis, on the one hand, often look back to the first days of Islam with nostalgia; some extremist Sunni groups such as the Taliban dream of a return to those days. Many pious Shiʿites, on the other hand, instead look forward to the last days, when the Hidden Imam will appear, and the light of true Islam will finally shine brilliantly throughout the world.

PART 2   THE QUR'AN

INTRODUCTION TO PART 2: HISTORY AND LITERATURE

At various points in the first part of this book, I reflect on the uncertain quality of the story of Islam's origins that I tell there. This uncertainty is a product of the Islamic sources on which this story is based. Ibn Ishaq, the earliest Islamic biographer of Muhammad, is said to have died in 767 CE, well over a century after the Prophet's death. Yet the earliest version of his biography is available to us only through the quotations of it by Ibn Hisham, who died in 833. Now Ibn Ishaq often attributes his narratives on the life of the Prophet to elders from the Prophet's own day. For example, before telling the story of the Battle of Badr, he relates,

Muhammad b. Muslim al-Zuhri and Asim b. ʿUmar b. Qatada and ʿAbdallah b. Abu Bakr and Yazid b. Ruman from ʿUrwa b. al-Zubayr, and other scholars of ours from Ibn ʿAbbas, each one of them told me some of this story and their account is collected in what I have drawn up of the story of Badr. (Ibn Ishaq, 370)

This list of names cannot be properly called a bibliography. Ibn Ishaq does not mention any book, or any document, that he read about the Battle of Badr. Instead, he gives the names of some (but not all) of the scholars from whom he has heard the story of the battle. He then notes that all of these scholars attributed their account to Ibn ʿAbbas, who is said to have been born three years before the Prophet's migration to Medina; he would have thus been only a young boy of five when

83

the Battle of Badr took place and could hardly have been an eyewitness to it. However, Ibn ʿAbbas later gained the reputation of being a great (if not the greatest) authority on the life of the Prophet and the meaning of the Qurʾan. Thus Ibn Ishaq here means to tell the reader how he has diligently listened to how the best scholars of his own day tell the story of Badr, and how he has confirmed that these scholars have a connection to Ibn ʿAbbas, the great historian of early Islam. This introduction to the account of the Battle of Badr, in other words, is meant to show that Ibn Ishaq has done his homework and that the reader can have confidence in the story he is about to tell.

Such declarations are also a common feature in the "Book of Raids," of Waqidi (d. 822), a second biography of the Prophet mentioned in the first part of the present volume. However, an interesting development appears in a third biography of the Prophet, that of Waqidi's student Ibn Saʿd (d. 845). At the opening of his description of the Prophet's raids, Ibn Saʿd presents a general list of his authorities similar to that of Ibn Ishaq above. However, when he comes to Badr itself, Ibn Saʿd adds a long series of specific reports (forty-one in all), preceded in each case by a precise list of transmitters. Regarding the date of Badr, for example, Ibn Saʿd recounts,

> ʿAffan Ibn Muslim and Saʿid Ibn Sulayman informed us: they said: Khalid Ibn ʿAbdallah informed us: ʿAmr Ibn Yahya informed me on the authority of ʿAmir Ibn ʿAbdallah Ibn Zubayr, he on the authority of his father, he on the authority of ʿAmir Ibn Rabiʿh al-Badri; he said: "The Battle of Badr took place

on Monday the seventeenth of [the month of] Ramadan." (Ibn Saʿd, 21)

In providing this list of transmitters, or **isnad**, Ibn Saʿd does not mean to show the reader that he has relied on the best-known scholars to investigate the question of the date of the Battle of Badr. Instead, he means to prove that he has a statement from an eyewitness. The *isnad* leads to a figure named ʿAmir Ibn Rabiʿah al-Badri. Unlike Ibn ʿAbbas, al-Badri has no status among the great scholars of Islam whatsoever (in fact, he is so obscure that a twelfth-century scholar named Ibn ʿAsakir devotes a paragraph in his book *On the History of Damascus* to the question, Who was ʿAmir Ibn Rabiʿah al-Badri?). Yet al-Badri has one virtue that Ibn ʿAbbas lacks: the name Badri, given to him because he is included among the lists of eyewitnesses to the Battle of Badr (Badri: "the one associated with Badr").

This *isnad*, then, suggests that Ibn Saʿd considers his report—that the Battle of Badr took place on Monday the seventeenth of the month of Ramadan—believable because it has been transmitted from someone who was there on that day. Of course, the absence of such precise *isnad*s in earlier works such as Ibn Ishaq suggests that Ibn Saʿd's *isnad* (and the report it leads to) may be his own creation.

By the ninth century, Muslim scholars had come to see reports like that of Ibn Saʿd, which collectively came to be known as *hadith*, as something more than historical records. In part due to the influence of a Sunni legal scholar named Shafiʿi (d. 820), a consensus began to emerge that *hadith* reporting the actions or the words of the Prophet are a source of divine instruction.

FROM A CLASSIC TEXT ❖ INTRO. 2.1

The *Hadith*: A Second Source of Revelation

Shafiʿi (d. 820) is known as the founder of one of the four principal schools of Sunni jurisprudence, yet his influence on the development of Islamic religious thought far exceeds legal matters. Shafiʿi argued that the Qurʾan itself binds Muslims to obey all of the instructions and to imitate all of the practices of the Prophet Muhammad—even those not found in the Qurʾan. His argument implies that the Prophet Muhammad was infallible and impeccable, that all of his words and all of his actions are a reliable manifestation of God's will for humanity.

By this way of thinking, hadith by or about Muhammad are useful not only as historical reports about the Prophet. Those hadith that can be validly traced back to the Prophet are in fact divine revelation; they are authentic indications of true Islam, the religion which God desires all people to follow. Determining which hadith are "valid" accordingly became one of the great scholarly activities of Sunni Islam. The importance of prophetic hadith in the religious thought of Shiʿite Muslims (who developed different hadith collections involving also the Imams) is also considerable, although Shiʿite hadith include reports from the Imams.

In the following example, Shafiʿi addresses the restrictions imposed upon a woman after her husband's death. A qurʾanic verse (Q 2:234) implies that a woman is not allowed to marry for a period (known in Islamic law as ʿidda) of four months and ten days after the death of her husband. The purpose of this period, according to the common understanding, is to determine whether the woman is pregnant with a child from her former husband (since the custody of the child would be given to his family, and not to her, according to Islamic law). Shafiʿi notes, however, that the hadith imposes other restrictions upon a widow during this period.

God said: "Those of you who die, leaving wives, let them keep to themselves for four months and ten [days]; when they reach the end of their term, then it is no fault in you what they may do with themselves honorably. God is aware of what you do" (Q 2:234). So God specified that [women] who [suffer] the death [of their husbands] are under obligation of the ʿidda and that upon the expiration of the term they shall be free to do honorably with themselves whatever they may wish, but He mentioned nothing else to be avoided during the ʿidda. The literal meaning of the divine communication is that [the widow] should abstain only from getting married during the ʿidda and that she should stay in her house.

[The communication] may [also] mean that [the widow] should [not only] abstain from marriage, but also from certain other things which were not forbidden to her before the ʿidda such as [the use of] perfume and [the wearing of] ornaments. Since the Prophet decreed that the widow must abstain from the use of perfume and the like, she is under obligation to do so [by virtue] of the duty imposed by the *sunna*, but her abstention from marriage and her stay in the house of her [deceased] husband are [imposed on her] by the Book and the sunna. (Shafiʿi, 172)

Shafiʿi argues that Muhammad's entire conduct, or *sunna*, was guided by God. Therefore the records of that conduct represent a source of revelation, a guide to Islamic law second only to the Qurʾan. To make this point, Shafiʿi turns to verses in the Qurʾan that describe the Prophet bringing both "the Book" and "the wisdom," such as Q 2:151: "We have sent among you, of yourselves, a Messenger, to recite Our signs to you and to purify you, and to teach you the Book and the Wisdom, and to teach you that you knew not." According to Shafiʿi, the "book" is the Qurʾan, and the "wisdom" is Muhammad's *sunna*. He concludes,

So it is not permissible to regard anything as a duty save that set forth in the Qurʾan and the *sunna* of His Apostle. For [God], as I have [just] stated, prescribed the belief in His Apostle. The *sunna* of the Apostle makes evident what God meant [in the text of His Book], indicating His general and particular [commands]. (Shafiʿi, 112)

According to Shafiʿi, the *hadith* are not, like the Qurʾan, the very words of God. However, those *hadith* that authentically preserve the *sunna* of Muhammad represent God's will for humanity no less than the Qurʾan. Thus, for example, the report of Ibn Saʿd that Muhammad launched the raid of Badr during Ramadan serves as evidence that fighting the holy war is permitted even during this holy month of fasting.

Shiʿites, it should be noted, expanded the idea of *hadith* to include the Imams. According to Shiʿite belief, the Imams were no less infallible than Muhammad. Accordingly, their words and deeds, like those of Muhammad, are a source of revelation and a guide for Islamic law. Thus Shiʿites developed their own collections of *hadith* in which traditions about Muhammad are joined with traditions about the Imams. Moreover, they look with skepticism on the *hadith* in Sunni collections (many of which were transmitted by the opponents of ʿAli and his family).

The basic problem for all Muslims, however, was figuring out which *hadith* are authentic. By the ninth century, *hadith* had begun to appear in such great numbers that all agreed many of them must be false. No individual, even if he were a prophet, could say or do all of the things attributed to Muhammad in one lifetime. Furthermore, many *hadith* contradict each other. In the *hadith* Muhammad blesses and condemns Shiʿism, supports and opposes the doctrine of free will, offers differing instructions on exactly how to pray, and permits and forbids the consumption of certain foods.

Evidently, the temptation to present one's personal view as a prophetic *hadith*—and thereby to convince others to accept it—was too difficult to resist. One sign that this was the case is a *hadith* in which Muhammad himself is made to warn against the multiplication of forged *hadith*: "After my departure the number of sayings ascribed to me will increase in the same way as sayings have been ascribed to previous prophets" (Goldziher, 2:56). Presumably, this *hadith* was forged by someone who hoped to convince Muslims to stop forging *hadith*.

Bukhari (d. 870), the author of the most authoritative Sunni collection of *hadith*, became famous for sorting out many of the authentic *hadith* from forged *hadith*. In a well-known tradition, Bukhari recounts having a dream in which he stands in front of Muhammad, who is fast asleep. Flies swarm around the Prophet's mouth while Bukhari shoos them away with a fan. Bukhari asked dream interpreters what this scene could mean, and they informed him that he would be the one to protect the Prophet from lies. Thus Bukhari made it his mission to identify *hadith* that had been wrongly put into Muhammad's mouth.

Bukhari and other *hadith* scholars after him determined a *hadith*'s authenticity by examining *isnad*s. They did not look for reports that are illogical, anachronistic, or inconsistent. Instead, they examined the list of transmitters in the *isnad* to see if anything was wrong. They asked whether each transmitter could in fact have passed on the *hadith* to the next one in the chain. This method of identification meant verifying the birth and death dates of the transmitters (as a dead person could no longer transmit *hadith*) and the region in which they lived (since, without telephones or the Internet, a Muslim in Spain could not have passed on a *hadith* to a Muslim in Iran).

They also asked whether the authorities mentioned in the *isnad* are to be believed, which meant examining the moral virtue and religious piety of each transmitter, since the absence of either might mean that this transmitter was willing to forge a *hadith*. These sorts of examinations, incidentally, led to the rise of an entire new field of research in Islam: "the science of men" (*'ilm al-rijal*). Through this science, Muslims produced remarkable biographical dictionaries the likes of which would not be found outside of the Islamic world until centuries later, and even then not on the same scale.

Scholars gave a *hadith* that passed the test of this *isnad* criticism the title *sahih*, or "valid." Bukhari thus gave the name *al-Sahih* ("The Valid") to his *hadith* collection. His biographers report that in his travels Bukhari learned over 600,000 *hadith*. Of these he determined that about 2,600 were valid.

Yet reliance on the *isnad* led Muslim scholars such as Bukhari to accept as valid *hadith* that, on the basis of their content, appear to be invalid. This was an old objection, made even by some early Muslims, and it was addressed in works such as the *Interpretation of Difference in Hadith* by Ibn Qutayba (d. 889). In the modern period, Ignaz Goldziher, a Hungarian author of the landmark work of Western scholarship on the *hadith*, argues that *hadith* believed to come from Muhammad on the basis of their *isnad* often, on the basis of their content, appear to come from well after his death.

This seems to be the case, for example, of the many *hadith* on the duty of Muslims to obey even a sinful and impious ruler. In one such *hadith*, the Prophet reports, "It is better to have a tyrannical government for a time than to have a period of revolution"; in another, he declares: "Hell has seven gates; one of them is destined for those who draw the sword upon my community" (Goldziher, 2:94). These "calming *hadiths*," as Goldziher describes them, would have had no place in the time of Muhammad, since the ruler at the time was the sinless and pious messenger of God. Yet they would have had a place in the Umayyad period, when caliphs such as Muʿawiya and his son Yazid were under threat from various religious movements which accused them of impiety.

Goldziher argues that these *hadith* were invented in order to convince the populace to remain docile. "All of them have the same purpose," Goldziher comments, "to teach that even a wicked government must be obeyed and that it must be left to God to cause the downfall of rulers of whom He disapproves" (Goldziher, 2:93–94). All of these *hadith* seem to have come from someone other than Muhammad, their impressive *isnads* notwithstanding.

In order to understand the importance of this point for the study of Islam's emergence, we must first note that *hadith* do not make up only one particular science of Islamic tradition, or one genre of Islamic literature (even if books, such as Bukhari's *Sahih*, are made up of *hadith*s organized by topic). The *hadith* (understood generally) are the basic building blocks of most Islamic sciences (including jurisprudence, history, mysticism, and even grammar). So too they are the building blocks of the Prophet's biography. Yet, as the contrast between Ibn Ishaq and Ibn Saʿd suggests, the *hadith* on Muhammad's biography (for example, regarding what day the battle of Badr took place) are systematic only in later works. Their connection with the Muhammad of history is questionable.

All in all, the problems with the Prophet's biography are significant enough to suggest that a different approach to the emergence of Islam is worth considering. In part 1 of the present volume, I examined the traditional biography of the Prophet and the first caliphs. Occasionally I noted verses of the Qurʾan that are cited or alluded to in that biography. Here in part 2, I will begin instead with the Qurʾan itself. Ignoring the links that the traditional biographers make between the Qurʾan and the life of Muhammad, I will ask what we can know about the emergence of Islam from the witness of the Qurʾan alone.

This approach is atypical. Most Western scholars insist that we can only properly understand the Qurʾan in the light of the Prophet Muhammad's biography, even when the Qurʾan makes no mention

BOX 4.1 ❖ MUSICAL INSTRUMENTS

Most classical Islamic manuals of law, on the basis of *hadith*, declare musical instruments forbidden. To this end a manual known as *Reliance of the Traveller* by Ahmad al-Misri (d. 1368) quotes a *hadith* in which the Prophet Muhammad declares, "Allah Mighty and Majestic sent me as a guidance and mercy to believers and commanded me to do away with musical instruments, flutes, strings, crucifixes, and the affair of the pre-Islamic period of ignorance," along with a second *hadith*, in which the Prophet declares, "On the Day of Resurrection, Allah will pour molten lead into the ears of whoever sits listening to a songstress." Al-Misri concludes, "All of this is explicit and compelling textual evidence that musical instruments of all types are unlawful." For his part, the "Qur'an Alone" Muslim Ahmad Subhi Mansour responds to a question on the permissibility of music with the following **fatwa**: "Music, songs, drama, and all the different kinds of art are *halal* [permitted]. It is prohibited to make them *haram* [forbidden]. As an Islamic rule, no one has the right to make anything *haram* unless it is mentioned clearly in the Qur'an" (http://ahl-alquran.com/arabic/show_fatwa.php?main_id=588). One might also note that music (with musical instruments) is widely accepted in the Islamic world today.

of him. Following a traditional Islamic idea, they argue that each sura of the Qur'an was proclaimed at a certain point during either the Meccan or the Medinan period of Muhammad's career. In order to understand a certain passage in the Qur'an, they insist, it is first necessary to identify its sura as "Meccan" or "Medinan." However, the Qur'an itself never names suras "Meccan" or "Medinan." Thus in part 2 of this work, I will base my narrative only on what is found in the Qur'an and thereby ask what the holy book of Islam itself might teach us.

As we will see, there is good reason to believe that the Qur'an comes from the period of Islam's origins, while the *hadith* (and the traditions that make up the Prophet's biography) do not. For this reason, I believe that we might gain a revealing view of Islam's emergence by relying above all on the scripture Muslims consider to be the very word of God brought down from heaven, the Qur'an.

Chapter 4

THE QURʾAN AND ITS MESSAGE

It is He who shows you the lightning, for fear and hope, and produces the heavy clouds; * the thunder proclaims His praise, and the angels, in awe of Him. He looses the thunderbolts, and smites with them whomsoever He will; yet they dispute about God, who is mighty in power. * To Him is the call of truth; and those upon whom they call, apart from Him, answer them nothing, but it is as a man who stretches out his hands to water that it may reach his mouth, and it reaches it not. The prayer of the unbelievers goes only astray.

—Qurʾan 13:12–14

The Nature of the Qurʾanic Text

Structure

The Qurʾan is a relatively short book (just over half the length of the New Testament). It is divided into 114 chapters, called suras, and each of these suras is divided into verses. According to Islamic tradition, the division into suras was revealed by God to the Prophet; the angel Gabriel taught Muhammad how to form suras from the pieces of revelation given to him by God. At the end of each year, Gabriel would visit Muhammad in order to review the suras that had thus far been compiled. (He had Muhammad review the suras twice during the last year of his life. The division into verses, however, was not revealed by God but was developed by later generations after the death of the Prophet. Before the standardization of the Qur'an in the early twentieth century, a good deal of variation in verse numbering existed. Nevertheless the verses appear to be an organic element of the text, as they generally are delineated according to Arabic rhyme, a prominent feature of the Qur'an.

All but two suras of the Qur'an are preceded by the invocation, "In the name of God the Merciful, the Compassionate." In *al-Fatiha*, the first sura of the Qu'ran, these words become part of the sura (verse 1); they are missing altogether in sura 9. Each sura also has a name, a feature similarly understood to be the work of Islamic tradition (on this, too, a good deal of variation existed). The traditional names are not like those of biblical books. The first book of the Bible is known to Christians as Genesis because it tells the story of origins, and to Jews as *Be-reshit* ("In the beginning . . . ") because it opens with these words. However, the names of the suras, for the most part, are neither their first words nor their main topics. Instead, they appear simply to be labels by which one sura might be distinguished from others. The first sura of the Qur'an is known as *al-Fatiha*, "The Opening," because it is the first sura. The second sura is known as "The Cow" not because it is about a cow but only because it refers briefly (verses 67–73) to a story in which Moses instructs his followers to touch a murdered man with the flesh of a sacrificed cow (that he may come

to life and, presumably, accuse his murderer; a story with connections to the Biblical passages Numbers 19:1–10 and Deuteronomy 21:1–9).

The Qur'an's 114 suras are organized, for the most part, in decreasing order of length (an ordering principle that has a precedent in the arrangement of Paul's letters in the New Testament). This principle is not applied precisely, however. Sura 2, and not sura 1, is the longest chapter of the Qur'an; the shortest sura (with only three verses) is 108, not 114.

In fact, the exceptions to this principle are telling. For the most part, the Qur'an speaks in the voice of God, like the sections of the Pentateuch or the Old Testament prophetic books in which God is quoted. However, the first sura—which has only seven verses—seems to be a prayer, the words of a believer speaking to God. The last two suras of the Qur'an—sometimes called "charm suras" because they seem to be incantations against evil—also seem to be in the voice of a believer (although they begin with the command "Say!" and thus are understood as the words of God, who is telling humans how to pray).

Meanwhile, in the middle of the text, the ordering principle of the suras seems to be broken in order to keep certain groups of suras together. Twenty-nine suras begin with a series of letters that in manuscripts are written individually (Arabic is otherwise written in a cursive script); for this reason, they are known in Islamic tradition as "the broken letters." Their precise meaning is unclear, which is why Western scholars have given them the more dramatic name "the mysterious letters."

However, their place in the text is not entirely mysterious. It seems clear at least that they served as labels for certain groupings of suras.

The broken letters *a.l.r.* appear at the beginning of suras 10–15 (sura 13 has *a.l.m.r.*). Yet suras 13–15 are all shorter than sura 16, in contrast to the larger organizing principle of the Qurʾan. Presumably, they were kept before sura 16 because the "*a.l.r.*" suras formed a unit of some kind even before the present Qurʾan was put together. (Similarly, sura 40—which is longer than sura 39—seems to be in its place because it opens with the letters *h.m.* along with suras 41–46.) This is one small hint into the way in which the Qurʾan was compiled, a process which is otherwise poorly known.

Rhyme

All of the Qurʾan's suras have some sort of rhyme (usually based on the penultimate letter of the last word of each verse). Yet Muslim scholars traditionally insist that the Qurʾan is not poetry, and understandably so. According to the classical understanding (evident in the Greek notion of "muses"), poets were not like other writers or storytellers, who told tales from their memory or created them with their wit. Instead, they were closer to oracles inspired by supernatural spirits. Thus the Qurʾan warns its audience against poets ("And the poets—the perverse follow them"; Q 26:224).

The attitude of later Islamic tradition to poetry is ambiguous. In the *hadith*, Muhammad both accepts and condemns poetry ("Some poetry contains wisdom" [Bukhari, 8:166]; "It is better for a man to fill the inside of his body with pus than to fill it with poetry" [Bukhari 8:175]). Muslim jurisprudents generally do not consider poetry forbidden (whereas many consider music forbidden), but the idea that poets are inspired either by a genie or a demon is widespread in classical Islamic sources. One of the Prophet's own companions, named Hassan b. Thabit, is said to have attributed his poems celebrating Muhammad's victories in battle to "his brother genie." This idea, not surprisingly, led Muslims to insist that the Qurʾan is not poetry. Accordingly, they are careful to use a special name for the Qurʾan's rhyme (*fasila*), a name which differentiates it from the rhyme of poetry (*qafiya*).

Yet rhyme, however it is named, clearly had a formative influence on the words, and the order of the words, in the Qurʾan. This influence is evident in the opening of sura 95.

(1) *Wa-l-tin wa-l-zaytun* (2) *wa-ṭuri sinin* (3) *wa-hadha l-baladi l-amin*

(1) By the fig and the olive, (2) the Mount Sinai (3) and this land secure!

The word *sinin* at the end of the second verse seems to be a version of the word *sayna*ʾ, or "Mount Sinai," in Q 23:20. However, it has been changed to fit the rhyme of *un/in* of sura 95 (although since the form *sinin* can also mean "years," one modern translation renders this verse "and the mount of ages").

We also see the importance of rhyme in the order in which the Qurʾan refers to Moses and his brother Aaron. Qurʾan 7:122 relates, "the Lord of Moses and Aaron [*harun*]," matching the rhyme of *un* in the following verse. Yet Qur'an 20:70 relates instead, "the Lord of Aaron and Moses [*musa*]," matching the rhyme of *a* in verses 69 and 71. Rhyme also seems to be a formative factor in sura 55. Here the Qur'an speaks of two heavenly gardens, although elsewhere it speaks of only one, as the dual form of gardens, *jannatani*, matches the *ani* rhyme of the sura.

These brief observations on the Qur'an's structure and rhyme suggest that at its origin the text was meant for public religious recitation and that the text was thoughtfully composed. The ordering of the text by the length of suras (and not by topic) and the choice of distinctive (and not descriptive) labels for the titles of those suras seem to be the product of a religious community with the practical goal of establishing a text that could be used conveniently by the one reciting it and remembered easily by his audience. Indeed, it could be the importance of recitation that led early Muslims to call their scripture *al-qur'an*, "the recitation," and not any of the other names (such as, for example, "the reminder" [*al-dhikr*]) that the Scripture gives itself.

The Traditional Account of the Qur'an's Development

Many Muslims, of course, would introduce the origin of the Qur'an in a different manner. Although the matter was an issue of fierce debate for some time in the medieval period, the prevailing Islamic tradition is that the Qur'an has always existed in heaven, along with God. This is the meaning, most commentators explain, of the final verses of sura 85: "Nay, but it is a glorious Qur'an, * in a guarded tablet" (Q 85:21–22). In this understanding, God did not "inspire" Muhammad. He sent down a preexisting book to him. Thus the Islamic view of the revelation of the Qur'an to Muhammad is closer to the Christian view of the incarnation of the Word of God in Jesus than it is to the Christian view of the Bible.

BOX 4.2 ❖ ETYMOLOGY OF THE WORD QUR'AN

The structure of the word *Qur'an* (in particular its ending *-an*) suggests that it was originally borrowed from Aramaic (which, unlike Arabic, regularly forms nouns with the ending *-an*) or, more specifically, a Christian form of Aramaic known as Syriac. Arabic and Aramaic/Syriac are both part of the Semitic language family (which includes also Hebrew and Ethiopic) and vocabulary exchange between Semitic languages is quite common. The possibility that the Arabic word *Qur'an* was taken from Syriac is especially intriguing, since in the centuries before Islam, Syriac-speaking Christians used a word quite close to Arabic *Qur'an*—*qeryana*—to refer to a book of Bible readings arranged for the sake of public recitation in churches.

The Revelation of the Text

This understanding of the Qurʾan's revelation is applied to the Sura of Destiny (Q 97), which opens with the verse, "We sent it down on the night of destiny" (my translation). Most Muslim commentators understand the pronoun "it" here as a reference to the Qurʾan. They explain that at the beginning of Muhammad's prophetic ministry, on a certain night of great holiness, God commissioned the angel Gabriel to transport the Qurʾan from the highest heaven to the lowest heaven.

The nature of most Islamic editions of the Arabic text evokes the Qurʾan's heavenly origin. They are generally decorated with ornate calligraphy and geometric patterns and bound in leather with a special flap for protection. Pious Muslims will often keep the Qurʾan on an ornate stand. They will be careful never to let it touch the ground, and they may kiss the text before reading it. This veneration of the text reflects the conviction that every Arabic edition of the Qurʾan *is* the very book brought down from heaven by the angel Gabriel.

FIGURE 4.1. *The opening chapter of the Qurʾan, and the beginning of the second chapter of the Qurʾan, in an ornate eighteenth-century Qurʾan written by hand in Persia. A flap intended to protect the text is visible to the left.*

To this end, it is revealing that such editions may include a brief guide to the symbols used to indicate proper recitation of the text, but they will not include an introduction to, or footnotes on, the Scripture's meaning (as one might find with an edition of the Bible). In other words, the most important thing about reading the Qurʾan in Arabic is to read it well. Muslims who recite the Qurʾan in Arabic are thereby performing a holy act and are assured of a certain spiritual benefit, whether or not they understand what they are reciting.

FROM A CLASSIC TEXT ❖ 4.1

How to Handle the Word of God

According to the majority view of Islamic tradition, the Qurʾan existed with God in heaven from the beginning of time. The angel Gabriel brought the book down from the highest heaven to the lowest heaven, and then disclosed the contents of the book to Muhammad in the form of oral revelations. These revelations were later assembled by Muhammad's followers in such a way that the Qurʾan read by Muslims today in Arabic is thought to be a perfect representation of the Arabic Qurʾan that exists still with God in heaven. From the perspective of pious Muslims, in other words, the Arabic Qurʾan (but not an English translation thereof) is a heavenly book to be treated with great reverence.

Over the centuries, this reverence was translated into precise rules regarding the proper handling of the Qurʾan. The passage below is an excerpt from a contemporary pamphlet meant to inform English-speaking Muslims on such rules.

The inviolability of the Qurʾan:

1. Not to touch the Qurʾan except in the state of ritual purity in ablution. Allah the Supreme states "None may touch it, except with ablution" (Q 56:79).
2. Not to recite it when in need of obligatory [ritual] bath.
3. It is unlawful for someone not in the state of ablution to carry a Qurʾan, even by a trap or in a box, or touch it, whether its writing, the spaces between its lines, its margins, binding, the carrying strap attached to it, or the bag or box it is in. States Allah the Supreme in "None may touch it, except with ablution" (Q 56:79). It is however permissible to carry books of Sacred Law (Shariʿah), Hadith, or Qurʾanic tafsir, provided that most of their text is not Qurʾan.

4. When one finishes reading the Qurʾan, not to leave it open.
5. Not to place other books upon the Qurʾan, which should always be higher than all other books, whether they are books of Sacred Knowledge or something else.
6. To place the Qurʾan on one's lap when reading; or on something in front of one, not on the floor.
7. Not to wipe it from a slate with spittle, but rather wash it off with water; and if one washes it off with water, to avoid putting the water where there are unclean substances or where people walk.
8. When writing the Qurʾan to do so in a clear, elegant hand.
9. Not to write it on the ground or on walls, as is done in some new mosques.
10. When passing it to someone, pass it with respect. Not to toss or throw it towards someone.
11. Not to enter the lavatory carrying the Noble Qurʾan. This is a great sin, and if done so on purpose, it is *kufr* (blasphemy).
12. Not to enter the lavatory wearing an amulet having words from the Qurʾan, unless it is encased in leather, silver, or other, for then it is as if kept in the heart.
13. If one writes it and then drinks it (for a cure or other purpose), one should say the "In the name of God" at every breath and make a noble and worthy intention, for Allah only gives to one according to one's intention.

The above amply illustrates the importance of handling the Qurʾan with the deepest respect. We hear some people say "Respect should be in the heart." True. But does this mean that there is no need to handle the Book with respect? Definitely incorrect to deem so. Actions reflect your inner feelings. Only a fool would claim to have respect in the heart if his actions are to the contrary!

There are some who also say, "The Qurʾan needs to [be] read or adhered to in practice." True. But does this mean that there is no need to handle the Book with respect? Definitely incorrect to deem so. Only an ignoramus would claim to be following the Qurʾan while going against the Qurʾan injunction of having deep respect for it. (www.ahlesunnat.biz/rukya.pdf [accessed September 22, 2021])

The idea of reading the Qurʾan in translation, a practice that was relatively rare before modern times, is quite different. Muslims today might do so, but the point of doing so is only to gain some sense of the Scripture's meaning. Therefore many Islamic translations—unlike editions of the Arabic text—do contain an introduction and footnotes. However, these translations are *not* the words of God, God spoke to Muhammad in Arabic.

The Collection of the Text

According to the tradition surrounding the "night of destiny," introduced above, the angel Gabriel did not bring the Qur'an to the Prophet directly but only to the lowest heaven. This tradition thus fits with a second notion about the revelation of the Qur'an—namely, that God (through the angel Gabriel) revealed individual, discrete passages to Muhammad according to the situation in which the Prophet found himself.

We have seen examples of this notion already in the first part of the present book: Qur'an 33:37 was revealed to inform Muhammad so that he could marry the divorced wife of his adopted son; Qur'an 2:144a was revealed to inform Muhammad, when he was in Medina, that the time had come to pray toward Mecca and no longer toward Jerusalem. In a similar fashion, the verse condemning poets mentioned above (Q 26:225) is said to have been revealed to Muhammad when he was still in Mecca and pagans accused him of being a poet himself. Thus Muslims generally hold that the Qur'an was brought down in two steps: first, in its entirety, from the highest to the lowest heaven; second, in pieces, from the lowest heaven to Muhammad.

Most traditions relate that the Prophet did not write down the Qur'an himself, and that he only had portions of it written down for him. However, he proclaimed all of the revelations publicly, and he learned the proper shape and order of the suras from the angel Gabriel (regarding which he instructed his followers). Thus when Muhammad died, the Qur'an existed in the hearts of the Muslims who had memorized it, and on scraps of various materials (such as the shoulder bones of camels, the leaves of palm trees, and pieces of parchment) where some of it had been recorded.

A number of traditions explain that during the bloody battles against Musaylima in Yamama, in the time of Abu Bakr's caliphate, a great number of Muslims who had memorized the Qur'an were killed. Abu Bakr accordingly became concerned that some of the divine revelation might soon be lost forever, so he commissioned a council to record the entire text. The council was led by Muhammad's personal scribe, a Medinan named Zayd b. Thabit, and contained a number of religious scholars from Mecca. After gathering all of the written fragments of the Qur'an and listening to the recitations of those who had memorized it, the council wrote an authoritative text on a collection of sheets. When Abu Bakr died, the sheets were passed down to ʿUmar, and when ʿUmar died, they were kept by his daughter (and the widow of the Prophet), Hafsa.

The traditional Islamic story of the Qur'an's collection, however, does not end here. As mentioned in part 1 of the present work, the third caliph, ʿUthman, is said to have established the official version of the Qur'an when his general Hudhayfa informed him that Muslim soldiers were fighting among themselves about the pronunciation of the text. To do the job, most Islamic traditions tell us, 'Uthman again convened a council with Zayd and the Meccan scholars. The council compared the sheets in Hafsa's possession to all of the other written and oral testimonies and established a second official text. This time, however, 'Uthman had the text bound and copied. He sent out the copies of his Qur'an to all of the major cities of Islam (and ordered that all other versions be burned). Accordingly, Muslim and Western scholars alike often refer to the Qur'an that exists today as the codex of 'Uthman.

Nevertheless, there is more than one reason to doubt this story. Western scholars such as Friedrich Schwally, by examining the traditional lists of the Muslim dead at the battle of Yamama, have shown that very few of the famous reciters of the Qur'an were among them. Moreover, it hardly makes sense that 'Uthman would gather together a council with many of the same members of Abu Bakr's council, a council which was to do essentially the same work. Finally, according to Islamic tradition, the text that 'Uthman codified did not include the vowels that indicate the Qur'an's pronunciation, and thus it would have hardly addressed the issue over which Muslim soldiers were supposedly fighting.

The "Readings" of the Qur'an

Indeed, for a scholarly appreciation of the Qur'an's collection, it is better to begin not with traditional stories about Abu Bakr and 'Uthman but rather with the physical evidence of ancient qur'anic manuscripts available to us today. These manuscripts are often written with few of the marks that indicate vowels in Arabic and with few—if any—of the marks that differentiate one consonant from another. With one famous exception (a manuscript discovered in Yemen in the 1970s), this basic, shorthand script—or *scriptio defectiva*, according to the Latin term—of the Qur'an is essentially consistent in the earliest manuscripts. Thus it seems possible that there was one central institution—such as a caliphate—that established the standard text of the Qur'an, for which reason there are few consonantal variations in the manuscripts. However, this leaves us with two questions. First, what did the Qur'an look like before it was standardized? Second, how does one go from the shorthand script, or *scriptio defectiva*, to a full script, or *scriptio plena*?

We know that later Muslim scholars did not agree over what the full script of the Qur'an should look like. The story that Hudhayfa's soldiers were fighting over the pronunciation of the Qur'an may be a legend, but by the tenth century, Muslim scholars were indeed fighting over how the Qur'an should be pronounced.

An example of this disagreement is found in an aforementioned phrase in Qur'an 2:119, which is read in a way to mean: "You will not be asked about those in hell." According to most Muslim commentators, this verse was revealed when Muhammad was distraught that the Jews of Medina had not accepted Islam; with this verse, God informed Muhammad that he would not be held responsible for their unbelief. This understanding, however, is based on reading an ambiguous word in the *scriptio defectiva* as *tus'al*, "you will not be asked."

Yet this same word can also be read as *tas'al*, meaning "Do not ask." Some Muslim scholars followed this reading and explained this verse with a different story, namely that God revealed it when Muhammad was worried about the fate of his parents (who died before Muhammad preached Islam), in order to inform him that he should not question the fate of those who died in unbelief, including his own parents.

To Ibn Mujahid (d. 936), a Qur'an and *hadith* scholar from Baghdad, such disagreements over the proper reading of the *scriptio defectiva* of the Qur'an were in need of an explanation. They complicated the basic Islamic assertion that the Qur'an had been passed down through a perfect oral transmission, from God to the angel Gabriel, to Muhammad, to his companions, and to each succeeding generation of Muslims who zealously memorized the proper pronunciation of every syllable of the Qur'an. To address this challenge, some later Muslim scholars argued that Muhammad himself had pronounced the Qur'an in seven different ways. In other words, they did not argue that Muhammad pronounced *tus'al* and that those scholars who pronounced *tas'al* had got it wrong (or the other way around). They insisted that Muhammad said both, and that both groups of scholars got it right. This was a change from the view of earlier Muslim scholars, as Shady Nasser explains:

> Early Muslim scholars did not look at the variant readings of the Qur'ān as divine revelation. They attributed the Qur'ānic variants to human origins; either to the reader's ijtihad ["independent reasoning"] in interpreting the consonantal outline of the Qur'ān or simply to an error in transmission. This position changed drastically in the later periods, especially after the 5th/11th century where the canonical Readings started to be treated as divine revelation, i.e. every single variant reading in the seven and ten eponymous Readings was revealed by God to Muhammad. (*Transmission of the Qur'an*, 77)

The idea that the Qur'an was revealed in seven "readings" (other Muslim scholars claimed that it was revealed in ten or fourteen readings) became a prominent idea in later Islamic doctrine, and today versions of the Qur'an can be purchased in the Islamic world that indicate each place in the text where there is any difference between the readings. However, the problem of the *scriptio defectiva* found another solution in 1924, when a committee in Cairo established a *scriptio plena* text based on the most popular of these seven readings (known as Hafs *'an* 'Asim after the two medieval Muslim authorities credited with the authoritative preservation of this reading). The Cairo text has since been promulgated throughout the world (in recent years thanks to the Saudi sponsorship of this text through a large publication enterprise in Medina). Thus today, with very few exceptions, Muslims throughout the world read precisely the same Arabic text of the Qur'an.

The Qur'an on Repentence and Belief

By now we've learned of the Islamic vision of the Qur'an as a book brought down from

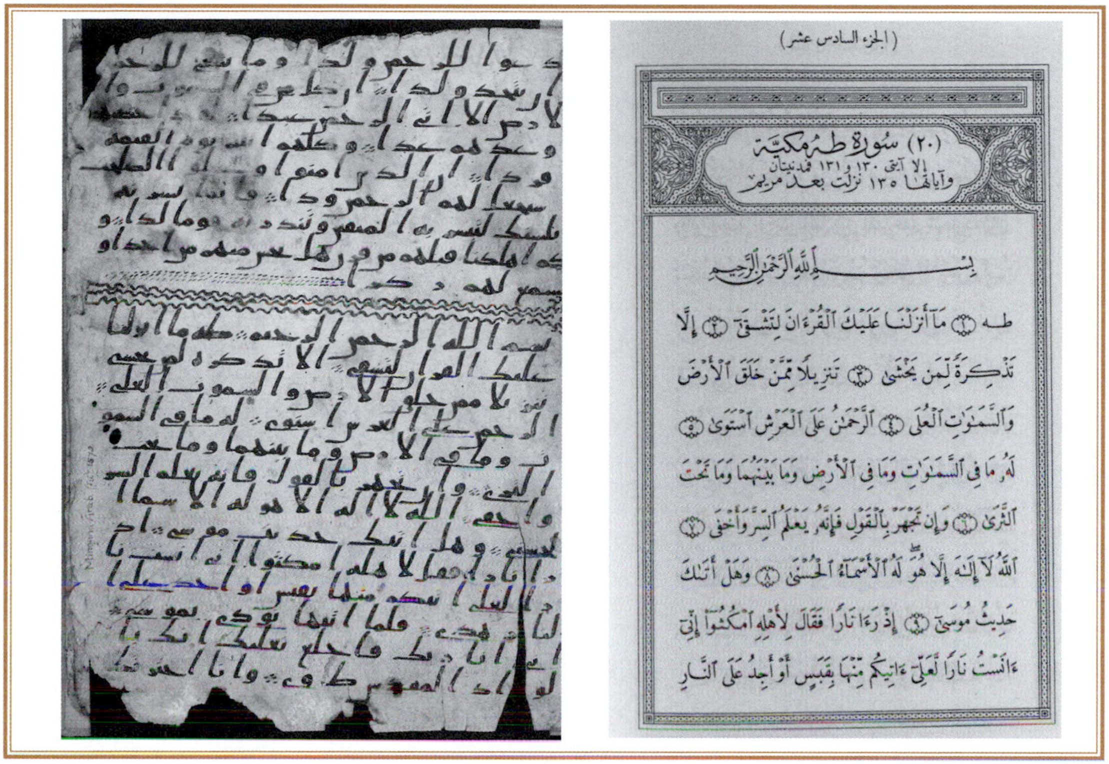

FIGURE 4.2. *Left. The opening of sura 20 of the Qurʾan (after the horizontal divider) in one of the earliest surviving Qurʾan manuscripts, perhaps dating to the late seventh century. Right. The opening of sura 20 of the Qurʾan in the Qurʾan edition prepared by the Egyptian Ministry of Education and published in 1924, the edition that has since become the standard text of the Qurʾan worldwide.*

heaven to earth, but what kind of book is the Qurʾan? One way to address this is to explain what the Qurʾan is *not*. The Qurʾan is not a book like the Bible, which is an account of God's relationship with the patriarchs, Israel, and finally (in the New Testament), with those who follow Jesus. The Qurʾan, however, is not an account at all. It is a book of God's direct speech, and in particular of his warnings and admonitions. The Qurʾan regularly moves back and forth between the warnings that God gave to earlier prophets and peoples, on the one hand, and the warnings that God is giving to Muhammad and the people of his time, on the other. Thus the style of the Qurʾan more closely resembles Christian homilies or sermons than it does the New Testament itself. Like a good preacher, the Qurʾan presents its audience with reasons to repent and believe in God. Three principal

BOX 4.3 ❖ PRINTING THE QUR'AN

The publication of the 1924 Qur'an was the culmination of a slow process by which printing of the Qur'an was accepted in the Islamic world. It was only in 1726 that the Ottoman Empire promulgated a fatwa ("legal opinion") that deemed printing itself acceptable. Even then, this fatwa was intended to cover only nonreligious works. In the early nineteenth century, religious scholars in Egypt delivered a series of fatwas against the printing of the Qur'an. Some fatwas expressed concern that a printing press used for the Qur'an (unlike a pious Muslim scribe) could be impure (for example, some product from an impure animal such as a pig could have come into contact with it, or an impure person—such as a non-Muslim or a woman in men-struation—could have touched it). Others argued that the very notion of applying pressure on the Qur'an—in the physical process of printing—especially in passages where the name of God appears, would be a sort of irreverent aggression against God. Still others maintained that the very idea of printing the Qur'an is the sort of innovation (Ar. **bid'a**) in religious matters that should be rejected.

Despite this opposition, the Qur'an began to be published in Cairo and other cities in the Islamic world in the second half of the nineteenth century. The committee that worked on the 1924 Qur'an was originally commissioned in 1907 by the Egyptian Ministry of Education in response to the discovery of differences between the various editions of the Qur'an being used in Egyptian public schools (some of which were imported from Istanbul and India, others printed in Cairo). At one point, the education ministry became so frustrated with the problem that they had a large quantity of imported Qur'ans (which they considered to have textual errors) loaded onto a boat and sunk in the Nile River. The job of the Qur'an committee was to establish an "error-free" Arabic text of the Qur'an for use in Egyptian public schools. By "error-free" they meant a version of the Qur'an that faithfully preserved one tradition of its proper recitation, not the evidence of ancient Qur'an manuscripts. This latter sort of a text—known as a critical edition—has still not yet been produced for the Qur'an.

reasons to this end are especially prominent in the Qur'an: punishment in this world, punishment—or reward—in the afterlife, and gratitude for the blessings of nature.

"Punishment Stories"

In the citation at the opening of this chapter, the Qur'an insists that God strikes unbelievers dead with thunderbolts (an idea also known in Jewish and Christian tradition). This sort of religious language, or rhetoric, is sometimes called "parenesis," by which a sort of moral exhortation is meant to terrify the audience and thereby lead them to piety. The Qur'an's reference to thunderbolts is connected to other passages in which the

Qur'an describes the destruction—through the forces of nature—of earlier peoples who stubbornly rejected the prophets. In sura 7, for example, the Qur'an relates prophet stories in quick succession, in a passage that might be paraphrased as follows (although keep in mind that the Arabic Qur'an rhymes, and so this passage has a literary quality that is not represented in what follows):

God sent Noah to his people. Noah called on them to acknowledge him as a prophet and to believe in God. They rejected his message and God destroyed them with a flood (v. 64).

God sent a prophet named Hud (not found in the Bible) to a nation named Ad. He called on them to acknowledge him as a prophet and to believe in God. They rejected his message and God destroyed them as well (v. 72; the Qur'an does not say how).

God sent a prophet named Salih (also not found in the Bible) to a nation named Thamud. Salih called on them to acknowledge him as a prophet and to believe in God. They rejected his message and God destroyed them with an earthquake (v. 78).

God sent Lot to his people. Lot called on them to acknowledge him as a prophet and to believe in God. They rejected his message and God destroyed them in a "rainstorm" (v. 84; presumably a rain of fire).

God sent a prophet named Shu'ayb (not found in the Bible) to the nation of Midian. He called on them to acknowledge him as a prophet and to believe in God. They rejected his message and God destroyed them in an earthquake (v. 91).

God sent Moses to Egypt. Moses called on them to acknowledge him as a prophet and to believe in God. They rejected his message and God struck the unbelieving people of Pharaoh with plagues (v. 130) and then drowned the forces of Pharaoh (v. 136) in the sea.

The Qur'an has very little concern with providing a precise historical account in these references to stories of punishment. Indeed, it offers no precise information on the geography or chronology of these events, and there is very little sense of a larger historical narrative. Indeed one could change the order of these narratives and without any logical problems in the resulting new order. Each nation, wherever and whenever they existed, faced the same choice, and suffered (more or less) the same fate. To this end, it is telling that both Noah and Lot, who in the book of Genesis are not called prophets and do not preach to their people, here appear as prophets like the others. They are recast in a Qur'anic mold. These stories, then, are not meant to form a salvation history but rather to serve as proofs, or signs, that the God who created humans also has the power to destroy them and that He is not afraid to use it. For this reason, the Qur'an has the Prophet aptly describe himself as a "warner" (e.g., Q 7:184; 11:12; 29:50).

Humans, the Qur'an relates elsewhere, have a natural tendency to forget that God controls their eternal fate. In 7:53 and 20:26, the Qur'an insists that the people who are "forgetful" on earth will be condemned to hell in the afterlife. Elsewhere (Q 6:68; 58:19), the Qur'an blames the devil for making humans forgetful. This tendency of humans to "forget" and to think that they have no need of God (except when they are in trouble) leads God, in his mercy, to send divine prophets with revelation to remind them that this is not the case. The Qur'an accordingly refers to itself as "a reminder" (see, e.g., Q 3:58; 6:90; 7:2).

Hell and Heaven

The Qur'an also refers to itself as a book sent "to warn the evildoers, and [to give] good tidings to the good-doers" (Q 46:12). Similarly, it describes the prophets as "messengers bearing good tidings, and warning" (e.g., Q 4:165; 5:19; 7:188). This double announcement of the prophets concerns the fate of humans in the afterlife, a second reason that the Qur'an presents to convince its audience to repent and believe. Not only do the prophets of the Qur'an warn their people that God might destroy them in this life, but they also announce that God will send them to hell, or heaven, in the next life. Some later Muslims accordingly describe the Qur'an as a book of *targhib* and *tarhib*, that is, "a book that instills fear [of hell] and desire [for heaven]."

The Qur'an pays particular attention to the punishment awaiting unbelievers in hell, which it describes in gruesome detail.

> Surely those who disbelieve in Our signs— We shall certainly roast them at a Fire; as often as their skins are wholly burned, We shall give them in exchange other skins, that they may taste the chastisement. Surely God is All-mighty, All-wise. (Q 4:56)

As for the unbelievers, for them garments of fire shall be cut, and there shall be poured over their heads boiling water, whereby whatsoever is in their bellies and their skins shall be melted; for them await hooked iron rods; as often as they desire in their anguish to come forth from it, they shall be restored into it, and: "Taste the chastisement of the burning!" (Q 22:19b–22)

> Therein they shall shout, "Our Lord, bring us forth, and we will do righteousness, other than what we have done." "What, did We not give you long life, enough to remember in for him who would remember? To you the warner came; taste you now! The evildoers shall have no helper." (Q 35:37)

> Is that better as a hospitality, or the Tree of Ez-Zakkoum? We have appointed it as a trial for the evildoers. It is a tree that comes forth in the root of Hell; its spathes are as the heads of Satans, and they eat of it, and of it fill their bellies, then on top of it they have a brew of boiling water (Q 37:62–67).

Many more verses describe hell, its horrors, and the remorse of those condemned to it. Some scholars, and many pious Muslims, attempt to present these verses in a way that offers a coherent vision of the Muslim hell, with details on exactly what punishments will be given to whom and in what order. Yet the nature of the Qur'an's language on hell suggests that it does not mean to give a systematic description at all but rather to present various terrifying images (such as the tree whose fruit is like the heads of demons) in order to lead its audience to repentance and belief. The Qur'an's concern with instilling fear is evident, for example, in Q 35:37 above, where the doomed cry "bring us forth!" and promise to repent, but God announces that their remorse has come too late.

The Qur'an's purpose in portraying such passages is to convince its own audience to make better choices than those made by the doomed. Thus it would be wrong to think that the Qur'an is a morbid book or that the God of the Qur'an is especially cruel. On the contrary, by presenting these terrible anecdotes, the Qur'an means to save souls from hellfire, and this is hardly a cruel act at all.

On the other hand, the Qur'an also offers vivid imagery of the pleasures of heaven. In order to inspire its audience with this desire for heaven, the Qur'an insists that its pleasures are better than anything to be found in this world.

> Decked out fair to men is the love of lusts— women, children, heaped-up heaps of gold and silver, horses of mark, cattle and tillage. That is the enjoyment of the present life; but God—with Him is the fairest resort. Say: "Shall I tell you of a better than that?" For those that are godfearing, with their Lord are gardens underneath which rivers flow, therein dwelling forever, and spouses purified, and God's good pleasure. And God sees His servants. (Q 3:14–15)

Here the Qur'an acknowledges that man (and here men in particular are meant) is naturally attracted to the things of this world that bring honor and pleasure: women, children, and wealth. In doing so, it does not demand that the audience give these things up by living a life of celibacy or poverty. Instead, it asks the audience to turn their thoughts to the pleasures of heaven so that they will live in obedience to God on earth. To this end, it describes heaven as a garden, where rivers and heavenly wives offer pleasure.

Elsewhere the Qur'an enters into further detail on this heavenly garden.

> Those are they brought nigh the Throne,
> * in the Gardens of Delight
> * (a throng of the ancients
> * and how few of the later folk)
> * upon close-wrought couches
> * reclining upon them, set face to face,
> * immortal youths going round about them
> * with goblets, and ewers, and a cup from a spring
> * (no brows throbbing, no intoxication)
> * and such fruits as they shall choose,
> * and such flesh of fowl as they desire,
> * and wide-eyed houris
> * as the likeness of hidden pearls,
> * a recompense for that they laboured.
> ^ Therein they shall hear no idle talk, no cause of sin,
> * only the saying "Peace, Peace!: (Q 56:11–26)

According to some scholars, Muhammad developed this image of heaven as a garden because he was preaching to a people who

---

BOX 4.4 ❖ *HOURIS* IN Q 56:22

In the Qur'an passage just quoted, the phrase "and wide-eyed houris" (Q 56:22) is a translation of only two Arabic words: *hur ʿin*. The term *hur* (a word that originated in Aramaic) means "white," while the term *ʿin* means "eyes" (the phrase is thought to allude to a contrast between the white of the eye with the black of the iris). According to the traditional Islamic interpretation of this verse, the Qur'an is here alluding to the "spouses" (see Q 2:25; 3:154; 4:57—the connection seems to be explicit in Q 44:54) whom God will give to the faithful (men) in paradise. Elsewhere (Q 37:48–9; 38:52; 55:56) the Qur'an speaks of women "of modest gaze" and insists that no man or "jinni" (or "genie") has touched (or deflowered) them before (Q 55:56). Since these women are described as hidden pearls (Q 56:23) or hidden eggs (Q 37:49), Islamic tradition generally describes them as white-skinned. Some scholars have noted that the presence of houris in the Qur'anic paradise seems to reflect the patriarchal society of late antique Arabia. At least one contemporary female Muslim scholar speculates that women, for their part, might find handsome male companions awaiting them in paradise. https://seekersguid-ance.org/answers/general-counsel/what-will-be-the-reward-of-women-in-paradise/

---

lived in the desert. He knew that the Arabs, who suffered from a mercilessly hot and arid climate, dreamed of well-watered, green oases. Thus Muhammad, in order to gain their attention, described heaven as just such an oasis.

The problem with this idea is that it ignores the identity of this heavenly garden. According to other passages in the Qur'an, the garden of paradise is the very garden in which Adam once dwelled: the Garden of Eden. "God has promised the believers, men and women, gardens underneath which rivers flow, forever therein to dwell, and goodly dwelling-places in the Gardens of Eden!" (Q 9:72a; see also, e.g., Q 13:23; 16:31; 18:31).

This idea of heaven as the Garden of Eden might be peculiar to those familiar with the biblical account of Eden. In Genesis, the Tigris and Euphrates rivers flow in Eden, and so Jews and Christians have often imagined Eden in Iraq or Jerusalem. Yet the Qur'an suggests that the Garden of Eden is rather at the top of a sort of cosmic mountain that reaches into heaven itself. For this reason Adam, his wife, and the devil are not cast *out* of the garden but rather *down* from Eden and into the world (Q 2:38; 7:18). On the Day of Resurrection, God will open again the gates of Eden. Believers will be brought *up* and welcomed into the garden from which Adam was banned.

Thus the Qur'an does not describe heaven as a spiritual realm (although some Muslims interpret the Qur'an in this way) but rather as a physical garden, where people enjoy physical pleasures. For this reason, the Qur'an relates that the dead will be judged and sent to heaven—or to hell—only on the Day of Resurrection, when God will give them a new body that will allow them to exist in a physical realm. (The martyrs in the holy war seem to mark an exception to this rule; the Qur'an insists that they are already in heaven; Q 2:154.) Later Muslim scholars accordingly taught that the souls of the dead fall into a sort of sleep until they are awakened on the Day of Resurrection.

The Qur'an's vision of heaven and hell is therefore dependent on a belief in the physical resurrection of bodies. Accordingly the Qur'an shows great interest in this topic. In fact, it quotes the doubts of the unbelievers on this point, "What, when we are dust shall we indeed then be raised up again in new creation?" (Q 13:5), and "What, when we are dead and become dust and bones, shall we indeed be raised up?" (Q 37:16).

To these questions the Qur'an has two answers. First, it insists that the God who created man has the power to raise him from the grave: "O men, if you are in doubt as to the Uprising, surely We created you of dust!" (Q 22:5). Just as God created Adam from dust,

FIGURE 4.3. *A view of the chamber underneath the Dome of the Rock in Jerusalem known as the "Well of Souls." According to a popular Islamic belief, the souls of the dead dwell around this chamber, awaiting their reunion with the body on the Day of Resurrection.*

the Qur'an implies, so he will "re-create" man when his body has returned to "dust" after death, when his bones have decomposed. Second, the Qur'an draws a parallel between the resurrection of the body and the return to life of a land that has grown barren (a common sight in the Middle East with the first rains after a hot, dry summer): "And We sent down out of heaven water blessed, and caused to grow thereby gardens and grain of harvest, * and tall palm-trees with spathes compact, * a provision for the servants, and thereby We revived a land that was dead. Even so is the coming forth" (Q 50:9–11). Just as grass mysteriously springs up from the ground after a rainfall, so man's body will rise up from his grave on the Day of Judgment.

The Blessings of Nature

Elsewhere the Qur'an describes the signs of God's work in nature without concern for any argument about the resurrection of the body. In such passages, which inevitably focus on divine blessings in nature, the Qur'an offers a third reason for repentance and belief. In its telling of punishment stories and discussion of the afterlife the Qur'an asks its audience to reflect on how God will respond to their choice to believe or not to believe. In its reflection on the good things in nature, however, the Qur'an asks its audience to reflect on how they will respond to the blessings that God has already given them.

> It is God who created the heavens and the earth, and sent down out of heaven water wherewith He brought forth fruits to be your sustenance. And He subjected to you the ships to run upon the sea at His commandment; and He subjected to you the rivers* and He subjected to you the sun and moon constant upon their courses, and He subjected to you the night and day. (Q 14:32–33)

* Let Man consider his nourishment.
* We poured out the rains abundantly,
* then We split the earth in fissures
* and therein made the grains to grow
* and vines, and reeds,
* and olives, and palms,
* and dense-tree'd gardens,
* and fruits, and pastures,
* an enjoyment for you and your flocks (Q 80:24–32).

Like the Qur'an's "punishment stories," such passages are shaped by the idea that God works through nature. In the punishment stories, the Qur'an describes how God uses the destructive forces of nature—such as floods and earthquakes—to punish unbelievers. In these passages the Qur'an describes how God blesses all people through nature. The rain, the rivers, the sea, the sun and the moon, and all the fruits of the earth are not simply signs of God's existence (the Qur'an seems to take the existence of God for granted); rather, they are blessings that God has given to humanity.

Yet the Qur'an also insists that most humans remain ungrateful: "And [God] gave you of all you asked Him. If you count God's blessing, you will never number it; surely man is sinful, unthankful!" (Q 14:34). This insistence appears to be a way of moving the reader's conscience, a way of asking: Are humans not ashamed to disregard the God who has done so much for them? It is important to note that the Qur'anic word for unbelief, *kufr*, can also mean "ingratitude."

This exhortation is of a different sort. In its reflections on the punishment stories and the afterlife, the Qur'an calls on the audience to think of their future well-being. Here, however, the Qur'an calls on the audience to examine their conscience.

The Qur'an on Divine Majesty

In its reflections on hell, the Qur'an occasionally describes the damned as wrongdoers and depicts them reflecting on their ill deeds (see Q 35:37 and 37:62–67, quoted above). More often, however, the Qur'an presents the damned as unbelievers (Ar. *kuffar*) in God's revelations or signs (see Q 4:56; 18:29; 22:19–22, quoted above). The judgment to which humans will be subjected on the Day of Resurrection will not simply be a question of weighing their good and evil deeds on a heavenly scale. The judgment will be above all about whether they have recognized, worshipped, and obeyed their creator.

The Importance of Theology

Accordingly, in Islamic tradition polytheism (Ar. *shirk*) is the worst possible sin, or better, the unforgivable sin. This doctrine is illustrated vividly in a *hadith* on the Day of Resurrection, which describes how all of those resurrected will be compelled to cross a bridge over the fires of hell.

Then a bridge will be laid over the (Hell) Fire. Allah's Apostle added, "I will be the first to cross it." And the invocation of the prophets on that Day, will be "O Allah, save us, save us!," and over that bridge there will be hooks. . . . These hooks will snatch the people according to their deeds. Some people will be ruined because of their evil deeds, and some will be cut into pieces and fall down in Hell, but will be saved afterwards, when Allah has finished the judgments among His slaves, and intends to take out of the Fire whoever He wishes to take out from among those who used to testify that none had the right to be worshipped but Allah. We will order the angels to take them out and the angels will know them by the mark of the traces of prostration (on their foreheads) for Allah banned the fire to consume the traces of prostration on the body of Adam's son. So they will take them out, and by then they would have been burnt, and then water, the water of life, will be poured on them, and they will spring out like a seed springs out on the bank of a rainwater stream. (Bukhari 8:577)

According to this *hadith*, many evildoers, both Muslim and non-Muslim, will be snatched down into hell. However, the angels of God will ultimately retrieve the believing Muslims among them, lifting them out of the infernal fire. The angels will be able to recognize the Muslims among the damned by a spot on their forehead, that is, a callous that forms on the heads of Muslims who pray frequently, pressing their heads to the ground in prostration (a feature sometimes seen today among religious Muslims).

This *hadith* reflects the qur'anic presentation of a God who demands that humans worship Him and Him alone. The God of the Qur'an insists that He alone is powerful, that no one and nothing can resist Him, and that He has no rivals.

> God there is no god but He, the Living, the Everlasting. Slumber seizes Him not, neither sleep; to Him belongs all that is in the heavens and the earth. Who is there that shall intercede with Him save by His leave? He knows what lies before them and what is after them, and they comprehend not anything of His knowledge save such as He wills. His Throne comprises the heavens and earth; the preserving of them oppresses Him not; He is the All-high, the All-glorious. (Q 2:255)

> Say: "O God, Master of the Kingdom, Thou givest the Kingdom to whom Thou wilt, and seizest the Kingdom from whom Thou wilt, Thou exaltest whom Thou wilt, and Thou abasest whom Thou wilt; in Thy hand is the good; Thou art powerful over everything." (Q 3:26)

Those who fail to recognize God's majesty—for example, by believing in more than one god—have failed the test that the Qur'an lays out for humanity. No matter how righteous their conduct, they will be among the lost on the Day of Judgment. In this regard, the Qur'an is a book with theology (literally, "a word about God"; from the Greek words *theos* and *logos*) at its center. The God of the Qur'an, in other words, speaks a lot about Himself.

The Qur'an's concern with divine majesty has had a profound impact on Islamic religious practice. The five daily prayers of Muslims, which are shaped around deep prostrations in which the believers touch their heads to the ground, embody humanity's humility before a majestic God. Muslims also emphasize divine majesty in their everyday speech: when pious Muslims mention the word "God," they often add the exclamation, *subhanahu wa-ta'ala* ("praiseworthy and exalted!").

This concern with divine majesty is also evident in the common slogan *Allahu akbar* ("God is greater!"). *Allahu akbar*, which is only the beginning of a comparative phrase, is grammatically peculiar. But the peculiarity is intentional: the point of the slogan is not to praise God but rather to insist on his superiority over any possible adversary. Thus, just as *Allahu akbar* was the rallying cry of Muhammad's army at Badr, it is also the rallying cry of Muslims today who gather to protest an oppressive ruler or an action deemed offensive to Islam. It is also an expression repeated in ritual prayer.

This pious act of defending God's majesty is perhaps nowhere better evident than in the ritual during the pilgrimage to Mecca, during which Muslims cast stones at pillars representing Satan. In the Qur'an, the devil's

FIGURE 4.4. *A Muslim man at prayer in a mosque in Sanliurfa, Turkey.*

sin is to resist God's authority. He is the original rebel, the original ingrate. By throwing stones at the devil during the Hajj, Muslim pilgrims rise to the defense of their majestic God (while imitating the action of Abraham to whom the original rites of the pilgrimage are attributed).

The Qur'an's Concern with Jesus

The Qur'an's concern with divine majesty also shapes its language on Jesus. The principal drama in the New Testament accounts of Jesus's life is the question of whether Jesus

of Nazareth is the Messiah, the Christ, the "anointed one" predicted by the prophets of the Old Testament. The reader knows from the beginning of the Gospels that this is Jesus's identity, but the characters in the story recognize his identity only gradually (or not at all). In the Qur'an, this drama does not exist. The Qur'an calls Jesus the Messiah, but it seems to imply nothing at all in doing so. Indeed, even Jews in the Qur'an call Jesus "the Messiah," although the very identity of Jews at the time was defined (in part) by the belief that the Messiah had not yet come. The

FIGURE 4.5. *Muslim pilgrims casting stones at "pillars" (today joined into a wall for the safety of pilgrims) meant to represent Satan during the annual pilgrimage.*

Qur'an in fact seems to use "Messiah" (Ar. *masih*) as a second name for Jesus, much as Christians today often use Christ and Jesus interchangeably.

Yet the Qur'an, like the New Testament, still reproaches the Jews for their rejection of Christ. Jesus's relationship with the Jews as depicted in the Qur'an appears to fit in some ways with the Qur'an's punishment stories. Jesus announces to his people, the Israelites, that he is a prophet of God, and he even produces signs to verify this claim. Nevertheless, they reject him.

Jesus, the son of Mary, said, "O Israelites, I am the messenger of God to you, confirming what is before me in the Torah, and giving you the news of a messenger to come after me whose name is 'the most-praised.'" Yet when he showed them miraculous signs, they said, "This is nothing but magic." (Q 61:6)

The Qur'an also insists, as in the punishment stories, that God punished the Israelites for their unbelief, though He did not destroy the Israelites as he destroyed other nations. Instead, their punishment was interior: God

Personalities in Islam 4.1
JESUS

Although the Qurʾan pays exceptional attention to Jesus (and is concerned with Christian teaching about him), its references to him hardly represent a complete biography. The Qurʾan essentially limits its remarks on his life to Jesus's birth and miracles. It insists that these miracles (such as the manner in which he formed a bird from clay and brought it to life with his breath) were signs given to him by God in order to verify his prophethood to the Jews. They are not proofs of his divinity. The passage on the crucifixion (Q 4:157)—which in fact affirms only that the Jews did not kill him, not that Jesus escaped into heaven without dying—similarly seems to be directed against the Jews. Later Muslims, however, tell stories about this passage that have God transform one of Jesus's friends—or one of his enemies—into his "likeness." This "Jesus look-alike" is then crucified in his place. Even today, however, Muslims disagree over exactly what took place on the day of the crucifixion, and accordingly the figure of the Muslim Jesus remains a mystery.

In other ways, however, Jesus became an important figure in Islamic religious lore. Qurʾan commentaries and books collecting "stories of the prophets" often portray Jesus as an ascetic (an idea perhaps suggested by the notion that he lived a celibate life, a practice generally foreign to Islamic ethics). Ibn Kathir relates that Jesus wore rough wool clothing, ate only leaves, and had no home. He taught his disciples to cry over their sins, to make life in the other world their only desire, and to think of themselves as guests in this world.

In other traditions, however, Jesus becomes a man of vengeance. The Qurʾan's reference to Jesus "cursing the Israelites" (Q 5:78) leads to stories of Jesus transforming a group of Jews into pigs. Traditions on Jesus's return in the last days (which have little basis in the Qurʾan) have him fight the enemies of Islam, break crosses, and slaughter all of the pigs on earth (an animal considered unclean by Islam).

cursed the Israelites for their unbelief (Q 2:88), set a seal over their hearts (Q 4:155), and hardened their hearts (Q 5:13).

Yet in the Qurʾan, Jesus also seems to be something more than a prophet in the line of punishment stories. One sign of this different status is the name the Qurʾan uses for him, as in the citation above: Jesus son of Mary. This locution is quite peculiar in Arabic, since men are generally referred to as the son of their father, not of their mother. Thus my eldest son, Luke, is known in the Arab world

FROM A CLASSIC TEXT ❖ 4.2

The Crucifixion

The only explicit mention of the crucifixion in the Qur'an is in verse 157 of sura 4. Here the Qur'an, after having made a number of other accusations against Jews, now accuses them of claiming to have killed Jesus. The Qur'an rejects this claim and then adds "wa-lakin shubbiha la-hum," an ambiguous Arabic phrase that might simply mean, "it seemed that way to them" (that is, God had ordained the death of Jesus, and the Jews were only his instruments), but most Muslim commentators take it to mean, "a likeness of Jesus was shown to them."

The Muslim commentators who follow this later interpretation often explain that God raised Jesus to heaven before the crucifixion and made someone else look like Jesus (according to some traditions, a faithful disciple such as Peter who volunteered to die in the place of Jesus; according to others, the traitor Judas, who was thereby punished for his treachery). This "substitute" was taken away and killed on the cross.

The texts below include Qur'an 4:155–58 and a tradition found in Islamic commentaries that reflects the traditional conviction that Jesus escaped death.

Qur'an 4:155–58

So, for their breaking the compact, and disbelieving in the signs of God, and slaying the Prophets without right, and for their saying, "Our hearts are uncircumcised"—nay, but God sealed them for their unbelief, so they believe not, except a few— * and for their unbelief, and their uttering against Mary a mighty calumny, * and for their saying, "We slew the Messiah, Jesus son of Mary, the Messenger of God"—yet they did not slay him, neither crucified him, only a likeness of that was shown to them [*wa-lakin shubbiha la-hum*]. Those who are at variance concerning him surely are in doubt regarding him; they have no knowledge of him, except the following of surmise; and they slew him not of a certainty—no indeed; * God raised him up to Him; God is All-mighty, All-wise.

On Jesus's Escape from Death

When Allah sent Jesus with proofs and guidance, the Jews, may Allah's curses, anger, torment and punishment be upon them, envied him because of his prophethood and obvious miracles; curing the blind and leprous and bringing the dead back to life, by Allah's leave. He also used to make the shape of a bird from clay and blow in it, and it became a bird by Allah's leave and flew. Jesus performed other miracles that Allah honored him with, yet the Jews defied and belied him and tried their best to harm him. Allah's Prophet Jesus could not live in any one city for long and he had to travel often with his mother, peace be upon them. Even so, the Jews were not satisfied, and they went to the king of Damascus at that time, a Greek polytheist who worshipped the stars. They told him that there was a man in Jerusalem misguiding and dividing the people in Jerusalem and stirring unrest among the king's subjects. The king became angry and wrote to his deputy in Jerusalem to arrest the rebel leader, stop him from causing unrest, crucify him and make him wear a crown of thorns.

When the king's deputy in Jerusalem received these orders, he went with some Jews to the house that Jesus was residing in, and he was then with twelve, thirteen or seventeen of his companions. That day was a Friday, in the evening. They surrounded Jesus in the house, and when he felt that they would soon enter the house or that he would sooner or later have to leave it, he said to his companions, "Who volunteers to be made to look like me, for which he will be my companion in Paradise?" A young man volunteered, but Jesus thought that he was too young. He asked the question a second and third time, each time the young man volunteering, prompting Jesus to say, "Well then, you will be that man." Allah made the young man look exactly like Jesus, while a hole opened in the roof of the house, and Jesus was made to sleep and ascended to heaven while asleep. Allah said (And [remember] when Allah said: "O Jesus! I will take you and raise you to Myself." Q 3:55)

When Jesus ascended, those who were in the house came out. When those surrounding the house saw the man who looked like Jesus, they thought that he was Jesus. So they took him at night, crucified him and placed a crown of thorns on his head. The Jews then boasted that they killed Jesus and some Christians accepted their false claim, due to their ignorance and lack of reason. As for those who were in the house with Jesus, they witnessed his ascension to heaven, while the rest thought that the Jews killed Jesus by crucifixion. They even said that Maryam sat under the corpse of the crucified man and cried, and they say that the dead man spoke to her. All this was a test from Allah for His servants out of His wisdom. Allah explained this matter in the Glorious Qur'an which He sent to His honorable Messenger, whom He supported with miracles and clear, unequivocal evidence. Allah is the Most Truthful, and He is the Lord of the worlds Who knows the secrets, what the hearts conceal, the hidden matters in heaven and earth, what has occurred, what will occur, and what would occur if it was decreed. (Ibn Kathir, on Q 4:157)

as "Luke son of Gabriel" and not "Luke son of (my wife) Lourdes." By employing this locution, the Qur'an affirms the virgin birth of Christ. Indeed, the Qur'an explains that Jesus was conceived by God's own spirit: "And [Mary] who guarded her virginity, so We breathed into her of Our spirit and appointed her and her son to be a sign unto all beings" (Q 21:91). Presumably, this is the reason why the Qur'an elsewhere (Q 4:171) names Jesus "a spirit" and "a word" (Q 3:45; 4:171) from God.

The Qur'an's use of the expression "word from God" is especially intriguing, since it is reminiscent of the language John uses in the opening of his Gospel to speak of Jesus's divinity: "In the beginning was the Word: the Word was with God and the Word was God" (John 1:1). By describing Christ as "the Word of God," John is invoking an idea of God as eternal truth and pure intelligence. The expression of this intelligence is God's Word (as the expression of human intelligence is speech), which came into the world in Jesus of Nazareth.

However, John's usage is evidently not what the Qur'an means by referring to Jesus in this way. Indeed, by calling Jesus "son of Mary," the Qur'an not only affirms the virgin birth, it also denies Christ's divinity. A Christian speaking in Arabic would have no hesitation in referring to Jesus as the son of his father, by calling him Jesus "Son of God." This the Qur'an does not do. To the Qur'an, the very idea of God as son, or God as father, belittles his majesty.

> Say: "He is God, One,
> * God, the Everlasting Refuge,
> * who has not begotten, and has not been begotten,
> * and equal to Him is not any one."
> (Q 112)

Thus the Qur'an reprimands Christians for their beliefs about Jesus.

> People of the Book, go not beyond the bounds in your religion, and say not as to God but the truth. The Messiah, Jesus son of Mary, was only the Messenger of God, and His Word that He committed to Mary, and a Spirit from Him. So believe in God and His Messengers, and say not, 'Three.' Refrain; better is it for you. God is only One God. Glory be to Him— That He should have a son! To Him belongs all that is in the heavens and in the earth; God suffices for a guardian. (Q 4:171)

In such passages, the Qur'an's concern is not Jesus but rather God. The Qur'an, ever concerned with theology, takes up the defense of God from a doctrine that—the Qur'an insists—belittles him. In some passages the Qur'an even has Jesus himself deny this doctrine:

> And when God said, "O Jesus son of Mary, didst thou say unto men, 'Take me and my mother as gods, apart from God'?" He said, "To Thee be glory! It is not mine to say what I have no right to. If I indeed said it, Thou knowest it, knowing what is within my soul, and I know not what is within Thy soul; Thou knowest the things unseen." (Q 5:116)

STUDY QUESTIONS

1 How are the suras of the Qur᾽an organized?

2 What does the Qur᾽an's use of rhyme tell us about its original function?

3 What is the traditional account of the Qur᾽an's "collection"? How have scholars challenged the historical accuracy of this account?

4 Why does the Qur᾽an tell stories of nations whom God destroyed?

5 What does it mean to say that the Qur᾽an's concern with Jesus is "theological"?

Chapter 5

THE QURʾAN AND THE BIBLE

So, if thou art in doubt regarding what We have sent down to thee, ask those who recite the Book before thee.

—Qurʾan 10:94

Biblical Literature and Qurʾanic Rhetoric

An important step to understanding the religious context in which the Qurʾan emerged is found in its close relationship with biblical literature. According to the traditional biography, Muhammad spent most of his life, and the first half of his prophetic career, in Mecca, the heart of a deeply entrenched pagan culture. He spent the second half of his prophetic career in Medina, a city with three Jewish tribes but otherwise similarly dominated by the same pagan culture. Accordingly, we might expect the Qurʾan to be filled with descriptions of pagan beliefs, rituals, and religious hierarchies. Yet this is not the case. Arthur Jeffery appropriately comments: "It comes, therefore, as no little surprise, to find how little of the religious life of this Arabian paganism is reflected in the pages of the Qurʾan" (Jeffery, *Foreign Vocabulary*, 1).

The Qurʾan and Paganism

One unambiguous reference to Arab paganism in the Qurʾan would seem to be the mention of Al-Lat, Al-ʿUzza, and Manat in sura 53 (a passage referred to in the "Satanic

Verses" story). In this passage, God denies that these three figures have any connection to him, insisting that they are nothing but names. According to most Western scholars, Al-Lat, Al-ʿUzza, and Manat were minor Meccan goddesses, whom the Meccans considered to be daughters of the high God, Allah. Today we know from pre-Islamic Arabian inscriptions that these three goddesses were indeed worshipped in Arabia, although only in the Qurʾan are the three mentioned together (see al-Jallad, *Linguistic Landscape*, 124). In any case, this one passage on Al-Lat, Al-ʿUzza, and Manat is exceptional. The Qurʾan is much more concerned with biblical characters and stories than it is with pagan gods and goddesses.

Moreover, the sorts of biblical characters and stories with which the Qurʾān is concerned is also surprising. If the Qurʾan referred only to stories found in the Old Testament, we might think of these passages as a reflection of Muhammad's interaction with the Jews of Medina. As we have seen, however, the Qurʾan is also interested in New Testament stories, and with the character of Jesus in particular. Moreover, many of the Old Testament material in the Qurʾan seems to have a Christian origin. For example, in the book of Genesis, a serpent tempts Adam and Eve in the Garden of Eden; Christians (but not Jews) later identified this serpent as Satan. The Qurʾan seems to accept the Christian interpretation: it does not even mention the serpent; only Satan appears in the qurʾanic garden. The Qurʾan's close relationship with

Christian traditions suggests that we might need to rethink the historical context in which it was proclaimed.

The Qurʾan and Scriptural Falsification

Yet the presence of biblical material in the Qurʾan also raises the question of what authority the Qurʾan gives to the Bible. The authors of the New Testament recognize the authority of the Hebrew Bible by quoting from it, and indeed the church simply added new Christian writings to the "Old Testament" to form its scripture. While the Qurʾan does not quote from the Bible in the same way that the New Testament authors quote from the Old Testament, it does refer frequently to biblical material. The Islamic community could—theoretically—have chosen to incorporate the Bible into its own scripture (which would have been a book in three parts), or into a canon of revelation (in the same way that the Church of Latter-day Saints accepts both the Bible, the Book of Mormon, and other books).

Instead the standard view of Islamic tradition is that the Bible is a corrupt, or falsified, version of an originally pure Islamic revelation. God sent down from heaven an Islamic book to Moses (*al-Tawrah*, from the Hebrew word *torah*) and an Islamic book to Jesus (*al-Injil*, from the Greek word *euangelion*, "gospel"), as he later sent down a book to Muhammad (*al-qurʾan*). The Jews destroyed or lost the book given to Moses and in its place wrote the Hebrew Bible/Old Testament. The Christians destroyed or lost the book given to Jesus and in its place wrote the New Testament. The true scriptures of Moses and Jesus, in other words, are lost. Only the Qur'an can be trusted.

The medieval Muslim theologian 'Abd al-Jabbar (d. 1025) exemplifies the Islamic view of scriptural falsification (Ar. *tahrif*) in his description of the Gospels.

> Know—May God have mercy on you—that these . . . Christian sects do not believe that God sent down to Christ the Injil, or a book of any kind. Rather, according to them Christ created the prophets and sent down to them the Books and sent down to them the angels. They only have four gospels from four individuals. Each one of them wrote his gospel in his era. Then another came after him and was not pleased with the [previous] gospel, [holding] his own gospel to be more proper. [The gospels] agree in some passages but differ in other passages. In some of them are things not found in others. They are made up of anecdotes about groups of men and women from the Jews, Romans and others, that they did this and said that. Yet there are many impossibilities, falsehoods, absurdities, manifest lies, and clear contradictions in them. ('Abd al-Jabbar, *Critique of Christian Origins*, 96–97)

Accordingly, while Christians bind the Hebrew Bible together with the New Testament in one book, it would be quite unusual for a Muslim even to keep the Bible next to the Qur'an in a mosque. Most Islamic bookstores will not sell the Bible at all, but they will sell books on the refutation of the Bible. On a popular site with Islamic legal opinions (fatwas), a Muslim posted the question "Is it permissible for me, as a Muslim, to read the Gospel out of curiosity, and not for any other purpose?" The Mufti responded, "The point is that the scholars who are well versed in Islamic teachings may need to look at the Torah or Gospel or Zaboor [Psalms] for Islamic purposes, such as refuting the enemies of Allah, or to highlight the virtue of the Qur'an and what it contains of truth and guidance. As for ordinary Muslims, they have no right to do that; rather if they have anything of the Torah or Gospel or Zaboor, what they must do is bury it in a clean place or burn it so that no one will be misguided by it" (https://islamqa.info/en/answers/128850/ruling-on-reading-the-gospel-and-torah).

Yet the position of the Qur'an itself in relation to earlier Scriptures is somewhat more complicated. The Qur'an does not present itself as a new covenant or testament, or the revelation of a new religion. It describes itself as a confirmation of the divine message found in earlier revelations: "This is a Book confirming, in Arabic tongue, to warn the evildoers, and good tidings to the good-doers" (Q 46:12). The description of the Qur'an as a book of confirmation matches what we have seen in the previous chapter of sacred history in the Qur'an. The prophets of the "punishment stories" all brought the same message, and the prophet of the Qur'an now brings this same message: believe in God and obey him, lest you be destroyed in this life or sent to hell in the next, and that you might live in bliss in a heavenly paradise.

BOX 5.1 ❖ GOSPEL OF BARNABAS

Many Islamic websites feature a work known as the *Gospel of Barnabas*, which tells the story of Jesus from an Islamic perspective (narrated by Barnabas, a disciple who appears in the Acts of Apostles). The only two existing manuscripts of the *Gospel of Barnabas* are in Italian and Spanish, and they date from the Renaissance period. Possibly the text was written by a Muslim who fled from the Spanish Reconquista to Venice, Italy. However, once the *Gospel of Barnabas* was published in an English translation in 1907, it became known to many Muslims as a text that proves that the Islamic version of the story of Jesus is the true and ancient one, and that early Christians suppressed this story. Among other things, the *Gospel of Barnabas* relates that God transformed Judas to look like Jesus and that Judas was subsequently crucified in his place (while Jesus ascended alive to heaven). This take on the crucifixion was later represented in a 2008 Iranian film titled *The Messiah*.

The Qurʾan connects in particular the revelation given to its prophet with that found in the "Torah" and the "Gospel": "He has sent down upon thee the Book with the truth, confirming what was before it, and He sent down the Torah and the Gospel * aforetime, as guidance to the people" (Q 3:3–4). The critical question, of course, is what the Qurʾan means by "Torah" and "Gospel." Does the Qurʾan mean the Bible that Jews and Christians were reading (or more likely, hearing) at the time of the Prophet Muhammad? In a tradition attributed to Ibn ʿAbbas (a young companion of Muhammad), the answer to this question is most definitely no.

> Ibn Abbas said, "O Muslims? How do you ask the People of the Scriptures, though your Book [i.e., the Quran] which was revealed to His Prophet is the most recent information from Allah and you recite it, the Book that has not been distorted? Allah has revealed to you that the People of the Scriptures have changed with their own hands what was revealed to them and they have said (as regards their changed Scriptures) 'This is from Allah,' in order to get some worldly benefit thereby." Ibn Abbas added: "Isn't the knowledge revealed to you sufficient to prevent you from asking them?" (Bukhari, 3:850)

In fact, it seems possible that this *hadith* does not come from the time of Muhammad himself but rather from a time when later Muslim scholars, eager to understand the biblical traditions of the Qurʾan, had begun asking Jews and Christians about them ("How do you ask the People of the Scriptures . . . ?"). The *hadith*, meant to condemn this practice, insists that the Jews and Christians ("the People of the Scriptures") cannot be trusted, since they "changed with their own hands what was revealed to them." This latter line is a reference to Qur᾽an 2:79: "Woe to those who write the Book with their hands, then say, 'This is from God.'"

The passage in which this verse occurs describes the infidelity of the Israelites, thus the accusation of writing "the Book"—and claiming that this writing comes from God—seems to be made against the Jews in particular. In a second passage, the Israelites doubt Moses's messages to them: "Moses, we will not believe thee till we see God openly" (Q 2:55), and then recounts, "The evildoers substituted a saying other than that which had been said to them" (Q 2:59). Elsewhere, the Qur᾽an accuses the Jews of falsifying the meanings (or perhaps "changing the places") of words (Q 2:78; 4:46; 5:13; 5:41). The Qur᾽an also accuses both Jews and Christians of hiding (Q 2:42, 140, passim) and forgetting (Q 5:13–14) revelation.

All in all, the Qur᾽an's idea of scriptural falsification does not seem to match the opinion of Ibn ῾Abbas in the hadith above. The Qur᾽an is certainly concerned with those (above all the Jews) who (it claims) misuse or misread scripture, or who consider their own writings to be divinely revealed. But the Qur᾽an does not actually argue that the Bible itself is a corrupt book. Indeed, the Qur᾽an's relative silence on this issue might be a reason why later Muslims felt the need to make this point explicit in a hadith.

In fact, the Qur᾽an suggests on several occasions that the Christians and Jews possess authentic revelation. In the fifth sura, the Qur᾽an describes Christians with the phrase "People of the Gospel" and commands them to "judge according to what God has sent down therein" (Q 5:47). Such a command would hardly make sense if the Qur᾽an did not believe in the Bible's authenticity.

At times, the Qur᾽an even insists that its audience follow the Bible, as when it proclaims: "O believers, believe in God and His Messenger and the Book He has sent down on His Messenger *and the Book which He sent down before*" (Q 4:136). The Arabic word translated here "Book" is *kitab*. In such passages, the word *kitab* seems to refer to something more than "book." It seems to refer to all of the divine truths, "written" in heaven, which God has revealed throughout the course of human history.

That the Bible is part of those divine truths is implied by the verse quoted at the opening of this chapter (Q 10:94), where the Qur᾽an tells the Prophet to consult those who recited "the Book" before him on matters regarding which he has doubts (in other words, God seems to instruct the Prophet to consult Jews and Christians when he has doubts about the revelations given to him). Elsewhere, the Qur᾽an even threatens those who are unfaithful to any revelation (and not only those given to Muhammad): "Those who cry lies to the Book and that wherewith We sent Our Messengers—soon they will know! When the fetters and chains are on their necks, and they are dragged into the boiling water, then into the Fire they are poured" (Q 40:70–72).

Thus the Qur᾽an does not present itself as the one true book. Instead it is the latest of God's revelations, and it calls on its audience to believe in all of them: "Say you: 'We believe in God, and in that which has been sent down on us and sent down on Abraham, Ishmael, Isaac and Jacob, and the Tribes, and that which was given to Moses and Jesus and the Prophets'" (Q 2:136).

The Qurʾan's Awareness of the Bible

At the same time, however, the Qurʾan does not seem to have a clear idea of the Bible's contents. The Qurʾan never mentions the Bible by name. Instead, the Qurʾan refers to the "Torah" and the "Gospel" (and on some occasions, *al-zabur*, a term that seems to refer to the Psalms). Yet even these terms are not used in a technical sense (that is, for the first five books of the Bible ["the Torah"] and one of four accounts of Jesus's life [a "Gospel"]) but rather as titles for Jewish and Christian revelation generally.

The Qurʾan's incomplete awareness of the Bible is also suggested by Qurʾan 7:157a (my translation): "Those who follow the messenger, the gentile [*ummi*] prophet, whom they find written in their Torah and Gospel, commanding them to do right, forbidding them to do wrong, permitting for them what is good, and prohibiting for them what is bad." "The gentile prophet" here is an allusion to Muhammad (he is the prophet from a "nation" [Ar. *umma*; Latin *gens*] that has never before received a revelation in its language). In other words, the Qurʾan is claiming that Muhammad appears in the Bible, and indeed that in the Bible he is said to give certain commands and prohibitions. However, Muhammad is not explicitly mentioned in the Bible (even if Muslims have

long argued that the Bible contains references to him, as when Jesus promises the coming of a paraclete, in John 14–16). It seems possible that this claim was made without a perfect awareness of the Bible's contents.

A similar conclusion might be made regarding a verse in the ninth sura: "God has bought from the believers their selves and their possessions against the gift of Paradise; they fight in the way of God; they kill, and are killed; that is a promise binding upon God in the Torah, and the Gospel, and the Qurʾan" (Q 9:111). The idea of God's promising heaven to those who are killed in a holy war, or who kill others in a holy war, fits neither the Old nor the New Testament. Heaven is missing from the Old Testament, and holy wars are missing from the New.

The Qurʾan's imperfect knowledge of the Bible is also suggested by the sorts of biblical traditions to which it refers. The Qurʾan refers frequently to the characters of the book of Genesis; it also refers to the stories of David, Solomon, and Jonah. Yet it has little to say about the wisdom or prophetic books of the Old Testament. The Qurʾan is quite interested in the birth and the miracles of Jesus, but it has little to say about the rest of his life. Moreover, it has nothing to say at all about the Acts of the Apostles, the letters of Paul, the Pastoral/catholic Epistles, or the book of Revelation.

This uneven distribution of biblical material suggests that the Qurʾan was aware of oral traditions about biblical characters but not of the Bible itself. It could be that the Qurʾan refers to the stories of Adam, Noah, Abraham, Joseph, David, Solomon, Jonah, and Jesus because these are the sorts of stories that were

FROM A CLASSIC TEXT ❖ 5.1

Qurʾan and Bible: *The Table from Heaven*

In sura 5 (titled "The Table") of the Qurʾan, the companions of Jesus ask whether his God is able to send down to them a table (Ar. maʾida) from heaven. Jesus at first refuses to answer their question, but the companions persist until Jesus makes the request they demand of him. God agrees, but he adds that the companions of Jesus will be punished severely if they disbelieve after having witnessed such a miraculous sign.

Western scholars have explained this unique qurʾanic episode by comparing it to a number of different Gospel passages, including Jesus's multiplication of fish and loaves, the Last Supper, and a passage in Acts 10 in which God sends down "something like a great sheet bound at the four corners" (Acts 10:11) filled with animals for Peter to eat. In fact, the qurʾanic passage on the table from heaven is most closely related to the passage in the Gospel of John in which Jesus gives the "Bread of Life" discourse, in which a crowd of followers approach Jesus the day after he multiplied the fish and loaves (John 6:10–13). They demand a sign from Jesus that would give them reason to believe in him, noting that their ancestors (who followed Moses from Egypt into the desert) received manna from heaven.

The qurʾanic passage on the table from heaven seems to integrate the motif of the followers of Jesus who demand a sign from him with the motif of the followers of Moses who demand food in the desert. The language of the Qurʾan seems to reflect in particular a reference in the Psalms to this latter motif, in which the followers of Moses are made to ask him whether God can set a "banquet" in the desert. In the Ethiopic translation of the Psalms, the word used for banquet is maʾedd (literally "table"), the Arabic form of which appears in the Qurʾan as maʾida.

Qurʾan 5:111–15	John 6:30–32
And when I inspired the Apostles: "Believe in Me and My Messenger"; they said, "We believe; witness Thou our submission." * And when the Apostles said, "O Jesus son of Mary, is thy Lord able to send down on us a Table [maʾida] out of heaven?" He said, "Fear you God, if you are believers." * They said, "We desire that we should eat of it and our hearts be at rest; and that we may know that thou hast spoken true to us, and that we may be among its witnesses."	So they said, "What sign will you yourself do, the sight of which will make us believe in you? What work will you do? * Our fathers ate manna in the desert; as scripture says: He gave them bread from heaven to eat." * Jesus answered them: "In all truth I tell you, it was not Moses who gave you the bread from heaven, it is my Father who gives you the bread from heaven, the true bread."

* Said Jesus son of Mary, "O God, our Lord, send down upon us a Table out of heaven, that shall be for us a festival, the first and last of us, and a sign from Thee. And provide for us; Thou art the best of providers." * God said, "Verily I do send it down on you; whoso of you hereafter disbelieves, verily I shall chastise him with a chastisement wherewith I chastise no other being."

Numbers 21:5
They spoke against God and against Moses, "Why did you bring us out of Egypt to die in the desert? For there is neither food nor water here; we are sick of this meagre diet."

Psalm 78:19–20
They insulted God by saying "Can God make a banquet [Ethiopic "table," *ma'edd*] in the desert? * True, when he struck the rock, waters gushed out and flowed in torrents; but what of bread? Can he give that, can he provide meat for his people?"

told (as they are now) in popular settings. The prophecies of Isaiah or Ezekiel, however, are not the stuff of storytellers.

Along these lines, it is telling that the Qur'an seems to make no distinction between traditions from the canonical Bible and those from Jewish and Christian legends, such as the story of the fall of the devil, of Alexander the Great (the "two-horned one" of Qur'an 18) or of Jesus's creating a bird from clay (which flies away when he blows in it; Q 3:49)—the sorts of legends that may have been told in popular settings along with the more entertaining stories from the Bible itself. It seems likely that the Qur'an was not aware of exactly which traditions came from the Bible and which from non-biblical legends. Nevertheless—and this is the most important point for our purposes—it is evident that the Qur'an was proclaimed in an

environment where biblical, and para-biblical, traditions were of great popular interest.

Indeed, the Qur'an seems to count on its audience's knowledge of biblical traditions when it uses nicknames for its characters. It refers to Pharaoh (associated in the Bible with building projects) as "the man of stakes" (Q 38:12; 89:10) and to Jonah as the "man of the fish" (Q 21:87; 68:48). The Qur'an refers to Potiphar from the story of Joseph (see Gen 37:36) only as al-'aziz, "the mighty one," a fitting nickname for the "commander" of Pharaoh's guard (Gen 39:1). It refers to Saul only as *talut* "the tall one" (Q 2:247, 9; the form of the name seems to have been chosen to rhyme with the qur'anic name for Goliath: *jalut* [Q 2:250]), a fitting nickname for a man who was "head and shoulders" taller than his people (1 Sam

10:23). In order for these references to have made any sense at all, the Qur'an's audience must have already been familiar with the biblical stories involving Potiphar (that is, the story of Joseph) and Saul.

The Qur'an's Conversation with Biblical Literature

This is not the only example of how the Qur'an depends on its audience's knowledge of biblical traditions. This dependence is also evident from the manner in which the Qur'an refers to biblical material, as the following cases might show.

Sarah's Laughter

Genesis 18 tells the story of three men who appear to Abraham (v. 2) while he is sitting near the entrance of his tent. After the men eat (v. 8), God speaks from their midst and announces that Sarah will soon give birth to her son. Hearing this, Sarah laughs, thinking to herself, "Now that I am past the age of childbearing, and my husband is an old man, is pleasure to come my way again?" (v. 12). In part, this story is meant to explain the name of her son Isaac, which in Hebrew means "he laughs" or (if it refers to God) "He makes [people] laugh."

When the Qur'an refers to this episode, however, it mentions the laughter of Abraham's wife (her name is not given—Mary is the only woman mentioned by name in the Qur'an) *before* the annunciation of a son (Q 11:71, my translation): "She laughed and we gave her the good news of Isaac and after Isaac, Jacob." The reason for this unusual order is clear enough:

the word for laughter (*dahikat*) does not match the rhyme of this section of the Qur'an (which requires a *u* or *i* as the penultimate letter). For this same reason the verse in question ends with "Jacob" (Arabic *ya'qub*), the son of Isaac (since Isaac, Ar. *ishaq*, also does not match the rhyme). Yet if the word order is different from the Bible, the idea is not: Sarah laughed *when* she received the good news.

In changing the word order for the sake of its rhyme, the Qur'an depends on its audience's knowledge of the biblical story of Sarah's laughter. Evidently, the Qur'an's original audience already knew why Sarah laughed and would not have been confused by the curious word order in the Qur'an.

However, this change did confuse medieval Muslim scholars, who were reluctant to refer to the Bible for such matters. Some were so troubled by this passage that they argued she did not laugh at all. Instead, they proposed that the Arabic word *dahikat* has a special meaning here: "to menstruate." By this interpretation Sarah menstruated just before she received the news that she would have a child. Her menstruation was a sign that gave her reason to believe the promise of a son in her old age. The logic of this interpretation is appealing. The only problem is that this special meaning for *dahikat* seems to have been invented in order to explain this passage. If the Qur'an is read in conversation with the Bible, however, no such invention is necessary.

Jonah

The Qur'an's references to the story of Jonah similarly troubled medieval Muslim interpreters. In the longest passage related to Jonah (Q 37:139–48), the Qur'an refers first to Jonah's departure from some place (v. 140), then his encounter with a fish (vv. 142–45), a tree that grew over him (v. 146), and his mission (v. 147–48). Muslim interpreters—following the order of this passage—were left wondering *where* Jonah departed from in the first place.

In their attempts to answer this question, most Muslim commentators relied on a second passage in the Qur'an (21:87), which relates, "The 'Man of the Fish' went off angry" (my translation). This seemed to hold the key to answering the question: Jonah left from some place where something happened that angered him. That place, they speculated, must have been the city to which he was sent by God: Nineveh. The people there did not believe him, and so he left Nineveh in anger. In other words, Jonah was not swallowed by a fish before he went to Nineveh, as in the Bible, but only *after* he left Nineveh (which, logically, is a bit hard to swallow, since Nineveh is in northern Mesopotamia and a long way from the sea, where big fish live).

But with this conclusion the commentators were confronted by a second problem: if Jonah's mission took place before he was swallowed, then why does the Qur'an mention that mission after (Q 37:147–48) it mentions the fish? One medieval commentator, named Ibn Kathir (d. 1373), has a solution: "There is no reason why he could not have returned to the people to whom he was first sent after he left the fish, and that they then believed him" (Ibn Kathir, *Commentary*, on Q 37:137–48).

In fact, if one reads the Qur'an alongside the Bible, then there is no problem to solve: Jonah departs not from Nineveh but Palestine, where he first received God's call (Jon 1:2–3; Q 37:140); he is swallowed by a fish (Jon 1–2; Q 37:142–45); he preaches in Nineveh (Jon 3); a vine grows over him (and then dies; Jon 4:6–8; Q 37:146); and finally he has a conversation with God about his mission to Nineveh (Jon 4:9–11; Q 37:147–48).

Mary's Nativity

The case of the nativity, or the birth story, of Mary is somewhat different. The Bible itself makes no mention of Mary's birth, but in the third sura, the Qur'an describes how Mary's mother (known in Christian tradition as Anne) dedicates her unborn child to God. When her baby girl is born, she names her Mary (Q 3:35–36). The Qur'an continues: "Her Lord received the child with gracious favour, and by His goodness she grew up comely, Zachariah taking charge of her. Whenever Zachariah went to her in the Sanctuary, he found her provisioned. 'Mary,' he said, 'how comes this to thee?' 'From God,' she said. Truly God provisions whomsoever He will without reckoning" (Q 3:37). Several verses later, after referring to the story of the birth of John (the Baptist), the Qur'an returns to the story of Mary: "That is of the tidings of the Unseen, that We reveal to thee; for thou wast not with them, when they were casting quills which of them should have charge of Mary; thou wast not with them, when they were disputing" (Q 3:47).

The Qur'an's references to Mary's nativity presented two questions to Muslim scholars.

First, what was the "Sanctuary" (Q 3:37) in which Mary resided? Some proposed that it was a sort of structure in which Mary was locked. This view seems to reflect a concern provoked by the traditional Islamic doctrine that Mary never married (a doctrine to which we will return). Others, however, proposed that the "Sanctuary" was a synagogue or a place of honor in a prayer hall or a court.

Second, what was the point of the contest, which apparently involved casting "quills," over "having charge" of Mary? In their answer to this question most Muslim scholars insisted that the Qur'an simply recounts the story of Mary out of order. The Qur'an's reference to a contest in verse 47 relates to a competition that Zachariah had already won, a competition which granted him the right to take Mary into his possession. This is the reason Mary is found in his care in verse 37.

In fact, both questions are better addressed by reading the Qur'an in light of an apocryphal Christian text known as the *Protoevangelium of James* (here *proto* means "first" or "early," an indication that this work tells the story of salvation before the birth of Jesus), written most likely in the mid or late second century CE (or earlier) and attributed to James, the half-brother of Jesus. In the *Protoevangelium*, Anne, who is barren, prays to God for a child, vowing that in return she will place this child, "whether male or female," into the service of the Jerusalem temple (*Protoevangelium* 4.1). When Mary is three years old, Anne accordingly brings her to the temple and delivers her into the care

of Zachariah (*Protoevangelium* 7:2). Thus we see that the "Sanctuary" of the Qur'an is the temple of Jerusalem.

The contest to which the Qur'an alludes (Q 3:47), however, takes place only when Mary approaches the age of puberty (and is in danger of defiling the temple with the blood of her menstruation). Because of this, Zachariah gathers the widowers of the land at the temple and instructs each one of them to bring his rod. They all give their rods to Zachariah, who prays over them until a dove emerges from the rod of Joseph (*Protoevangelium* 9.1). Thus God revealed that Mary was to marry Joseph, and so it was. The Qur'an refers to the "rods" of this contest as *aqlam*, an Arabic word that can also mean "pens" (for which reason Arberry [incorrectly] translates "quills"). The word, however, is derived from the Greek word for "reed (≈ 'rod', such as the rod put in the right hand of Jesus in Matthew 27)" and the Qur'an uses it in this ancient sense. Thus we understand why the Qur'an refers to a contest over Mary.

Most Islamic accounts of the lives of Mary and Jesus, following the standard interpretation of this passage, never mention Joseph at all. According to these accounts, Mary never married. For its part the Qur'an—by referring to the ancient Christian story of Mary's engagement to Joseph—suggests that she did indeed marry. Its reference to the story of Mary's engagement is admittedly subtle; but then it is the very subtlety of the reference which suggests that the Qur'an's audience already knew the story, and did not need to hear it again.

The Seven Sleepers and Their Dog

A final example of the Qur'an's conversation with biblical literature is found in sura 18:9–26, where the Qur'an refers to the "companions of the Cave," a group of young men who flee a city of pagans and hide in a cave (Q 18:16). There God casts sleep upon them, and they wake up 309 years later (Q 18:25), although they think they have slept for a day or less (Q 18:19). The whole affair, the Qur'an announces, took place so that the people of the city would believe that God has the power to raise the dead (Q 18:21).

In the midst of the Qur'an's account, however, is a reference to a dog who stayed with the companions in the cave (Q 18:18). The dog is a problem to some Muslim interpreters, since according to Islamic law dogs are unclean animals and they assume (although the text does not actually say so) that these

FIGURE 5.1. *Seven Sleepers (Islamic art): Falnama (The Book of Divination); Seven Sleepers of Ephesus. Mid-sixteenth century. Ink, colors and gold on paper, 23 × 17 3/4 in. (58.4 × 45.1 cm). Rogers Fund, 1935 (35.64.3). Location: The Metropolitan Museum of Art, New York, NY, U.S.A.*

companions must have been holy men. Accordingly, Ibn Kathir insists that the dog was with the companions but remained *outside* of the cave (*Commentary* on Q 18:18). Others proposed that the Arabic word "dog" (*kalb*) should be *kali'*, to make it mean "guardian," thus doing away with the dog completely. In fact, the dog plays an important role in this episode.

Here the Qur'an follows a popular Christian tradition, widespread in the Middle East before Islam, according to which a group of seven young Christian men flee the city of Ephesus (in modern day Turkey) when they hear that the emperor Decius (r. 249–51) is planning to force all Christians there to perform pagan sacrifices. They flee to a cave where God casts a miraculous sleep upon them (or, to be more precise, God takes their souls to heaven while their bodies remain in the cave). The "seven sleepers" wake up only during the reign of the Christian emperor Theodosius II (r. 408–50). The emperor, hearing of the miraculous story of the seven sleepers, rushes to Ephesus to meet them. Now in Theodosius's time, some Christians were denying the doctrine of the resurrection of the body (arguing that the soul alone experiences the afterlife). The seven sleepers accordingly inform the emperor that they have been "awoken" in order to convince him of the resurrection of the body.

In recounting this legend, Jacob of Serugh (d. 521 CE) describes the sleepers as "blessed lambs" and the evil king Decius as a "wolf who thirsts for blood." He adds that God placed a "watcher" in the cave to guard their bodies (Griffith, 128). Jacob never describes this "watcher" as a dog, but the allusion seems clear enough: sheepdogs watch over sheep. And in fact, a dog is mentioned by a pilgrim—also named Theodosius—who traveled to the holy land in the year 530. This Theodosius describes Ephesus as the city famous for "the seven sleeping brothers, *and the dog Viricanus at their feet*" (Theodosius, 16). Thanks to Theodosius, we know why the Qur'an refers to a dog in the eighteenth sura, and we even know his name.

STUDY QUESTIONS

1   What is the position of the Qur'an on the authority of the Bible? What is the later Islamic view of "scriptural falsification" (*tahrif*)?

2   What are some indications that the Qur'an is aware of the Bible's contents?

3   What does it mean to say that the Qur'an has a "conversation" with biblical literature? How do the examples cited in this chapter illustrate that?

Chapter 6

THE QUR'AN AND THE BIOGRAPHY OF THE PROPHET

The Muslim scripture and Muhammad's prophetic experience are so closely linked that one cannot be fully understood without the other.

—"The Ku'ran," *Encyclopaedia of Islam* by Alfred Welch

The Biography of Muhammad and Exegesis of the Qur'an

In the previous two chapters, I suggest that the Qur'an was proclaimed in a milieu where people were hotly debating theology, and in particular theology involving Christ (that is, Christology), and where they knew the literature of Jews and Christians well. However, according to the traditional biography of Muhammad, the Qur'an was proclaimed for the first twelve years of the Prophet's mission in the pagan city of Mecca, where theology would not have been a major concern, Christology would have no place at all, and the Bible would have been irrelevant. For the last ten years of the Prophet's mission, according to the traditional biography, the Qur'an was proclaimed in the city of Mecca, where the young Muslim community competed with Jewish tribes (at least initially), but where Christians are nowhere to be found. Thus the Qur'an's remarkable interest in Christ, and its use of Christian traditions (such as that found in the *Protoevangelium of James*) seems to clash with the picture of

Islam's emergence painted by the traditional biography of Muhammad.

Western Scholarship and the Traditional Biography of the Prophet

Nevertheless, Western scholars such as Alfred Welch (who is quoted at the opening of this chapter) generally assume that the traditional biography is basically correct, that Muhammad was the sole author of the Qur'an, and that the key to understanding the Qur'an is understanding his life. In light of these assumptions, they have long sought to explain the Qur'an's interest in Judaism and Christianity by finding Jews and Christians in the traditional biography of the Prophet. Those scholars interested in Judaism focused on the reports of Muhammad's contacts with the Jews of Medina. This was the focus of the first important book of critical qur'anic studies (published in 1833), Abraham Geiger's "What did Muhammad Take from Judaism?" (in German: *Was hat Mohammed aus dem Judenthume aufgenommen?*).

Other scholars, such as the Austrian Aloys Sprenger or the Swede Tor Andrae, were more interested in Christianity and the Qur'an. This interest meant looking further afield, since in the traditional biography, Muhammad has less frequent contact with Christians. Thus these scholars tended to speculate on Christians whom the Prophet might conceivably have met. Taking their lead from the nature of the Qur'an's discourse on Christ and Mary, they often imagined that Muhammad met heretical Christians, perhaps wandering monks from Ethiopia or Syria who rejected the divinity of Christ (or believed in the divinity of his mother; see Q 5:116). At its worst, their approach reflects the medieval Christian polemical portrait of Muhammad as a Christian heretic (a gruesome example of which is found in Dante's *Inferno*).

The Qur'an and Storytelling

But were these scholars right to think of the Qur'an in light of the traditional biography of the Prophet? What if that biography was itself written by early Muslim scholars as a way of explaining the Qur'an? This possibility is raised by Francis Peters:

> Once they began to interest themselves in Muhammad's life, they took up the task of matching Qur'anic verses with remembered incidents of the Prophet's life. Or perhaps it was the other way around: the Qur'anic verses, repeated over and over again, promoted wonder at what was happening behind the naked revelation" (Peters, *Jesus and Muhammad*, 28)

If the biography of Muhammad was written by scholars who did not know the story of how the Qur'an was proclaimed and written down, but who were "wondering" how this came to be, then it would be perfectly circular to explain the Qur'an according to that biography.

One reason to believe that this is how the biography of the Prophet was written—at least in part—is the way in which early Muslim scholars offer different stories to explain different possibilities of reading the same qurʾanic verse. For example, those who read Qurʾan 2:119 to mean, "You will not be asked about those in hell," explain that it was revealed when the Prophet grew distraught about the refusal of the Jews to believe in him. God revealed this verse so that Muhammad would not feel responsible for their disbelief. Those scholars who follow the alternative reading, and understand this verse to mean, "Do not ask about those in hell," insist that God revealed this verse when Muhammad was worried about the eternal fate of his parents (who had died before he preached Islam). Now one of these two stories could be right and the other wrong. On the other hand, it could be that neither story is right, that both stories were written after Muhammad's life by Muslims who were wondering why this phrase appeared in the Qurʾan in the first place.

The same phenomenon is found with the stories meant to explain a phrase found in both Qurʾan 2:88 and 4:155: "Our hearts are sealed [ghulf]," or, according to another way of reading the same phrase, "Our hearts are containers [ghuluf]." Those Muslim scholars who follow the first reading explain that one day the Jews of Medina—exasperated at the Prophet's preaching—told him, "Our hearts are sealed" (that is, "we will not listen to what you say"). Those who follow the second reading explain that one day the Jews of Medina—wanting to flaunt their religious knowledge—told Muhammad, "Our hearts are containers" (of the wisdom found in the Torah). It is worth asking whether the Jews of Medina said one of these two things, both of them, or neither.

These cases suggest that many stories in the Prophet's biography are not memories of historical events but rather stories told to explain material in the Qurʾan. This may be the case with the report that one of Muhammad's followers refused to join the attack against the Byzantine forces at Tabuk because he knew that he would lose control if he saw Byzantine women. This story seems to have been written to explain Qurʾan 9:49: "Among them is the one who says, 'Give me leave and do not tempt me!'" (my translation). The report that *several* Muslims (and not just "one") refused to join the attack because of the heat of the journey seems to have been written to explain Qurʾan 9:81: "*They* said, 'Go not forth in the heat!'"

In this light, we might consider again an account found in the story of Muhammad and the monk Bahira, referred to in the first chapter. Ibn Ishaq reports that Bahira found a birthmark between the shoulder blades of Muhammad; this was a sign that proved the boy to be a prophet. Presumably it is no accident that the word Ibn Ishaq uses for birthmark is *khatam*, which literally means not birthmark but "seal." His word choice suggests that this account was inspired by Qurʾan 33:40, which describes Muhammad as the "seal [*khatam*]" of the prophets. This story turns the symbolic word "seal" into a physical feature of Muhammad's body.

The manner in which stories about Muhammad seem to be built from material found in the Qurʾan seems fundamentally similar to the manner in which the early Islamic sources tell stories about other prophets. In the second sura, God announces to the angels his intention to create Adam by declaring: "Indeed I am setting on the earth a *khalifa*" (Q 2:30). The Arabic term *khalifa* (traditionally rendered in English as "caliph") can mean either "vicegerent/viceroy" or "successor." (Early Muslim rulers used it in this later sense as their title, since they presented themselves as the successors to the Prophet.) Most Muslim scholars prefer the second meaning, since the idea that God would have a "vicegerent" (that is, a "substitute") seems to conflict with the traditional Islamic notion of a God who is wholly unlike humanity. Yet by choosing the second meaning ("successor") these scholars were compelled to explain how Adam—who after all was the first

human—could succeed someone else. They did so by telling a story.

> The first to inhabit the earth were the *jinn*. They spread corruption thereon and shed blood, and killed each other. So God sent Iblis [the devil] against them with an army of angels, and Iblis and those with him killed them pursuing them as far as the islands of the oceans and the summits of the mountains. Then He created Adam and settled him thereon. That is why He has said: "I am about to place a *khalifa* on earth." (Tabari [commentary], 209)

According to this story, Adam was a successor not to humans but to *jinn* (the genies of

---

BOX 6.1 ❖ JINN

A widespread Islamic tradition relates that God created angels from light, humans from dirt, and creatures known as the *jinn* from fire. This tradition seems to be inspired by the Qur'an, which in one place (Q 18:50) describes the devil as one of the *jinn* and elsewhere (Q 7:12; 38:76) has him declare that he was made from fire. In fact, the Qur'an seems to present the *jinn* as a certain type of demon, or fallen angel. The Qur'an also has God order the devil—who is one of the *jinn*—to bow down before Adam with the angels. (When he refuses to do so, he is cast out of heaven.) The Qur'an describes how the *jinn*, like the demons, seek to enter into heaven and are chased away when missiles are cast at them from above.

Yet the Qur'an also has the *jinn* themselves declare that some of them are righteous (Q 72:11), a declaration which suggests to most Muslims (who generally understand demons to be purely evil) that the *jinn* are a special type of creature. In Islamic literature, the *jinn* indeed have a special place as magical creatures who are often up to mischief but who can also be compelled to grant favors to humans. The tales in the *Arabian* (or *One Thousand and One) Nights* about the *jinn* led to the Western idea of "genies" who can be trapped in a bottle and (as Aladdin found out) grant three wishes to their masters.

the *Arabian Nights*), the creatures whom God had originally put on earth (but who behaved so badly that they lost God's favor). This story—its fantastic nature notwithstanding—explains rather logically why the Qur'an would call Adam a "successor" (*khalifa*). A similar "exegetical" logic is found in the story (mentioned in the previous chapter) that Sarah menstruated at the moment she heard the promise of a child in her old age.

Such stories are common in early Muslim commentaries on the Qur'an. Indeed, it seems likely that the earliest stage of Islamic exegesis (that is, commentary on the Qur'an) involved above all the telling of stories meant to explain the turns of phrase found in the Qur'an. But exactly how much of Muhammad's biography was written in this way? Was such "exegetical storytelling" a process that only added details (such as a birthmark) to a basic, historically authentic account? Or was storytelling a process that shaped even the core of Muhammad's biography? We find an answer to these questions in one of the most controversial elements of that biography.

The Satanic Verses Reconsidered

In part 1 of the present work, I mention the tradition according to which Muhammad, while he was still in Mecca and eager to win the hearts of the Meccan pagans for Islam, heard a revelation from Satan, which he mistook for a revelation from God. According to this story, Muhammad heard these "satanic verses" just after he proclaimed two verses found in sura 53:

> Have you considered El-Lat and El-ʿUzza
> * and Manat the third, the other? (Q 53:19–20)

When Muhammad finished proclaiming these verses, Satan whispered to him: "These are the exalted cranes, whose intercession is approved." When Muhammad proclaimed aloud that which Satan had whispered and the Meccan pagans heard him praise their goddesses, they rejoiced. The angel Gabriel, however, rushed down from heaven, reprimanded Muhammad, and informed him of the verses God had intended him to proclaim.

> What, have you males, and He females?
> * That were indeed an unjust division.
> * They are naught but names yourselves have named, and your fathers; God has sent down no authority touching them. They follow only surmise, and what the souls desire; and yet guidance has come to them from their Lord. (Q 53:21–23).

The story of the satanic verses became well known in the 1990s because of the controversy following the publication of an English novel by an Indian Muslim, Salman Rushdie, by this title. Even before this controversy, however, modern Muslim scholars had largely come to reject this story (although it is widely reported in classical Islamic sources), since it seems to call into question both the infallibility of Muhammad and the reliability of the Qur'an.

FIGURE 6.1. *A first century statue from Syria of the Arabian goddess Al-Lat.*

BOX 6.2 ❖ THE SATANIC VERSES

The story of the satanic verses is possibly a manner to explain Qur'an 22:52: "We sent not ever any Messenger or Prophet before thee, but that Satan cast into his fancy, when he was fancying; but God annuls what Satan casts, then God confirms His signs—surely God is All-knowing, All-wise." This verse seems to call out for a story that would have Satan "cast" and God "annul." One suspects that the story was written around Qur'an 53:23 ("They are naught but names yourselves have named . . .") in part because that verse is longer than what comes after and calls attention to itself. If this suspicion is correct, then one need not imagine that Muhammad really made a "temporary concession" to paganism, but rather that later biographers of the Prophet wove a tale about him with threads they found in two different qur'anic suras.

For their part, Western scholars largely accept the story (some argue that at this point in his prophetic career Muhammad had become desperate to win the support of the Meccans). Indeed, some scholars maintain that the story of the satanic verses is precisely the sort of report that is most likely to be accurate, since a Muslim would never fabricate a story that puts Muhammad in such a bad light. William Montgomery Watt comments, "It is unthinkable that the story could have been invented by Muslims, or foisted upon them by non-Muslims" (Watt, *Muhammad at Mecca*, 103).

Watt's ideas about what is unthinkable reflect his general approach to the biography of the Prophet. According to Watt, Muslim scholars such as Ibn Ishaq inherited a large body of traditions about Muhammad's life. Many of these traditions were authentic reports that had been passed down from Muhammad's companions and other eyewitnesses; others—notably those with supernatural occurrences or those that seem designed to prove that Muhammad was a prophet—were invented at some point by well-meaning, pious Muslims and then added to the larger body of reports. The job of a critical scholar, in his view, is to remove those additions, so that what is left is the authentic core of Muhammad's biography. The story of the satanic verses, Watt concludes, must have been part of that authentic core.

Yet Watt's conclusion follows only because of his initial assumption. What if early scholars such as Ibn Ishaq and Tabari received a body of traditions that did not include eyewitness reports? What if the traditions about Muhammad were something like the traditions about Adam (successor to the *jinn*)? That is, what if they were written largely on the basis of turns of phrase in the Qur'an? One sign that suggests this is the case for the tradition of the satanic verses is its place in the Qur'an commentary of Tabari. When tabari discusses sura 53 (with its mention of Al-Lat, Manat, and Al-'Uzza), he does not mention the story of the satanic verses at all. Instead, he tells the story in his commentary on sura 22 (verse 52): "We sent not ever any Messenger or Prophet before thee, but that Satan cast into his fancy, when he was fancying; but God annuls what Satan casts, then God confirms His signs—surely God is All-knowing, All-wise." It seems quite likely, in other words, that the story of the satanic verses was written in order to explain this verse. It was written for the same reason that the stories surrounding Qur'an 2:119 ("You will not be asked" or "Do not ask" "about those in hell") and Qur'an 9:49 ("Among them is the one who says, 'Give me leave and do not tempt me!'") were written: to provide an otherwise ambiguous verse in the Qur'an a place in the story of Muhammad's life. Evidently, it was written at a stage in the emergence of Islam when there was little concern for the infallibility of Muhammad. What mattered was the story.

The Night Journey Reconsidered

For many Western scholars, the story of Muhammad's night journey from Mecca to Jerusalem is quite unlike the story of the satanic verses. It is precisely the sort of story that scholars such as Watt are prone to consider invented, since it involves both supernatural occurrences (Muhammad flies on a winged beast) and it serves to prove that Muhammad is a prophet (when he arrives in Jerusalem, all of the earlier prophets pray behind him). As we saw in part 1 of this book, however, one Islamic tradition (associated with ʿAʾisha) reports that the Prophet visited Jerusalem only in a dream or a vision, and not on the back of a magical animal. To Watt, this latter report represents the authentic core of the tradition around Muhammad's night journey. Muhammad, he argues, claimed only that he had a spiritual journey to, and vision of, Jerusalem. His overzealous followers added the legend of his journey through the night skies on a magical beast.

Yet even here, Watt, for all of his concern to be rigorous, seems to miss the relationship between this story of the verse on which it is based, namely Qurʾan 17:1: "Glory be to Him, who carried His servant by night from the Holy Mosque to the Further Mosque the precincts of which We have blessed, that We might show him some of Our signs. He is the All-hearing, the All-seeing." Again, we are dealing with a verse marked by ambiguity. This verse names neither the one who "carried" nor the one who was "carried" (and as this is the first verse of the sura; there is no way to look back in the text to understand the pronouns). Nor indeed are the two locations mentioned in the verse identified geographically; they are simply the "holy mosque" (Ar.

masjid, literally, "place of prostration") and the "further mosque."

On the one hand, the explanation of Islamic tradition—that this verse refers to Muhammad's journey from Mecca to Jerusalem—is quite reasonable. Muhammad might indeed be referred to as a "servant"; Mecca might be thought of as a "holy mosque," and Jerusalem as a "further mosque" (after all, it is quite a long way from Mecca) with blessed precincts. Yet on the other hand, one could imagine other ways of interpreting this passage. For example, the "further mosque" could be heaven and the verse could be about a mystical or supernatural ascent into the divine realm by Muhammad (or someone else). Now the Jerusalem story seems to fit Qurʾan 17:1 particularly well, of course, but this is precisely what we would expect if it were written as a way of explaining this passage.

The Battle of Badr Reconsidered

These examples suggest that at least some of the Prophet's biography is the product of exegesis. But it may be that this is an insight that applies only to elements of the Prophet's biography that involve religious matters, such as the "satanic verses" and the "night journey." Perhaps the episodes in the biography that recount more mundane matters, such as the Battle of Badr, are not stories told on the basis of the Qurʾan, but rather relatively faithful records of events that were truly remembered and passed down through the generations.

In his article on Badr in the *Encyclopaedia of the Qurʾan*, John Nawas relates, "Badr is mentioned explicitly only a single time in the Qur'an (Q 3:123), but there are allusions to it in at least thirty-two other verses. Almost all of these references are found in the eighth sura, "The Spoils." The "explicit" mention of Badr to which he refers is as follows.

> God most surely helped you at Badr, when you were utterly abject. So fear God, and perhaps you Will be thankful. * When thou saidst to the believers, "Is it not enough for you that your Lord should reinforce you with three thousand angels sent down upon you? * Yea; if you are patient and godfearing, and the foe come against you instantly, your Lord will reinforce you with five thousand swooping angels." (Q 3:123–25)

The Qur'an does indeed seem to be referring to a battle here at a place named Badr. However, on the basis of this verse alone, it is not clear whether the Qur'an refers to a historical event that is recounted in Muhammad's biography or if the story of Badr in that biography was written to explain this verse. That story, of course, includes the detail of angels coming to the aid of the believers, a detail that might have been inspired by the reference to angels in the passage above.

Other features of the story seem to have been inspired by passages in the eighth sura. In part 1 of the present work, I quote an account in which Muhammad prays persistently to God before the battle, imploring his help (to the point where Abu Bakr interrupts his prayer to assure him that God would be with him). This account seems to follow

Qur'an 8:9: "When you were calling upon your Lord for succour, and He answered you, 'I shall reinforce you with a thousand angels riding behind you.'" I mention there the tradition that a miraculous rain fell before Badr (a rain that impeded the progress of the polytheists but not the believers). This tradition seems to follow from Qur'an 8:11: "When He was causing slumber to overcome you as a security from Him, and sending down on you water from heaven, to purify you thereby, and to put away from you the defilement of Satan, and to strengthen your hearts, and to confirm your feet." In other words, it seems possible that the tradition that it rained before the Battle of Badr was not passed down by eyewitnesses who saw the Meccans get wet that day. Instead, a storyteller who found a way to explain the phrase "sending down on you water from heaven" in Qur'an 8:11 passed it down (although the verse speaks of a rain that fell on the believers, not unbelievers).

To this end, it is worth noting that this same verse begins, "When He was causing slumber to overcome you as a security from Him . . . ." This phrase, too, seems to have inspired part of the Badr story. According to a tradition in Ibn Ishaq on Badr, "While the apostle was in the hut [from which he observed the battle] he slept a light sleep" (Ibn Ishaq, 300). Moreover, Ibn Ishaq tells us that during his sleep, the Prophet had a vision of the angel Gabriel "holding the rein of a horse and leading it." This vision reassured Muhammad that angels would fight alongside the Muslims at Badr, a detail that explains how his sleep brought "security from Him." Now if the story of Badr were in fact the product of an ancient tradition, passed down by those who were there on that day, it might seem curious that the Prophet (who was also the general that day) would go to sleep just before a decisive battle was about to take place. At such a time, most commanders would typically be busy instead with battle plans. However, if the story of Badr was written on the basis of references in the eighth chapter of the Qur'an, then it is perfectly understandable: the line "when He made the slumber fall upon you" would have compelled those who wrote the story to have the Prophet sleep.

Meanwhile, the detail of the angels' involvement in the Battle of Badr reflects not only the reference to "three thousand" and "five thousand" angels in Qur'an 3:124 and 125 (cited above) but also a reference in the following verse (Qur'an 8:12): "When thy Lord was revealing to the angels, 'I am with you; so confirm the believers. I shall cast into the unbelievers' hearts terror; so smite above the necks, and smite every finger of them!'" Here God seems to instruct the angels to attack the unbelievers. In light of this verse, it is understandable why Ibn Ishaq reports a tradition (quoted in part 1 of the present work) that a veteran of Badr recalled how he was pursuing a polytheist during the battle but "his head fell off before I could get at him with my sword" (Ibn Ishaq, 303).

Even the detail of the prophet throwing a handful of pebbles at the polytheists (Ibn Ishaq, 303)—which by itself may seem like a curious thing to do before a big battle—seems to be a way of explaining Qur'an 8:17: "It was not thyself that threw, but God threw."

A Chronology of Revelation?

All of this suggests that the traditional method of reading the Qur'an is backwards. Pious Muslims and Western scholars alike generally read the Qur'an by connecting a certain passage with a certain incident from Muhammad's biography that seems to offer information on when and why this passage was proclaimed. By mapping out various passages onto the traditional story of Muhammad's prophetic career they give the Qur'an a chronological order. Most modern scholars also follow the traditional notion that entire suras can be taken as complete units of revelation, for which reason they argue that all of the suras can be lined up according to the order in which they were proclaimed. This method is evident in most recent translations of the Qur'an into English. Muhammad Abdel Haleem, for example, includes an introductory paragraph before each sura in his translation where he inevitably identifies the sura that follows as "Meccan" (that is, revealed during the period of Muhammad's prophetic career that took place in Mecca, traditionally 610–22 CE) or Medinan (622–33 CE). Often, his chronological observations are more specific still. For example, Abdel Haleem opens his introductory paragraph to Qur'an 8 with the explanation: "The main part of this Medinan Sura is a comment on the Battle of Badr." Some translations of the Qur'an (including the first edition of Blachère's French translation) actually rearrange the suras so that they might be read according to the supposed order in which Muhammad proclaimed

FIGURE 6.2. *The first sura of the Qur'an in the famous 1698 Latin translation (and Arabic edition) of Ludovico Marraci (d. 1700). The sura is labeled "Meccan" in both the Arabic and Latin text.*

FIGURE 6.3. *The title page of a Qur'an in which the suras are rearranged according to the supposed chronology in which the Prophet proclaimed them.*

them. This rearrangement—which would hardly be acceptable to pious Muslims—is meant to help readers to gain a critical sense of the development of Muhammad's religious thought, in light of the ups and downs of his biography.

Incidentally, the method of reading the Qur'an according to the chronology of Muhammad's biography offers a certain privilege to those passages of the Qur'an that contain strict religious laws and advocate aggression toward non-Muslims. These sorts of passages are traditionally placed in the Medinan period of Muhammad's biography, since only in Medina did Muhammad have the responsibility of making laws for a community, and only in Medina did Muhammad lead military raids against infidels. The chronological reading of the Qur'an has made it difficult for new, liberal interpretations of the Qur'an to gain a large following, since according to Islamic law the message of "later" passages may abrogate, or "overrule," the message of "earlier" passages.

The chronological reading of the Qur'an is also problematic on scholarly grounds. If the stories that make up Muhammad's biography—such as the accounts of the satanic verses, the night journey, and the Battle of Badr—were written as a way of explaining the Qur'an, then the very idea of a chronology of revelation would seem to inhibit a critical understanding of the text. The proper critical method, it would seem, would be to do things the other way around. Instead of providing a historical context for the Qur'an on the basis of the stories in Muhammad's biography,

---

BOX 6.3 ❖ CONFLICTS WITHIN THE QUR'AN

Muslim scholars often address apparent conflicts within the Qur'an by arguing that God revealed certain verses in order to replace, or "abrogate," the teaching of verses revealed earlier in the life of Muhammad. But as a rule, those verses that are judged to abrogate are more strict than those verses judged to be abrogated. For example, Q 2:62, which relates that believing Jews and Christians are, like Muslims, promised admission into heaven, is generally considered to have been abrogated by Q 3:85: "Whoso desires another religion than Islam, it shall not be accepted of him; in the next world he shall be among the losers." Q 2:256, which relates, "No compulsion is there in religion," is generally considered to be abrogated by Q 9:5: "Then, when the sacred months are drawn away, slay the idolaters wherever you find them, and take them, and confine them, and lie in wait for them at every place of ambush." Q 2:219, which notes that there is good and bad in drinking wine, is generally considered to be abrogated by Q 5:90: "O believers, wine and arrow-shuffling, idols and divining-arrows are an abomination, some of Satan's work."

we might provide a historical context for Muhammad's biography (or, more broadly, for the emergence of Islam) on the basis of the Qur'an. This is precisely what we propose to do in the chapter that follows.

The Sectarian Milieu

Before doing so, however, we should give some attention to a second feature of the Prophet's biography: religious apology (that is, the effort to convince others of one's religious teaching). The context of the medieval Islamic world in which the biographers of the Prophet lived was not perfectly Islamic. After all, the Islamic conquests left Muslims in control over the entire Middle East and North Africa, a region that was overwhelmingly populated by Christians (with smaller populations of Zoroastrians, Jews, and other religious groups). To Muslim scholars, the very presence of Christians was a challenge to Islamic claims about Muhammad. Christians who believed those claims, who accepted that Muhammad was a prophet, became Muslims. Those who refused to become Muslims, therefore, had implicitly rejected the prophethood of Muhammad.

Some Christians, moreover, made their rejection explicit. Saint John of Damascus (d. ca. 750), an elder contemporary of Ibn Ishaq, describes Muhammad as a false prophet in his work on heresies: "Muhammad, the founder of Islam, is a false prophet who, by chance, came across the Old and New Testament and who, also, pretended that he encountered an Arian monk and thus he devised his own heresy" (translation from D. Sahas, *John of Damascus on Islam*, p. 73).

Muhammad's Miracles

With such views in the air, Muslims were understandably eager to find ways to prove that Muhammad was a prophet. This eagerness shows through in the many accounts of Muhammad's miracles that were included in his biography, many of which have already been mentioned. The case of the tree that walked over to Muhammad when he called out to it is a telling example. According to Ibn Ishaq, Muhammad performed this miracle in order to prove his prophethood to a skeptic, an Arab named Rukana. Rukana was convinced by this miracle and became a Muslim. Presumably the skeptical reader was meant to have the same reaction. Other miracle accounts seem designed to prove that Muhammad was like biblical prophets (only better). At the birth of Jesus, a star shone brightly in the sky, but while Muhammad's mother Amina was pregnant with him a light came forth from her body by which she could see the castles in Syria (Ibn Ishaq, 69). Moses produced water from a rock for the Israelites in the desert (Exod 17:6; Num 20:11), but Muhammad produced water from his own fingertips (Bukhari, 4:779).

Muhammad, Mecca, and Abraham

We also find the apologetical shaping of Muhammad's biography in the portrayal of Mecca as a pagan city and the doctrine that Muhammad was illiterate. At first, these two ideas may seem unrelated, but both were put to use to prove Muhammad's prophethood. Since his city was pagan, his knowledge of biblical figures (evident already in passages traditionally dated to the Meccan period of his career) could not have come from a Jew or a Christian. Since he was illiterate, that knowledge could not have come from books. In his tenth-century work *The Critique of Christian Origins*, ʿAbd al-Jabbar makes precisely that point: "You will also find that [Muhammad]—God's blessing and peace be upon him—related the truth of [Christian] teachings. Yet he was not a debater or a diviner. He did not read [Christian] books or encounter [Christians]. He was not a rehearsed man. [Christians] could not be found in Mecca or the Hijaz [the region around Mecca] at that time" (ʿAbd al-Jabbar, 3). The image of pagan Mecca, though useful for arguing that Muhammad truly received revelation, also served to present Muhammad as a new Abraham. According to the biblical account, God chose Abraham and brought him out of Ur (Gen 15:7; Neh 9:7; Acts 7:2–4). Jews and Christians had long thought of Ur as a pagan city; indeed, many believed Abraham's own father to have been a pagan (something suggested by Josh 24:2 and made explicit in Q 6:74).

The Qur'an in turn compares its Prophet to Abraham: "Surely the people standing closest to Abraham are those who followed him, and *this Prophet*, and those who believe; and God is the Protector of the believers" (Q 3:68). The biographers of the Prophet, it seems, were eager to tell the story of this Prophet in a way that emphasizes this comparison. Thus, like Abraham, Muhammad comes from a pagan city and indeed from a pagan family (his parents are both said to have died before he preached Islam); like Abraham, Muhammad is called by God; like Abraham, Muhammad migrates from that city to establish his religion elsewhere.

The Place of Christians in Muhammad's Biography

Ibn Ishaq also uses the biography of Muhammad to send a message to the Christians of his day. This he does through the portrayal of wise and holy Christians who recognize the prophethood of Muhammad (and defy their own community in doing so). Bahira, the monk who lives a secluded existence in his cell in the desert of Syria, is one such Christian. The good king of Ethiopia, who recognizes the truth of Islam after hearing a passage of the Qur'an, is another.

A third such character is Salman the Persian (the same figure who is said to have suggested to the Muslims that they build a trench to protect the city of Medina against a Meccan attack). Salman, according to Ibn Ishaq, is raised a Zoroastrian in his native Iran, but after hearing Christians praying in a church one day, he embraces Christianity and leaves with a group of Christians for Syria. In Syria, he gets to know a Christian bishop who is robbing his people (a detail perhaps meant to explain Q 9:34: "O believers, many of the rabbis and monks indeed consume the goods of the people in vanity"). He reveals the bishop's crime to the local community of Christians,

Personalities in Islam 6.1
ABRAHAM

In sura 6 of the Qur'an, Abraham condemns his own father, and his own people, for their idol worship (Q 6.74). The Qur'an then has God show Abraham the "kingdom of the heavens and earth" (Q 6.75). When Abraham sees a star, he thinks, "This is my Lord," but when it sets he realizes that it cannot be so (Q 6.76). When he sees the moon rise, he thinks, "This is my Lord," but when it sets he realizes that it cannot be so (Q 6.77). Thereafter, he sees the sun and thinks, "This is my Lord" (Q 6.78). When it sets, however, he realizes that it cannot be so and finally proclaims, "I have turned my face to Him who originated the heavens and the earth, a man of pure faith; I am not of the idolaters" (Q 6:79). This passage (which refers to a story that, although not in the Bible, is widespread in earlier Jewish and Christian writings) presents Abraham as a "pure monotheist." In the midst of pagans, Abraham learns to worship the one true God. With no scriptures to read and no religious teachers to guide him, he receives inspiration directly from God. In all of this, he is understood to be the model of the Prophet Muhammad himself.

In their explanations of this passage, most classical Muslim commentators add more details. They have Abraham grow up in a pagan city of Iraq, a city ruled by an evil king named Nimrod (cf. Gen 10:8–11). When his astrologers predict that a child will soon be born who will ruin the pagan religion of the city, Nimrod orders that all newborn boys be put to death. Abraham's mother, however, gives birth to her son in secret, hides him in a cave, and leaves him there. Yet Abraham does not die. He finds nourishment by sucking his thumb, from which milk miraculously flows, and he grows in a day as other babies grow in a month. In this way, Abraham lives in perfect seclusion. Finally, he emerges one night from his cave, sees a star, the moon, and then the sun. Rejecting the worship of these heavenly bodies, Abraham declares his belief in the one true God and departs for the city of the evil king Nimrod. There he debates with the pagans and condemns their false beliefs. This story seems to be a sort of model for the story of Muhammad, who likewise receives his first inspiration in a cave and then departs to debate with the pagan people of Mecca.

who promptly stone and crucify the bishop (although it is hard to imagine Christians crucifying their bishop) and appoint another in his place. This new bishop is pious and honest. Eventually, he takes Salman aside to tell him, "My dear son, I do not know anyone who is as I am. Men have died and have either altered or abandoned most of their true religion" (Ibn Ishaq, 96). Salman continues his travels and later finds another "true Christian," who sends him to another. This third "true Christian" sends Salman to look for a prophet in Arabia. In this way he finds Muhammad. The "true Christian," it turns out, is a proto-Muslim.

The figure of the "true Christian" in the biography of Muhammad might be thought of as a response to the polemic of Christians such as John of Damascus. To John of Damascus, Muhammad was a false prophet, a Christian heretic. To Ibn Ishaq, Muhammad is a true prophet, and true Christians would recognize him as such.

The role of Jesus in the *hadith* on the end of the world, recorded by Bukhari, also seems to be a response to the refusal of Christians to accept Muhammad. According to these *hadith*, Jesus will return to earth in the end times to complete his life (since he did not die on the cross according to Islamic understanding). Before doing so, however, he will set things straight with Christians: "Allah's Apostle said, 'By Him in Whose Hands my soul is, surely [Jesus] the son of Mary will soon descend amongst you and will judge mankind justly (as a Just Ruler); he will break the Cross and kill the pigs and there will be no *jizya*" (Bukhari, 4:657). The *jizya* is the tax that non-Muslims are compelled to pay in an Islamic society. It will no longer exist when Jesus returns, because all people will accept Islam.

STUDY QUESTIONS

1   What does it mean to say that Muhammad's biography is exegetical or a sort of explanation of the Qur'an? How does the story of the satanic verses exhibit this exegetical quality?

2   What is meant by a "chronology of revelation" in the Qur'an? How is the concept of a chronology of revelation in the Qur'an useful to Muslim scholars?

3   What is meant by "sectarian milieu"? What elements of the Prophet's biography seem to respond to the sectarian milieu in which Islam developed?

Chapter 7

THE HISTORICAL CONTEXT OF THE QURʾAN

At that time a certain man from among those same sons of Ishmael whose name was Mahmet, a merchant, as if by God's command appeared to [the Arabs] as a preacher [and] the path of truth. He taught them to recognize the God of Abraham, especially because he was learned and informed in the history of Moses. Now because the command was from on high, at a single order they all came together in unity of religion. Abandoning their vain cults, they turned to the living God who had appeared to their father Abraham. So Mahmet legislated for them: not to eat carrion, not to drink wine, not to speak falsely, and not to engage in fornication. He said: "With an oath God promised this land to Abraham and his seed after him forever. And he brought about as he promised during that time while he loved Israel. But now you are the sons of Abraham, and God is accomplishing his promise to Abraham and his seed for you. Love sincerely only the God of Abraham, and go and seize your land which God gave to your father Abraham. No one will be able to resist you in battle, because God is with you."

— *The Armenian History*
Attributed to Sebeos

Qurʾanic Evidence

Most introductory books on Islam begin with the biography of Muhammad and then explain the Qurʾan according to that biography. In the present chapter, we will do things the other way around. Instead of asking what the biography of the Prophet can teach us about the Qur'an, we will ask what the Qur'an can tell us about the biography of the Prophet, and about the emergence of Islam in general.

In fact, our study of the Qur'an in chapter 5 has already taught us two lessons about the historical context of Islam's origins. First, the Qur'an's interest in taking Christians to task for their doctrines about Christ suggests that Islam emerged in an environment where theology and Christology were topics of general interest. Second, the Qur'an's frequent reference to biblical traditions (and the allusive nature of those references) suggests that Islam emerged in a context where biblical literature was well known (including later Christian works such as the *Protoevangelium of James* and the Syriac *Cave of Treasures*).

An Arabic Qur'an

In the present chapter, we turn to a quality of the Qur'an—its Arabic language—that offers us a third lesson on Islam's origins. The point here is not simply that the Qur'an is written in Arabic (although, as we will see, this is indeed remarkable). Instead, the point is that the Qur'an itself repeatedly emphasizes that it is written in Arabic. Neither the Old Testament, written (mostly) in Hebrew, nor the New Testament, written in Greek, boasts much about its language. The Qur'an, however, most certainly does.

In sura 16, the Qur'an refers to its language while refuting the accusation that the Prophet has an informant: "And We know very well that they say, 'Only a mortal is teaching him.' The speech of him at whom they hint is barbarous; and *this is speech Arabic, manifest*" (Q 16:103). The Qur'an does not reveal here the name of the person rumored to have been teaching the Prophet (if indeed the "him" in "teaching him" is a reference to Muhammad). The Qur'an does declare, however, that this person did not speak Arabic; his tongue was "barbarous." This declaration is revealing. Apparently, there were non-Arabic speakers in the Prophet's milieu (although according to the traditional biography both the Meccans and the Medinans spoke Arabic).

Elsewhere, the divine voice of the Qur'an presents the Arabic language as one of its fundamental qualities: "Truly it is the revelation of the Lord of all Being, * brought down by the Faithful Spirit * upon thy heart, that thou mayest be one of the warners, * *in a clear, Arabic tongue*" (Q 26:192–95). In sura 12:2, the Qur'an has God explain why He has chosen to send a revelation in Arabic: "We have sent it down as an Arabic Qur'an, so that you [plural] might understand" (Q 12:2, my translation). This is a revelation, in other words, for the Arabs. The same conclusion can be made about Qur'an 42:7: "And so We have revealed to thee an Arabic Qur'an, that thou mayest warn the Mother of Cities and those who dwell about it, and that thou mayest warn of the Day of Gathering, wherein is no doubt—a party in Paradise, and a party in the Blaze." Islamic tradition identifies the "Mother of the Cities" as Mecca. Whether or not this identification is correct, it was certainly a place where Arabs lived.

Elsewhere, the Qurʾan insists that the message it brings is not new. What is new is the language in which it is delivered: "This is a Book confirming, *in Arabic tongue*, to warn the evildoers, and good tidings to the good-doers" (Q 46:12). Here the Qurʾan presents itself as an Arabic version of the very same revelation given to other nations in early times. At last the time has come, the Qurʾan declares, that God has chosen to share a revelation with the Arabs, that they too might be saved from His wrath and enter into the heavenly paradise (see Qurʾan 42:7).

In this light, the importance of Arabic to the Qurʾan might be compared to the importance of German to Martin Luther's translation of the Bible. Luther (although he was not actually the first to do so) provided the Germans with a Bible in German so that they were able to read God's word in their own language. The Qurʾan's preoccupation with its own Arabic language suggests that a similar dynamic existed in its own historical context. The Arabs, the Qurʾan suggests, had heard God's word before, but they had not heard it in their own language. This suggestion happens to match what we know about the early history of Arab Christianity.

Arab Christianity before Islam

The New Testament itself implies that Arabic speakers were among the first converts to

---

BOX 7.1 ❖ "PEOPLE OF THE BOOK"

The Qurʾan refers regularly to the "People of the Book," a phrase that seems to refer to Jews and Christians. For example, the Qurʾan reprimands Jews for various sins in sura 5, verse 13, and then reprimands Christians for some of the same sins in verse 14. In verse 15, it apparently refers to both groups when it proclaims: "People of the Book, now there has come to you Our Messenger, making clear to you many things you have been concealing of the Book, and effacing many things. There has come to you from God a light, and a Book Manifest."

Muslim and Western scholars alike have often imagined that with this phrase the Qurʾan is distinguishing Jews and Christians from pagans by their possession of a written Scripture, the Bible. Yet by "Book," the Qurʾan means the revelation written not on earth but in heaven, or in the mind of God, which is transmitted *orally* to prophets (note, for example, that at the end of the verse quoted above the Qurʾan speaks of a "Book Manifest" coming now from God, even though the Qurʾan was evidently not yet a complete book when these words were proclaimed). Thus the Qurʾan seems to mean that Jews and Christians are "People of the Book" because they are nations to whom God has *already* given revelation—a chapter of the heavenly "book"—in the past. With the Qurʾan, a new nation, the Arabs, has received their messenger, and their "Book," in the present.

Christianity. The Acts of the Apostles reports that Arabs, among other people, heard the apostles praising God (in their own tongue [!]) on the day of Pentecost (Acts 2:11). The Apostle Paul reports in his letter to the Galatians (1:17) that after leaving Damascus—where he had come to believe in Jesus—he went to Arabia (although it is not clear exactly what place he means with this reference).

Between the time of Paul and the rise of Islam in the seventh century, Christianity

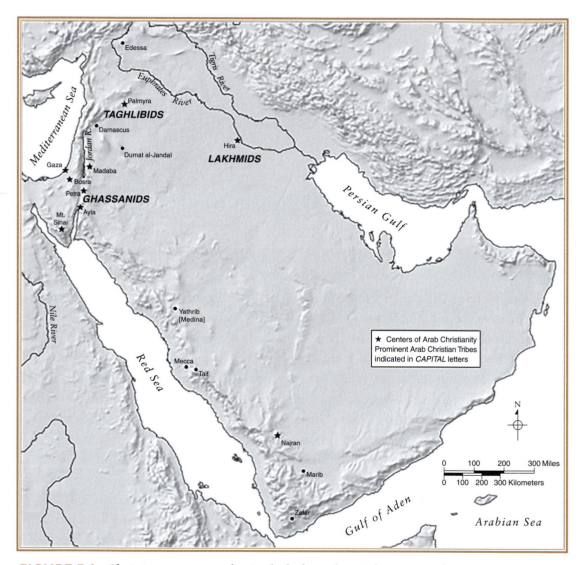

FIGURE 7.1. *Christianity among the Arabs before Islam. The names of prominent Christian Arab tribes are written in capital letters in their principal territories. Settlements with a sizeable Arab Christian population are indicated with stars.*

spread into the Arab Peninsula from three directions.

Eastern Arabia, including the islands and the coastlands around modern-day Bahrain, became home to a thriving Christian culture by the year 400. Recent archaeological expeditions have uncovered numerous churches and monasteries in this region, and ecclesiastical records note the presence of bishops from this area at church councils before the rise of Islam. Already in 325, a bishop named David is said to have represented an Arab community on the northern shore of the Persian Gulf at the Council of Seleucia-Ctesiphon (the capital of the Sassanian Persian Empire).

Southern Arabia, including modern-day Yemen, was largely Christian at the time of Islam's rise. (It was also home to a sizeable Jewish community.) The majority of Christians there were miaphysites and had close links with the miaphysite Ethiopian Church. Around the year 523, a large number of Christians were massacred by a Jewish ruler in the South Arabian city of Najran, an event recorded both in Arabic rock inscriptions by local Christians and in Greek and Latin historical accounts. Jacob of Serugh, the Syriac author mentioned in chapter 5, wrote a work entitled "the martyrs of Najran" to honor these Christians. In response to the massacre, the Ethiopian king Kaleb of Axum

FIGURE 7.2. *The ruins of an ancient Arab church in Qusair, southern Iraq.*

invaded Yemen and placed a Christian ruler on the throne. The successor to this ruler was Abraha, who is said in Islamic tradition to have attacked Mecca with an elephant.

Northern Arabia, meaning the territory of much of modern Syria, Jordan, and northern Saudi Arabia, was also largely Christian at the time of Islam's rise. The church historian Eusebius of Caesarea (d. 339) refers to two local church meetings—which he calls the "Councils of Arabia"—that took place in 246 and 247 in the southern Syrian city (largely populated by Arabs) of Bostra (the same city Muhammad is said to have passed by when he met the hermit Bahira). The most famous early inscription in Arabic (although it is written in Nabatean, not Arabic, letters) is found near a fort named Nemara in the desert southeast of Damascus. The Nemara inscription, which is dated to 328 CE, is an epitaph for a king named Imruʾ al-Qays, whom it describes as "king of all the Arabs." Tabari reports that Imruʾ al-Qays was a Christian, and the presence of his tomb in Christian Byzantine territory suggests that this was indeed the case. Recently an increasing number of pre-Islamic inscriptions—some written in the Arabic script—have been discovered in northern Arabia with Christian language or even ornamented with the Cross, including an inscription dated to around AD 550 recently found in northern Saudi Arabia.

Many northern Arabs would convert to Christianity in the centuries before Islam. In some cases, entire tribes seem to have embraced the faith en masse. The Palestinian Christian historian Sozomen (d. ca. 450) tells the story of an Arab ("Saracen") tribe that was converted by a holy monk.

Some of the Saracens were converted to Christianity not long before the present reign. They shared in the faith of Christ by intercourse with the priests and monks who dwelt near them, and practiced philosophy in the neighboring deserts, and who were distinguished by the excellence of their life, and by their miraculous works. It is said that a whole tribe, and Zocomus, their chief, were converted to Christianity and baptized about this period, under the following circumstances: Zocomus was childless, and went to a certain monk of great celebrity to complain to him of this calamity; for among the Saracens, and I believe other barbarian nations, it was accounted of great importance to have children. The monk desired Zocomus to be of good cheer, engaged in prayer on his behalf, and sent him away with the promise that if he would believe in Christ, he would have a son. When this promise was confirmed by God, and when a son was born to him, Zocomus was initiated, and all his subjects with him. From that period this tribe was peculiarly fortunate, and became strong in point of number, and formidable to the Persians as well as to the other Saracens. (Sozomen, 375)

In the centuries before Islam, some Arab tribes were even known for their devotion to a particular saint. The Tanukhids (whose territory spread from southwestern Iraq to

FIGURE 7.3. *A rock with a pre-Islamic Arabic inscription near Dumat al-Jandal in north-west Saudi Arabia analyzed by Prof. Leila Nehmé. The inscription (on the left side, mid-height) concludes with a cross. Permission: Saudi-Italian-French archaeological project in Dûmat al-Jandal, G. Charloux (DJ2016a0150)*

southern Syria) were known for their devotion to Saint Thomas, the Ghassanids (whose territory was in Palestine and Syria) for their devotion to Saint Sergius. By the sixth century, so many Arabs had converted to Christianity that the Palestinian monk Cyril of Scythopolis (d. 558) would observe: "Those who were formerly called the wolves of Arabia became members of the spiritual flock of Christ" (cited in Hoyland, 148).

Thus Christianity was widespread among the Arabs before Islam (although since the written sources say very little about the interior of the Arabian Peninsula, it is difficult to say much about Christianity there), and it seems proper to speak of a pre-Islamic Arab Christian culture. The Greek, Latin, and Syriac historical sources for this period do not describe any significant Arab pagan religion, but they describe in detail the Christian faith of the Arabs. For this reason, it is all the more remarkable that there is still no compelling evidence of an Arabic translation of the Bible before Islam. Indeed, it appears that the earliest Arabic book was the Qur'an itself. In other words, when Muhammad preached Islam, many Arabs had long been believers in the one God, the creator of heaven and earth. Yet until now they heard about this God in a foreign tongue. Most likely, the Bible was read in churches in Syriac and then translated orally so that the Arab worshipers could understand it. Indeed, it is tempting to think that this scenario explains Qur'an 16:103 (quoted above), which quotes an accusation that someone who spoke a language other than Arabic was teaching the Prophet. Perhaps that language was Syriac or another form of Aramaic.

In any case, in this light it is understandable why the Qur'an repeatedly boasts that it is a scripture in Arabic. In the Qur'an, God finally speaks to the Arabs in their own language: "We have sent it down as an Arabic Qur'an, haply ["that perhaps"] you will understand" (Q 12:2).

The Arabs as Heirs of Abraham

In the quotation at the opening of this chapter, from a work attributed to the Armenian historian Sebeos (d. late seventh century), connects the rise of Islam to the preaching of Muhammad (whose name he gives as Mahmet), who reminded the Arabs, the children of Ishmael, that they, too, are the descendants of Abraham. With this conviction, he urged them to conquer the holy land, the rightful inheritance of Abraham.

We should be careful not to take this account as "the true" account of Islam's emergence. Like the medieval Muslim authors who wrote the traditional biography of Muhammad, Sebeos (or Pseudo-Sebeos) shapes his account according to a religious vision. In the Bible, Abraham exiles his son Ishmael to the wilderness (Gen 21:14). This is presumably the reason why Sebeos (or Pseudo-Sebeos), a Christian who knew the Bible well, presents the Islamic conquests as the "return" of the Ishmaelites from the wilderness of the Arabian desert. Nevertheless, if this presentation of the Islamic conquests appears mythical, it still might teach us something about the emergence of Islam.

In this regard, we should note that the association between Arabs and Ishamel is not very ancient. As mentioned in the introduction to part 1 of the present work, the very idea of the Arabs as a single, unified people seems to have developed only gradually. Jewish, Christian, and Zoroastrian sources generally refer to individual Arab tribes, but not to a single Arab people. But at some point Jews and Christians in the Middle East began to associate all Arabic-speaking nomads with Ishmael, the son of the wilderness. They understood Genesis 37:25, in which traveling "Ishmaelites" take Joseph to Egypt, as a reference to these nomads.

Eventually, the idea emerged that *all* of the Arabic-speaking tribes (who were only in part nomadic) are the descendants of these Ishmaelites (just as the tribes of Israel represented the descendants of Isaac). Exactly when this idea emerged is difficult to establish,

FIGURE 7.4. *Two coins from the Umayyad (661–750 CE) period that illustrate the developing Islamic and Arabic ideology of the empire. The first coin (top) dates between 692–94 and was minted in Damascus (indicated by the Greek letters DAM, which can be seen on the bottom of the reverse of the coin [to the right]). This coin is based on the Byzantine coin of the emperor Heraclius, and includes Christian symbolism (notice the crosses on the obverse of the coin [to the left]). The minting of a coin with crosses may suggest that Islam had not yet clearly separated itself from Christianity. In later Umayyad coinage, as is evident from the second coin (dated to 740–41, and from the Caucasus), all traces of Byzantine Christian imagery have been removed. Indeed, this second coin is free of all figures whatsoever, which suggests that the Islamic doctrine on the prohibition of figural representation had developed in the intervening years. In the place of Byzantine Christian imagery, Arabic Islamic slogans now appear. The obverse of the coin (to the right), contains sura 112 of the Qurʾan in the center. The inscription in the margin around this citation is related to Qurʾan 9:33. However, while this qurʾanic verse begins, "[God] sent his messenger with guidance," the coin provides the name of Islam's Prophet: "Muhammad is the messenger of God. [God] sent him with guidance."*

but it is tempting to connect it with the time of Imru' al-Qays, whose funeral inscription (dated 328 CE) describes him as the "king of all the Arabs."

More telling, perhaps, is the evidence offered by Sozomen. According to Sozomen, some Arabs of his day (whom he calls Saracens) followed religious practices like those of the Jews.

> As their mother Hagar was a slave, they afterwards, to conceal the opprobrium of their origin, assumed the name of Saracens, as if they were descended from Sara, the wife of Abraham. Such being their origin, they practice circumcision like the Jews, refrain from the use of pork, and observe many other Jewish rites and customs. If, indeed, they deviate in any respect from the observances of that nation, it must be ascribed to the lapse of time, and to their intercourse with the neighboring nations. Moses, who lived many centuries after Abraham, only legislated for those whom he led out of Egypt. The inhabitants of the neighboring countries, being strongly addicted to superstition, probably soon corrupted the laws imposed upon them by their forefather Ishmael. (Sozomen, 375)

Sozomen goes on to explain how the "Saracens" "rediscovered" their Abrahamic roots: "Some of their tribe afterwards happening to come in contact with the Jews, gathered from them the facts of their true origin, returned to their kinsmen, and inclined to the Hebrew customs and laws. From that time on, until now, many of them regulate their lives according to the Jewish precepts" (Sozomen, 375). Like the work attributed to Sebeos, Sozomen sees the Arabs through a biblical lens. We might doubt the idea that the Arabs rediscovered their Abrahamic origins by speaking with the Jews. This idea seems to originate from a Christian notion of a natural alliance between the Arabs and Jews. According to this notion, Jews are children of Abraham by blood, but Christians are the children of Abraham by faith (see Gal 3:29: "And simply by being Christ's, you are that progeny of Abraham, the heirs named in the promise.").

Nevertheless, it is quite likely that some authentic historical occurrence lies behind Sozomen's narrative. Although Sozomen was a Greek speaker, he lived in Palestine and claims to have confirmed his reports with the Arabs of the region (see Shahid, 276). It seems reasonable to think that in the course of the fourth and fifth centuries, Arabic speakers themselves began to adopt the label of Ishmaelite given to them by Christians. By adopting this label, they necessarily gained a conception of nationhood: all Arabic speakers, whatever their tribe, are children of Abraham through Ishmael. They are all Ishmaelites.

In fact, the notion of an Abrahamic nation seems to be at the center of the Qur'an's message. The Qur'an is the Arabic scripture given to Abraham's children. To this end the Qur'an has Abraham and Ishmael pray together that God will form a holy nation from their offspring and raise up a divine messenger from that nation.

> And when Abraham, and Ishmael with him, raised up the foundations of the House:

"Our Lord, receive this from us; Thou art the All-hearing, the All-knowing; * and, our Lord, make us submissive [*muslimayn*] to Thee, and of our seed a nation submissive to Thee; and show us our holy rites, and turn towards us; surely Thou turnest, and art All-compassionate. * Our Lord, send to them a messenger who is one of them, a messenger who will recount the signs that give witness to you, who will teach them revelation and wisdom and who will purify them. Indeed you are the all-powerful, the all-wise. (Q 2:127–29)

According to this vision, the Arabs are that holy nation, and their messenger is Muhammad.

Islam and Theological Rivalries

The notion of the Arabs as a holy nation, the children of Abraham, seems to have prepared the way for the preaching of the Qur'an. It seems likely that by the early seventh century the Arabs were largely Christianized, but that their attachment to Christianity was qualified by two factors. First, Christianity, in cultural terms, remained a foreign faith. It had been brought to them by foreign (whether Greek-, Syriac-, Persian-, or Ethiopic-speaking) missionaries, and the Bible remained in a foreign tongue.

Second, the idea that they were the descendants of Abraham like the Jews—an idea developed largely by Greek- and Syriac-speaking Christians—must have given them a special identity within the church. They had become children of Abraham by faith, but they were *still* children of Abraham by blood. It is no surprise, then, that the Arabs welcomed a prophet who came to them with a message in Arabic and who insisted that their true faith is neither Judaism nor Christianity but rather the faith of Abraham: "And they say, 'Be Jews or Christians and you shall be guided.' Say thou: 'Nay, rather the creed of Abraham, a man of pure faith; he was no idolater'" (Q 2:135).

This is not, however, the full story of the emergence of Islam. As we have seen, the Qur'an also has a distinct theology. It is this theology that definitively separated the faith of Muslims from that of Christians. It was through this theological message that the formation of a distinct Islamic identity was assured. Yet this theological message was not entirely new.

The Legacy of Christian Theological Debate

The early centuries of the history of church are marked by a series of disputes over the nature of Christ and the nature of God. These disputes were most intense in the Eastern Roman Empire, that is, in the Middle East, where Islam would later emerge. The protagonists in these debates, and the particular questions at issue, varied. Nevertheless, we can identify two competing styles of theological thought throughout this long period of intense intellectual and religious debate.

One current of theological style involved a celebration of the particular story of divine immanence—that is, God's intimate connection with his creation—in Christian revelation. This idea is already emphasized by Saint Paul, when in the book of Philippians he celebrates the willingness of Christ to sacrifice his divine majesty for the sake of humanity.

> Make your own the mind of Christ Jesus: * Who, being in the form of God, did not count equality with God something to be grasped. * But he emptied himself, taking the form of a slave, becoming as human beings are; and being in every way like a human being, * he was humbler yet, even to accepting death, death on a cross. * And for this God raised him high, and gave him the name which is above all other names. (Phil 2:5–9)

Paul seemed to recognize that some people found the Christian doctrine of divine immanence—the message of an omnipotent God who was willing to be born a human and to die a human—to be ludicrous. Yet to Paul the very point of the gospel, this "good news," is that it surpasses human reasoning. God's love for humanity led him to act in a way that humans find incredible: "We are preaching a crucified Christ: to the Jews an obstacle they cannot get over, to the gentiles foolishness, * but to those who have been called, whether they are Jews or Greeks, a Christ who is both the power of God and the wisdom of God. * God's folly is wiser than human wisdom, and God's weakness is stronger than human strength" (1 Cor 1:23–25). The language of the Latin-speaking theologian Tertullian (d. 220) is similar. In his refutation of a heretic named Marcion, who contended that the Son of God did not truly become incarnate, Tertullian begins by asking:

"To the extent that you [Marcion] consider yourself competent to judge in this matter, you must have thought either that birth is impossible for God or that it is unsuitable for him" (*On the Flesh of Christ* 3 [Norton, 65]). After arguing that such a thing could not be impossible for God, since even the angels are able to take on human flesh (as in the story of Gen 18, when three heavenly figures appear to Abraham), Tertullian continues,

> So then, if [birth] is neither as impossible nor as dangerous to God that you repudiate his becoming embodied, it remains for you to reject and denounce it on the ground that it is unworthy of him. Come, then, start from the birth itself, the object of aversion, and run through your catalog, the filth of the generative seeds within the womb, of the bodily fluid and the blood. . . . Undoubtedly you are also horrified at the infant, which has been brought into the world together with its afterbirth. Christ loved that human being, that lump curdled in the womb in the midst of impurities, that creature brought into the world through unmentionable organs, that child nourished on mockery. On his account Christ came down. On his account Christ preached. On his account Christ, in all humility, brought himself down to death, the death on a cross. (Tertullian, *On the Flesh of Christ* 4 [Norton, 67–68])

Tertullian, like Paul, begins his theological thinking with the Christian teaching that God so loved humanity that he became a man. Marcion, along with other Christians known as gnostics, represented an early (and unorthodox) version of the second current of theological thought. They began their theological thinking with the rational understanding of God as a transcendent and perfect being and their practical experience of the world as an imperfect place. Therefore they felt compelled to explain Christian teaching in a way that kept God above and beyond this world. God, by their way of thinking, is perfectly other, perfectly transcendent; He has no true contact with this world of imperfection and impurity. The idea of God himself being born (and being "brought into the world through unmentionable organs") is an offense against the majesty of a transcendent God.

Nestorians, Jacobites, and Melkites

In the centuries that followed, these two theological styles of thinking remained in competition. Eventually, the theological style centered on divine immanence became associated with the city of Alexandria in Egypt, and in particular with Athanasius (d. 373), Apollinaris (d. 390), and Cyril (d. 444). The theological style centered on divine transcendence would become associated with the city of Antioch in Syria, and in particular with Theodore of Mopsuestia (d. 428) and Nestorius (d. 451).

In the early fifth century, Cyril and Nestorius engaged in a momentous theological debate that would have a lasting impact on the shape of Middle Eastern Christianity. By this time, of course, the Eastern Roman Empire had become the Byzantine Christian Empire. In 412, Cyril became bishop of Alexandria, and in 428 Nestorius (a student of Theodore) was named bishop of Constantinople (the most powerful position in the church at the time, since Constantinople was also the capital of the empire). The next year, Nestorius gave a series of sermons in which he argued that Mary should not be referred to with the title *theotokos*, "Mother of God." He did not preach such a thing out of a disdain for Mary but rather out of a concern for divine transcendence. The idea of God being a "child" seemed to him an insult to God. "Does God have a mother?!" Nestorius asks rhetorically in one of his sermons (*First Sermon against Theotokos* [Norton, 124]).

Upon hearing of these sermons, Cyril wrote Nestorius from Alexandria, insisting that he rethink the matter. To Cyril, Nestorius's concern for divine transcendence had led him to stray from the central message of the Christian faith. By rejecting the title *theotokos*, Nestorius was looking for a way to avoid the conclusion that God was born. By this same token, Nestorius did not accept that God suffered or that God died. Only the human nature in Jesus, he explained, experienced these things. Cyril, however, insisted that the very point of the Christian faith is that God embraced all of the things that humans experience (although exactly how He did so is beyond human understanding) so that we would come to know His love for us. Thus Cyril insists that the point of the gospel is not that the Son of God "united to Himself the person of a human being" but rather that God Himself "became flesh" (*Second Letter to Nestorius* [Norton, 134]).

In 431 the emperor Theodosius II called for a church council in the city of Ephesus to settle this dispute. Instead of a unified council, however, the supporters of Nestorius and Cyril met separately (and each condemned the other). Two years later, however, Cyril agreed to a common declaration, the "Formula of Reunion," with certain followers of Nestorius. These followers of Nestorius agreed to the title *theotokos* for Mary, while Cyril acknowledged that Christ had a human nature (body *and* soul) and a divine nature (some of his earlier writings suggested that Christ did not have a human nature, only a human body). Nestorius, however, rejected the Formula of Reunion and was forced into exile. Some of Cyril's more ardent supporters also rejected the Formula of Reunion, insisting that Christ has only one nature.

Ultimately, the disputes between Cyril and Nestorius led to the first lasting divisions in the church. Those bishops (primarily in Iraq and Iran, beyond the borders of the Byzantine Empire) who supported Nestorius throughout were labeled "Nestorian" (although they never accepted this label, but rather often referred to themselves simply as the Church of the East). The ardent supporters of Cyril would be called "Miaphysites" (from a Greek word meaning "one nature") and would later call themselves "Jacobites" due to the influence of a bishop named Jacob Baradaeus (d. 578). Those who followed the Formula of Reunion (which was affirmed at the Council of Chalcedon in 451) became known in the Arabic-speaking world as Melkites, or followers of the king (Ar. *malik*).

It is telling for our purposes that, at the dawn of Islam, the principal issue that divided Christians was not the organization of the church hierarchy (an issue that would lead to the schism between Orthodox and Catholics in the eleventh century) or Christian teaching on grace, Scripture, or the Eucharist (which would lead to the Reformation in the sixteenth century). Instead, the issue was theology.

Throughout the fifth, sixth, and seventh centuries, an intense theological debate continued to rage among the "Nestorians" Jacobites, and Melkites. Theologians from each of these churches continuously sought to convince the faithful that their teaching was orthodox while the teaching of the other two churches was heterodox. The Byzantine emperors alternatively sought compromise or used political pressure and social discrimination to encourage Jacobite churches to abandon their position. (The Nestorians were largely out of the emperor's reach.) But each of the churches had developed a strong attachment to their theological position, and efforts at compromise or compulsion failed. The resolve of each community was hardened by ethnic rivalries. The Nestorians were largely Syriac (but also Persian) speakers living in Mesopotamia and Iran. The Jacobites were largely ethnic Copts, Arabs, Ethiopians, Syriac speakers, and Armenians. The Melkites (even if some were Syriac or Arabic speakers) were generally associated with the Greek-speaking imperial regime.

This is the background against which we might properly envision Islam's emergence. Islam represented a *fourth* theological/christological position within the religious milieu of the seventh-century Middle East. Like the doctrine of Nestorius, the doctrine of Islam was shaped around an insistence on divine transcendence. Islam, however, went much further. Nestorius insisted that the divine nature of Christ was not involved with his birth or death, but the Qur'an insists that Christ had no divine nature at all. Indeed, the Qur'an insisted that humans *must* accept this point. If Christianity is ultimately about what God has done in human history, Islam is ultimately about what *humans* do: will they, or will they not, recognize his transcendence above all else? Will they hold an "orthodox" theological position, or a "heterodox" position? This is precisely the sort of concern that was common in the Christian theological debates at the time of Islam.

It could very well be that the particular theological position of the Qur'an, in which Christ loses his divine nature entirely, is a reflection of the Qur'an's conviction that it preaches the same religion as Abraham. On four different occasions (2:135; 3:67; 6:79, 161), the Qur'an emphasizes that Abraham was not an idolater. It generally presents Abraham as a man who believed in a transcendent God and who knew nothing of a divine Christ. Meanwhile, the Qur'an also suggests that Muhammad was sent with the teaching of Abraham: "Surely the people standing closest to Abraham are those who followed him, *and this Prophet*, and those who believe; and God is the Protector of the believers" (Q 3:68).

STUDY QUESTIONS

1 Why does the Qur'an emphasize that it is written in Arabic?

2 How did the idea of the Arabs as children of Abraham and Ishmael emerge?

3 What were the major divisions in the Christian community of the Middle East at the time of Islam's rise? What sort of issues divided Christians there?

CONCLUSION TO PART TWO

At this point, the reader who had hoped for a year-by-year description of the rise of Islam might justifiably feel disappointed. Due to the nature of our sources, a precise history of Islam's emergence has proven to be elusive. The Islamic sources on the life of the Prophet are late; moreover, they consist of stories written to explain the Qur'an, and they are shaped by the apologetical goals of authors working in a sectarian environment. The non-Islamic sources (for example, the work attributed to Sebeos) are much earlier, yet they, too, are affected by religious apology.

It turns out that the most intriguing source for the emergence of Islam is the Qur'an itself. The trouble that Muslim interpreters have had in understanding material in the Qur'an (for example, its material on Jonah or the sleepers of Ephesus) seems to confirm that a good deal of time elapsed between the time the Qur'an was proclaimed and the time that those interpreters set to work. In other words, there is every reason to think of the Qur'an as an ancient work.

Western scholars have often thought that the Qur'an—even if it is an ancient work—is a poor source of history, since it includes few references to events, places, or people that we might compare with other sources. But if the Qur'an lacks such references, it does contain other features that make it a surprisingly useful source of history.

The Qur'an's description of itself as a revelation given by God in Arabic, a message given to the Arabs so that they might now understand His "Book" (which He had given before to other peoples), seems to be (in part at least) a response to the absence of any translation of the Bible into Arabic. The Qur'an's presentation of the Arabs as the children of Abraham seems to be a response to the way in which earlier Christians identified Arabic-speaking nomads with Ishmael. The Qur'an's insistence on a transcendent God, who punishes those who fail to recognize Him as such, seems to be a response to the religious context at the time in the Middle East, where churches were divided over precisely these theological issues. Indeed, the case of Jesus in particular teaches us a very important lesson about the Qur'an, namely, that it is a book above all concerned with the defense of a majestic God.

This concern offers us an important insight into the historical and religious context in which Islam emerged. Indeed, it suggests that the story of Islam's emergence is closely connected to the history of Christianity. Of course it should be remembered that the Qur'an is also a book with claims about a new prophet. The voice of God in the Qur'an offers advice to Muhammad and responses to his opponents. Thus if the Qur'an is connected to Christian history it is also an original and distinctive work. Yet instead of thinking of Islam as a religion that emerges abruptly from a pagan background, the Qur'an suggests that we should think of Islam's emergence in terms of its place in the larger religious history of the Middle East.

At the same time, students of Islam should learn to appreciate the traditional story of Islam's emergence, for that is the story that is so dear to Muslims around the world. Indeed, many Muslims are convinced that Islamic societies today should be modeled on the society that Muhammad once established in Medina, and it is to this conviction that we will now turn.

PART 3

CONTEMPORARY PERSPECTIVES

INTRODUCTION TO PART 3: CLASSICAL TEXTS AND CONTEMPORARY RELIGION

The conviction that Muslim societies today should be modeled on that of the Prophet Muhammad in Medina reflects a notion about the Prophet himself—namely, that he was the perfect man. Muhammad was impeccable ("free from sin") and infallible ("free from error"). Each of his actions, and each of his words, offers humanity a source of guidance no less valid in the twenty-first century than it was in the seventh. Thus Muslims have two guides for their lives: the Qur᾿an and the life of the Prophet.

Through the Qur᾿an and the life of Muhammad (as preserved in the *hadith*), Muslims may know the sharia, the divine law that covers every aspect of life. If the mass media tends to bring up sharia only in regard to controversial questions of war and peace, or laws for criminal offenses, pious Muslims bring up sharia even in regard to the smallest questions of their daily life.

Thus satellite television stations (such as Al-Jazeera) in the Islamic world regularly host "Ask the Mufti" programs, in which callers inquire about the position of the sharia on basic questions, from marriage and divorce, to proper dress, to the permissibility of playing poker. Similarly, the Internet is filled with "Ask the Mufti" websites (in various Islamic and Western languages) and forums in which Muslims of all walks of life discuss the classical sources of Islam.

The importance of sharia to the lives of Muslims today is evident from the Islam Question and Answer website (islamqa.com;

published in sixteen languages), which is devoted to the teachings of the conservative Palestinian scholar Muhammad Al-Munajjid. In "Fatwa number 72313," for example, Al-Munajjid addresses the following concern, submitted over the Internet by an anonymous Muslim: "I have the problem of yawning a great deal whilst praying, even though I do not yawn outside of prayer. Please advise me, may Allah bless you."

In his response, Al-Munajjid does not advise the anonymous questioner to get more sleep, or suggest that he look into the medical causes of yawning. Instead, he turns immediately to the Qur'an and the *hadith*.

Praise be to Allah.

Allah has praised His believing slaves, and He says that one of their greatest characteristics is that they "offer their [prayers] with all solemnity and full submissiveness" [Q 23:2]. The Prophet (peace and blessings of Allah be upon him) stated that the [the devil] strives to distract the worshipper from his prayer, and Allah is testing the believers with that. One of the ways in which [the devil] distracts the worshipper is by distracting his thoughts and whispering to him when he is praying. Another method is to make him yawn so much that this distracts him from his prayer. The Prophet (peace and blessings of Allah be upon him) stated that yawning comes from the Shaytaan, and he told us to suppress yawning as much as we can, but if yawning overtakes us, then he told us to put our hands over our mouths.

Al-Munajjid goes on to quote the following *hadith* (the first is from the collection of Muslim, and the second from the collection of Bukhari).

(1) It was narrated that Abu Sa'eed al-Khudri (may Allah be pleased with him) said: The Messenger of Allah (peace and blessings of Allah be upon him) said: "If one of you yawns [according to another report: "whilst praying"]—let him suppress it as much as he can, for the [devil] comes in."

(2) It was narrated from Abu Hurayrah (may Allah be pleased with him) that the Prophet (peace and blessings of Allah be upon him) said: "Yawning comes from the [devil], so if one of you feels the urge to yawn, let him suppress it as much as he can, for if one of you says 'ha' (the sound made when yawning), the [devil] laughs."

In quoting this fatwa ("juridical opinion") I do not mean to emphasize the importance of the Islamic teaching on yawning, but rather to illustrate a larger point: as Muslims today confront daily questions and challenges, they often do so by calling on the classical sources formed during the period of Islam's emergence. As we will see, this is true not only for conservative Muslims such as al-Munajjid, but also for the growing movement of progressive Muslims in the West. And this is true not only for apparently minor questions like yawning, but also for questions related to issues of significant political and social importance, as we will discover in the final chapter of our work.

Chapter 8

CONTEMPORARY MUSLIM NARRATIVES OF ISLAM'S EMERGENCE

Islam is the solution.

—slogan of the Muslim Brotherhood

The Struggle for an Islamic Society Today: Egypt, Pakistan, Afghanistan, and Iran

The story of Islam in the modern era is a story of remarkable growth. In the year 1900, the global population of Muslims was 200 million; by 2020 this number had risen to 1.9 billion. Even in terms of percentage of world population, the number of Muslims has grown considerably, doubling from approximately 12.5 percent in 1900 to 25 percent in 2020.

This same period also witnessed the remarkable growth of a particular movement of Islamic thought, namely Islamism. Some "Islamist" groups (often the more rigorist, and as a rule Sunnis) refer to themselves with the Arabic term *salafi*, in light of their conviction that Muslims today should base themselves only on the example of the Prophet Muhammad and *al-salaf al-salih* (or the "Pious Forebearers"), generally considered to be the first three generations of Muslims. Islamists typically hold that the Prophet Muhammad and the first four (or "rightly guided") caliphs established an Islamic state in conformity with God's decrees and that this state should be the model for Muslims today.

In order to work toward (re-)establishing this pure Islamic state, Muslims are called to purge Islam from any "innovation" (*bidʿa*), any religious doctrine or practice of a non-Islamic origin, that wrongly entered into Islam after this period.

Ibn Taymiyya, Sayyid Qutb, and Islamic Society

One great authority for Islamists is Ibn Taymiyya (d. 1328), a scholar who spent most of his career in Damascus, where he was known for his fatwas (legal opinions) against "innovations," his condemnations of heretical movements, and his calls for jihad. In addition, he wrote extremely influential treatises on theological topics, such as the relation between reason and revelation, and the possibility that hellfire could not be eternal in light of divine mercy. Ibn Taymiyya gathered a large circle of disciples around him, but his combative preaching and his constant promulgation of new fatwas did nothing to endear him to the ruling Mamluk dynasty of the time. Ibn Taymiyya suffered imprisonment six times during his public career, and his life ended during the last of these imprisonments. To many Islamists today, Ibn Taymiyya's willingness to suffer imprisonment for the sake of the purification of Islam testifies to his piety, and makes him a model that all Muslims should aspire to imitate.

Ibn Taymiyya appeared on the public scene after he performed the Hajj to Mecca in 1292–93 and began to condemn what he saw as innovations in the ceremonies of the pilgrimage in his day. (He would later write a polemical work entitled *The Ceremonies of the Hajj*.) Soon after, he wrote a treatise arguing that a Syrian Christian accused of insulting the Prophet Muhammad should be put to death for this blasphemy (the Christian had converted to Islam hoping that this would save him).

Ibn Taymiyya's subsequent writings are similarly marked by polemics against non-Muslims or against those Muslims who, as he saw it, taught a corrupt form of Islam. Around 1298, Ibn Taymiyya preached a jihad in Damascus against the Christian Armenian kingdom of Cilicia. The following year, he wrote a work against rationalist Muslim theologians, whom he accused of relying on vain intellectual speculation while neglecting the example—or *sunna*—of Muhammad as preserved in the *hadith*. He wrote works against the Shiʿites as well (and, in 1300 and 1305, joined military expeditions against the Shiʿites of Mount Lebanon), condemning their devotion to the Imams as an "innovation." Although he was personally interested in Islamic mysticism, Ibn Taymiyya was also interested in condemning the errors of certain Muslim mystics, or "Sufis." Some Sufis, he argued, insulted the God of Islam by teaching that the divine being encompasses all things (a doctrine known as monism, and which may seem close to pantheism), disobeyed the Prophet of Islam by teaching that spiritual enlightenment is more important than following the dictates of the sharia, and introduced illicit innovations in Islamic worship.

Personalities in Islam 8.1
IBN TAYMIYYA

To sharia-minded Sunni Muslims today, Ibn Taymiyya (d. 1328) is a figure of immense importance. He is cherished for fighting tirelessly, and aggressively, against innovations to the pure religion of Islam passed down from the Prophet and his companions (and preserved in Sunni *hadith* literature). He is no less cherished for his assertive view of Islam as a political force, for demanding that the Muslim rulers of his day fight the jihad against non-Muslims or Muslim "heretics", and for demanding that those who insult the Prophet Muhammad be punished in the strictest manner permissible. For all of these things, Ibn Taymiyya was acclaimed by later Sunnis as "Shaykh al-Islam" ("The Authoritative Teacher for All of Islam").

Originally from the city of Harran (the city from which Abraham departed for Canaan) in modern-day Turkey, he later settled in Damascus, which at the time was controlled by the staunchly Sunni Mamluk dynasty. Damascus, and indeed all of the Islamic Middle East, was threatened in his day by the Mongols. Ibn Taymiyya, who is said on one occasion to have rebuked the great Mongol leader Ghazan Khan publicly, sought to rally Mamluk leaders against the Mongols (only some of whom had converted to Islam by this time). Yet the Mongols were not his only opponent. He wrote a long treatise against Christian doctrine and another to demand the execution of a Christian accused of insulting Muhammad. In yet another treatise, he demanded that the Mamluks launch a jihad against the Shi'ite Muslims of Lebanon. Ibn Taymiyya also delivered numerous fatwas condemning the practices and beliefs of philosophers, rationally minded theologians, tradition-minded legal scholars, mystics ("Sufis"), and any Muslim who followed a practice (such as worshiping at tomb-shrines) that appeared to him to be something borrowed from Jews or Christians, and thus an innovation of pure Islam. At the same time, he believed in divine mercy and in the possibility that hellfire would be only temporary.

Eventually, all of this treatise-writing, and all of these fatwas, won Ibn Taymiyya a considerable amount of enemies, even among the Sunni Mamluks. In 1326, he was arrested and imprisoned in the Citadel of Damascus. He was banned by a decree of the Sultan from writing fatwas, but he continued to do so until his guards removed the paper and ink in his cell. In that same cell, Ibn Taymiyya died, after an imprisonment of two years.

FROM A CLASSIC TEXT ❖ 8.1

Fatwas Today

The idea of sharia, or Islamic law, is based on the conviction that Islam is an eternal and universal religion. From the moment of creation, God willed that humanity would follow a certain code which covers every aspect of life, from clothing to food, prayer, recreation, washing, sex, and war. In other words, Islam is not only a set of spiritual teachings. Islam is a code of living established by God himself. The challenge for Muslims, however, is discovering just what this code consists of.

The Qurʾan contains precious few instructions on proper Islamic conduct. The hadith have many more, but individual hadith frequently seem to give different views on the same question. Moreover, new questions appear in every age that find no clear answer in the hadith (for example, whether loudspeakers can be attached to the outside of mosques, or whether smoking, or vaping, is permitted by Islam).

When faced with such questions, pious Muslims will often request a fatwa, or "legal opinion," from a mufti ("one who gives a fatwa"), a scholar known for his expertise in Islamic law. The fatwas they receive generally do not have any binding legal force. Individuals unhappy with a particular fatwa are free to seek out a new fatwa on the same question from a different mufti. For his part, the mufti's goal is not to come up with a reasonable answer to an individual's question. Instead, the mufti seeks to come up with the Islamic answer—the answer God himself would give to such a question—by referring to the Qurʾan, the hadith, and by using certain techniques such as reasoning by analogy.

Below is a collection of fatwas quoted in response to a question on the permissibility of statues, submitted to the website (www.islamonline.net) of the prominent Sunni mufti Yusuf al-Qaradawi (b. 1926), an Egyptian scholar based in Qatar.

Islamic Views on Erecting Statues

Question
Dear scholars, As-Salamu ʿalaykum ["Peace be with you"]. How does Islam view the issue of making statues for leaders, thinkers, or scientists?

Date
03/Apr/2006

Name of Counselor
IOL [Islam Online] Shariʿah Researchers

In the Name of Allah, Most Gracious, Most Merciful.

All thanks and praise are due to Allah and peace and blessings be upon His Messenger.

Dear questioner, we would like to thank you for the great confidence you place in us, and we implore Allah Almighty to help us serve His cause and render our work for His sake. Muslim scholars have unanimously agreed on the prohibition of making statues with the purpose of worshipping or revering them. If this is the case, the sin of making statues involves the sculptor, the buyer, the worshipper, and deifiers. There is also an agreement among scholars that the statues made to be an object for training and children toys, i.e. dolls of animals and humans are not included in the prohibition.

However, scholars have differed regarding some other points as follows: The majority of scholars are of the opinion that defaced or incomplete statues are not prohibited so long as they are not worshipped. However, some scholars prohibit the use of statues under any circumstances whatsoever.

On the other hand, the full-figured statues are, according to the majority of scholars, prohibited, even if they are not worshipped or revered. By the passage of time, there is a possibility of people turning such statutes into objects of worship as did the people of Noah (peace be upon him) who made statues of their pious ancestors in order to remember them, and they ended up worshipping such statues. Some scholars, however, hold the view that making statues is permissible if they are not deemed to be worshipped. Deep thinking will show that it is more haram [forbidden] to erect statues commemorating tyrant rulers. Perpetuating the memories of rulers, thinkers, and scientists is best achieved through establishing organizations carrying their names or issuing books about their efforts and achievements. In this regard, the prominent Muslim scholar Sheikh Yusuf Al-Qaradawi states:

> Islam prohibits statues and three-dimensional figures of the living creatures. The prohibition is even more stressed in case the statue is for a being already dignified i.e. Angels, prophets, the Virgin, or idols like cows for Hindus. We need to understand the Islam's stand on this issue as a means of safeguarding the concept of monotheism. Some people may argue that such ruling belongs to the old ages when paganism was rampant, not in these days that worshipping idols exist no more. Such argument is weak especially as we know idolatry and paganism still keep their traces in some people's minds and are rejected in their conduct. People do still believe in myths and even the educated ones sometimes fall in such errors. Therefore, the statues of ancient Egyptians are prohibited. Some people may use busts like the head of some ancient Egyptian queens as an amulet to protect against evil eye or evil souls, in which case the prohibition of amulets is added to that of the statues. The only type of statues that is permitted is children [sic] dolls. (fatwa published on April 3, 2006, at www.islamonline.net);)

Ibn Taymiyya's career of religious polemic was inspired by two beliefs: first, that Islam is the only religion God has ever revealed to humanity and, second, that Islam necessarily involves the imposition of the sharia. The first belief involves the conviction that non-Islamic religions (such as Christianity) are falsifications of the Islamic messages taught by earlier prophets (such as Jesus).

The second belief involves the conviction that God revealed to the Prophet Muhammad detailed instructions on both otherworldly matters (such as the nature of God, the angels, the jinn, heaven and hell) *and* worldly matters, including religious practice (such as how to pray, fast, and perform the pilgrimage), personal conduct (such as how to eat, wash, dress, and have sexual relations), and statecraft (such as how to manage an economy, treat non-Muslims, and conduct wars). The Prophet Muhammad passed on these instructions unchanged to his companions. His companions and the following generations of Muslims (the "Pious Forebearers") preserved these instructions faithfully, but subsequent generations deviated from it. Some deviated so far that they cannot be considered Muslims; they falsified the teaching of Muhammad, just as Christians falsified the teaching of Jesus.

The goal of Ibn Taymiyya, therefore, was not to develop new interpretations of Islam appropriate to his time and place; instead, he sought to recover the Islam of Muhammad's Medina by purging the religion of non-Islamic innovations. In order to do so, he wrote treatises, preached sermons, and promulgated fatwas condemning any teaching or practice that he deemed unfaithful to Muhammad's teaching. At the same time, he looked to the state (in his case, the Mamluk sultanate) to enforce the punishments Muhammad himself had established against those who violated the sharia or taught false doctrines. It was not enough to teach and preach Islam; it was also necessary to enforce Islam.

In Ibn Taymiyya's religious vision, very little separates the teaching of Muhammad from the revelation of God. Only the Qur'an can be considered the very speech of God, of course, but the teachings of Muhammad preserved in authentic *hadith* are no less divinely revealed. It might even be said that in a way the *hadith* are more important to the religious vision of Ibn Taymiyya than the Qur'an. After all, the Qur'an offers little instruction on religious conduct, and while it is filled with pious exhortations, it hardly offers a systematic presentation of religious doctrine. These instructions, and that presentation, are found instead in the *hadith*, where they are attributed to the Prophet Muhammad.

Later Muslims remember Ibn Taymiyya for his fidelity to the Prophet. One of his disciples, named Abu Hafs al-Bazzar (d. 1349), describes Ibn Taymiyya as "the defender of the pure sharia and the conduct of the Prophet" (*The Lofty Virtues of Ibn Taymiyya*, 6). To Islamists, Ibn Taymiyya's defense of Islam as taught by the Prophet is exemplary. As Ibn Taymiyya fought to purify Islam from innovations and heresies in his day, so Muslims today are called to take up this same fight.

The teachings of Ibn Taymiyya are particularly important to the Muslim Brotherhood, a Sunni movement founded in Egypt by Hassan al-Banna (d. 1949) in 1928, whose influence later spread throughout the Arab world. The slogan the Muslim Brotherhood frequently invokes is: "Islam is the solution." By invoking this slogan, the Brotherhood suggests that the political, economic, and social problems of the Arab world are due largely to "innovations" in doctrine and practice. The solution to these problems, accordingly, is a return to pure Islam.

The most famous spokesman for the ideals of the Muslim Brotherhood was Sayyid Qutb, an Islamist leader executed by the Egyptian regime of Gamal Abdel Nasser in 1966. In his younger years, Qutb worked in the Egyptian Ministry of Education. In this capacity he traveled between 1948 and 1950 to the United States, where he studied at the Colorado State College of Education. Although there is some dispute over the exact nature of Qutb's religious development, most scholars argue that Qutb had relatively moderate religious ideas toward the beginning of his career, and that his time in America played a significant role in his radicalization. In fact, in a brief memoir titled *The America I Have Seen*, Qutb presents America as a den of immorality (and the America he knew was still two decades away from the "summer of love").

FIGURE 8.1. *A famous image of Sayyid Qutb taken during his imprisonment under Egyptian president Gamal Abdel Nasser. Qutb was executed by hanging in 1966.*

He illustrates this immorality with an anecdote about a church dance in Colorado, during which boys and girls danced in the dark. To Qutb's amazement, the church minister seemed satisfied with all of this. Indeed, at one point, Qutb explains, the minister himself played "But Baby It's Cold Outside," a song in which Dean Martin tries to convince his date to let him stay awhile.

Elsewhere, Qutb presents America as a society that is notable at once for material advancement and moral savagery.

> The researcher of American life will stand at first puzzled before a wondrous phenomenon, a phenomenon that exists nowhere else on earth. It is the case of a people who have reached the peak of growth and elevation in the world of science and productivity, while remaining abysmally primitive in the world of the senses, feelings, and behavior. A people who have not exceeded the most primordial levels of existence, and indeed, remain far below them in certain areas of feelings and behavior. (Qutb, *The America I Have Seen*, 11)

In *Milestones* (published in 1964), an influential work he wrote from a prison cell in Egypt, Qutb argues that Egyptian society had begun to suffer from a similar sort of moral primitiveness because of the way it had embraced non-Islamic values and habits. By abandoning the God-given sharia for Western practices, Egyptian society had become something like the "ignorant" (Ar. *jahili*) society of pre-Islamic pagan Arabia.

Islam knows only two kinds of societies, the Islamic and the *jahili*. The Islamic society is that which follows Islam in belief and ways of worship, in law and organization, in morals and manners. The *jahili* society is that which does not follow Islam and in which neither the Islamic belief and concepts, nor Islamic values or standards, Islamic laws and regulations, or Islamic morals and manners are cared for.

> The Islamic society is not one in which people call themselves "Muslims" but in which the Islamic law has no status, even though prayer, fasting and Hajj are regularly observed; and the Islamic society is not one in which people invent their own version of Islam, other than what God and His Messenger—peace be on him—have prescribed and explained, and call it, for example, "progressive Islam." (Sayyid Qutb, *Milestones*, 63)

This Islamist vision, according to which Muslim societies today are called to follow the law of Islam as it was followed in Muhammad's Medina, is not only an Egyptian phenomenon. In recent decades, this vision has become increasingly popular in much of the Islamic world. In the case of Pakistan, to which we now turn, this sort of vision has effectively replaced the vision given to the country by its founding father.

Islam in South Asia: India, Pakistan, and the Taliban

The country of Pakistan was founded in 1947 when the British left India and the country was partitioned between a Muslim-majority state (Pakistan) and a Hindu-majority state (India). However, in order to understand Pakistan's development—and especially its religious development—we must go much further back in time. Indian Islam was fundamentally shaped by a culture of religious learning centered in the central Indian city of Deoband.

The "Deobandi" movement grew out of reformism in India connected with the thinking of the scholar Wali Allah of Delhi (d. 1762; and his son ʿAbd al-Aziz). The movement was later centered at Dar al-ʿUlum, a school (or madrasa) established in Deoband in 1867. In part the movement was known for its modern techniques of delivering the content of the traditional Islamic sciences. Instrumental to the foundation of the Deoband madrasa were two scholars Muhammad Qasim Nanautawi (1833–79) and Rashid Ahmad Gangohi (1829–1905). Matthew Kuiper, writing about Deoband, has emphasized the interest of the Deoband movement in Islamic missions (daʿwa) and in publishing fatwas (juridical opinions) as vehicles for their teaching (Daʿwa and Other Religions, 122–27). That teaching involved a response to the Hindu majority in India and to Christian missions by articulating arguments for Islam. It also involved questioning traditional elements of Indian Islam, including music, the celebration of certain festivals such as the commemoration of the Prophet's birthday (or mawlid), and the belief in the ability of Muhammad to intercede for his community after his death (Defending Muhammad, 173–78).

However, Deobandi Islam was not the only religious current in India. Indeed, the Deobandis had a fierce and formidable opponent in Ahmad Raza Khan, the founder of a movement known as the Barelvis. Ahmad held that the campaigns of the Deobandis against traditional Islamic practices (such as the mawlid) were violations of the longstanding consensus of the Islamic community. Khan presents his readers with a thought exercise in which he imagines what it would be like if the Deobandis were insolently to confront generations of Muslim scholars with their criticism of the mawlid ceremonies (Defending Muhammad, 277). Khan even went so far as to say that the Deobandis might escape punishment in this world since the British would not interfere with them, but that they would not escape punishment in the next.

Yet Khan was not a "liberal" in religious matters as one might be tempted to imagine on the basis of his opposition to the Deobandis. Like the Deobandis, he, too, was worried about certain "aberrant" practices of Indian Muslims. He was particularly concerned about syncretism, such as participating in Hindu festivals (unless one went with the goal of converting Hindus to Islam), and he was also no fan of leisure activities such as flying kites and playing chess. Khan was also distinctly worried about the way in which some of his opponents were cooperating with Hindus (and Gandhi in particular) in their anti-British political campaigns.

A more liberal voice in South Asia was an older contemporary of Ahmed Raza Khan and a man with a similar name: Syed Ahmad Khan (or Sir Syed Khan after he was knighted in 1888). Syed Ahmad was an early leader of the Muslim nationalist movement that eventually led to partition. He also advocated for a reformist vision of Islam in which the hadith—which for Deobandis and Barelvis alike were an unimpeachable source of Islamic teaching—were to be read critically and in the light of reason. Syed Ahmad founded a university known as Aligarh, which continues on today. His method of interpreting Islam might be understood from his teaching that interest (traditionally considered forbidden on the basis of the Qur'an and the hadith) was only forbidden when it was taken from (and harmed) the poor. Interest could be charged to rich investors. They can afford it, and the practice can benefit the growth of industry in Islamic societies. Thus for Syed Ahmad, principles like the common good played a role in thinking through social and religious questions.

The founding father of Pakistan—known to Pakistanis as *baba-e qawm* ("Father of the Nation") or *qaed-e azam* ("The Great Leader")—was Muhammad ʿAli Jinnah, a Shiʿite Muslim lawyer and intellectual who led the struggle for an independent Muslim homeland during the final years of British colonial rule of India. In 1936, Jinnah was elected President of the Parliamentary Board of the Muslim League on India. Four years later, under Jinnah's leadership, the Muslim League announced its demand for a separate Muslim state upon Indian independence. The popularity of this position among Indian Muslims, and indeed Jinnah's own popularity,

was validated by the 1946 Indian parliamentary elections—the final elections of the colonial era—in which the league won the great majority of Muslim seats. When Pakistan came into existence in 1947, Jinnah became its first "governor-general." The following year he passed away.

Pakistanis remember Jinnah with reverence for his struggle to establish a separate state for Indian Muslims. He did not struggle, however, to establish a state based on the sharia. Jinnah was raised in a family of the Ismaʿili Shiʿite tradition, a form of Shiʿism marked more by the pursuit of wisdom and moral refinement than any notion of a religious law. And while Jinnah later converted to the majority ("Imami" or "Twelver") Shiʿite tradition, he remained wary of conservative Islamic movements (which in the Indian context were overwhelmingly Sunni). He opposed, for example, the Indian Khilafat movement, the goal of which was to unify Muslims worldwide under a renewed caliphate.

To Jinnah, Pakistan was to be a state where Muslims would be protected from a Hindu majority that might deprive them of their rights or obstruct their religious practice; it was not to be a state where the Qur'an and the *hadith* would be the fundamental source of law, or where non-Muslims would find their own religious practice obstructed. These convictions are evident in Jinnah's public address on April 11, 1947, three days before the country of Pakistan was born.

You are free; you are free to go to your temples, you are free to go to your mosques or

FIGURE 8.2. *Muhammad ʿAli Jinnah with Mahatma Gandhi in 1944.*

to any other place or worship in this State of Pakistan. You may belong to any religion or caste or creed that has nothing to do with the business of the State. As you know, history shows that in England, conditions, some time ago, were much worse than those prevailing in India today. The Roman Catholics and the Protestants persecuted each other. Even now there are some States in existence where there are discriminations made and bars imposed against a particular class. Thank God, we are not starting in those days. We are starting in the days where there is no discrimination, no distinction between one community and another, no discrimination between one caste or creed and another. We are starting with this fundamental principle that we are all citizens and equal citizens of one State. (Muhammad ʿAli Jinnah, Speech to the Constituent Assembly, April 11, 1947)

Jinnah's view of citizenship is far removed from the spirit of the founding constitution of Pakistan, enacted in 1956, and the current constitution, enacted in 1973. This constitution declares that "no law shall be enacted which is repugnant to the Injunctions of Islam as laid down in the Holy Quran and Sunna" (paragraph 198), and that "steps shall be taken to enable the Muslims of Pakistan individually and collectively to order their lives in accordance with the Holy Quran and Sunna" (paragraph 25).

The constitution of Pakistan effectively made the state an Islamic institution. Indeed, the provision that the state should "enable" Muslims to live according to the Holy Qurʾan and Sunna—for all of its ambiguity—is reminiscent of the teaching of Ibn Taymiyya, who looked to the Mamluk sultanate to punish those who violated Islamic morals or doctrine and thereby to inculcate Islam. Such provisions evidently are hardly consistent with the teaching of Muhammad ʿAli Jinnah, who insisted that the state not take sides, that it treat all Pakistanis as citizens, with no regard for their religious affiliation. The Islamist spirit of the constitution of Pakistan reflects the influence of conservative Sunni Muslims in the years following the death of Jinnah, and in particular of Abu al-ʿAla al-Mawdudi (d. 1979), founder of the powerful movement (and later political party) *Jamaat-e Islami* ("The Islamic Congregation").

In the 1920s, while still in Hyderabad, India, Mawdudi had been part of the Khilafat movement that Jinnah opposed. In 1932, he founded a journal (*Tarjuman al-Quran*) dedicated to the renewal of Islamic religious thought. Mawdudi's understanding of renewal involved above all the reestablishment of Islamic principles in public life. In a later memoir, Mawdudi explained that he sought from the beginning to "break the hold which Western culture and ideas had come to acquire over the Muslim intelligentsia, and to instill in them the fact that Islam has a code of

life of its own, its own culture, its own political and economic systems and a philosophy and an education system which are all superior to anything that Western civilization could offer" (Mawdudi, "Twenty-Nine Years of the Jamaat-e Islami," *The Criterion*, 45).

Mawdudi was also active in political affairs and to this end founded *Jamaat-e Islami* in 1941. Originally, the *Jamaat-e Islami* fought against the call of the Muslim League for an independent Islamic state, insisting that the very notion of a nation-state is foreign to Islam. Muslims worldwide, Mawdudi argued, should think of themselves *already* as one nation and should together work to spread Islam in whatever state they find themselves. But when the nation-state of Pakistan emerged in 1947, Mawdudi embraced the new country and worked to shape it into an Islamic state. To this end, in 1951, the *Jamaat-e Islami* organized a declaration of Muslim clerics (Ar. *ulama*ʿ) demanding that Pakistan be declared an Islamic state faithful to the sharia. Five years later, their demand was enshrined in a new constitution.

Mawdudi's understanding of the sharia led him to a distinctive notion of citizenship. Whereas Jinnah hoped that all citizens, regardless of creed, would have equal rights in Pakistan, Mawdudi led campaigns (in 1952–53 and again in 1974) to ostracize and punish Pakistani citizens belonging to a religious community known as the Ahmadiyya. Members of the Ahmadiyya, a movement founded by an Indian Muslim named Ghulam Ahmad (d. 1908), understand themselves to be Muslims, but they insist that Ahmad was

FROM A CLASSIC TEXT ❖ 8.2

The Sharia Today

Muslims understand the sharia to be a code of conduct that God himself has decreed for the organization of every aspect of human life. Many Muslims conclude that Islamic states should be run by this code of conduct and not by any system of law developed by humans (whether in the West or elsewhere). God, they might say, knows more than humans about such things.

A number of Islamic states acknowledge the sharia in their constitution, although the actual meaning of this acknowledgment for the laws and policies of these states varies, since there is no one book that contains the sharia in its entirety. Two different Islamic states might both insist that their laws and policies are based in the sharia, but their laws and policies may have very little in common.

However, religious scholars—even when they are not in a position of political leadership—tend to exercise considerable authority in all states that acknowledge sharia as the source of law. Since these scholars can claim the position as the only proper interpreters of Islamic law, they are always able to criticize the state for its infidelity to Islam (or to justify the state when others criticize it).

The excerpts below illustrate how three Islamic countries, two Sunni (Pakistan, Saudi Arabia) and one Shiʿite (Iran), express the relationship between the state and Islam in the opening sections of their present constitutions.

The Constitution of Pakistan (April 12, 1973)
Preamble

In the Name of God, the Merciful, the Benevolent,

Whereas sovereignty over the entire Universe belongs to Almighty Allah alone, and the authority to be exercised by the people of Pakistan within the limits prescribed by Him is a sacred trust;

And whereas it is the will of the people of Pakistan to establish an order;

Wherein the State shall exercise its powers and authority through the chosen representatives of the people;

Wherein the principles of democracy, freedom, equality, tolerance and social justice, as enunciated by Islam, shall be fully observed;

Wherein the Muslims shall be enabled to order their lives in the individual and collective spheres in accordance with the teachings and requirements of Islam as set out in the Holy Quran and Sunnah;

Wherein adequate provision shall be made for the minorities freely to profess and practise their religions and develop their cultures;

Wherein the territories now included in or in accession with Pakistan and such other territories as may hereafter be included in or accede to Pakistan shall form a Federation wherein the units will be autonomous with such boundaries and limitations on their powers and authority as may be prescribed;

Therein shall be guaranteed fundamental rights, including equality of status, of opportunity and before law, social, economic and political justice, and freedom of thought, expression, belief, faith, worship and association, subject to law and public morality;

Wherein adequate provision shall be made to safeguard the legitimate interests of minorities and backward and depressed classes;

Wherein the independence of the judiciary shall be fully secured;

Wherein the integrity of the territories of the Federation, its independence and all its rights, including its sovereign rights on land, sea and air, shall be safeguarded;

So that the people of Pakistan may prosper and attain their rightful and honoured place amongst the nations of the World and make their full contribution towards international peace and progress and happiness of humanity Now, therefore, we, the people of Pakistan,

Cognisant of our responsibility before Almighty Allah and men;

Cognisant of the sacrifices made by the people in the cause of Pakistan;

Faithful to the declaration made by the Founder of Pakistan, Quaid-i-Azam Mohammad ʿAli Jinnah, that Pakistan would be a democratic State based on Islamic principles of social justice;

Dedicated to the preservation of democracy achieved by the unremitting struggle of the people against oppression and tyranny;

Inspired by the resolve to protect our national and political unity and solidarity by creating an egalitarian society through a new order;

Do hereby, through our representatives in the National Assembly, adopt, enact and give to ourselves, this Constitution.

The Constitution of Saudi Arabia (January 31, 1992)

Chapter 1: General Principles

Article 1

The Kingdom of Saudi Arabia is a sovereign Arab Islamic state with Islam as its religion; God's Book and the Sunnah of His Prophet, God's prayers and peace be upon him, are its constitution, Arabic is its language and Riyadh is its capital.

Article 2

The state's public holidays are Id al-Fitr and Id al-Adha. Its calendar is the Hegira calendar.

Article 3

The state's flag shall be as follows:

(a) It shall be green.
(b) Its width shall be equal to two-thirds of it's [sic] length.
(c) The words *"There is but one God and Mohammed is His Prophet"* shall be inscribed in the center with a drawn sword under it. The statute shall define the rules pertaining to it.

Article 4

The state's emblem shall consist of two crossed swords with a palm tree in the upper space between them. The statute shall define the state's anthem and its medals.

The Constitution of Iran (April 12, 1983)

Chapter 1: General Principles

Article 1

The form of government of Iran is that of an Islamic Republic, endorsed by the people of Iran on the basis of their longstanding belief in the sovereignty of truth and Qur'anic justice, in the referendum of Farwardin 9 and 10 in the year 1358 of the solar Islamic calendar, corresponding to Jamadi al-'Awwal 1 and 2 in the year 1399 of the lunar Islamic calendar (March 29 and 30, 1979], through the affirmative vote of a majority of 98.2% of eligible voters, held after the victorious Islamic Revolution led by the eminent marjiʿ al-taqlid [religious authority], Ayatullah al-Uzma [the Grand Ayatollah] Imam Khumayni.

Article 2

The Islamic Republic is a system based on belief in:

1. The One God (as stated in the phrase "There is no god except Allah"), His exclusive sovereignty and the right to legislate, and the necessity of submission to His commands;
2. Divine revelation and its fundamental role in setting forth the laws;
3. The return to God in the Hereafter, and the constructive role of this belief in the course of man's ascent towards God;
4. The justice of God in creation and legislation;
5. Continuous leadership [by the imams descended from ʿAli] and perpetual guidance, and its fundamental role in ensuring the uninterrupted process of the revolution of Islam;

6. The exalted dignity and value of man, and his freedom coupled with responsibility before God; in which equity, justice, political, economic, social, and cultural independence, and national solidarity are secured by recourse to:

1. Continuous legal reasoning of the Muslim jurisprudents possessing necessary qualifications, exercised on the basis of the Qurʾan and the Sunnah of the Infallible imams, upon all of whom be peace;

2. Sciences and arts and the most advanced results of human experience, together with the effort to advance them further;

3. Negation of all forms of oppression, both the infliction of and the submission to it, and of dominance, both its imposition and its acceptance.

sent by God to renew the Islamic community. Most Ahmadis consider him to have fulfilled prophecies associated with Jesus, and some of them call him a prophet.

The Qurʾan (33:40), as we have seen, describes Muhammad as the "seal of the prophets," and Muslims have long understood this to mean that there can be no prophets after him (a view made explicit in the hadith). By contradicting this doctrine, Mawdudi argued, the Ahmadiyya had become apostates. In a treatise titled "The Finality of Prophethood," Mawdudi explicitly compares the case of Ghulam Ahmad with the "false prophet" Musaylima of the Prophet Muhammad's day. Muhammad, he continues, declared Musaylima an apostate, and Abu Bakr's forces later attacked and killed Musaylima during the Wars of Apostasy. Mawdudi concludes that the policy of the Islamic state of Pakistan toward the Ahmadiyya should be modeled on the conduct of Muhammad, and of Abu Bakr, toward Musaylima. In fact, in large part due to the influence of Mawdudi and the *Jamaat-e Islami*, Pakistan has applied an increasing number of restrictions and policies meant to inhibit the activities of the Ahmadiyya.

Mawdudi, in other words, held with Ibn Taymiyya that an Islamic state is responsible not only to teach Islam in its educational institutions but also to use compelling force in order to ensure that none of its citizens act in a way contrary to Islam. It is this same notion (sometimes referred to with the qurʾanic slogan "commanding right and forbidding wrong") that helped inspire the enactment of the "blasphemy laws" in Pakistan after the death of Mawdudi, during the rule of Zia ul-Haqq (president of Pakistan from 1977 to his death in a suspicious plane crash in 1988).

Zia ul-Haqq generally sought the political support of Islamic groups such as *Jamaat-e Islami*. To this end he furthered the process of Islamization in Pakistan. In the course of this process, Zia ul-Haqq's government sponsored the passage of laws in 1980 in which

BOX 8.1 ❖ AHMADIS' STATUS AS MUSLIMS

On May 28, 2010, two mosques belonging to the Ahmadiyya Muslim Community in Lahore, Pakistan, were attacked with grenades and gunfire, killing eighty-six people. This attack was the culmination of a long history of violence and persecution suffered by the Ahmadis in Pakistan. In 1974, the Pakistani parliament amended the constitution to define Ahmadis as non-Muslims, and indeed in Pakistan Ahmadis are widely described as heretics or apostates. *Jamaat-e Islami* in particular has repeatedly campaigned against the Ahmadis. In 1984 the government, under pressure from *Jamaat-e Islami,* passed a law by which Ahmadis are subject to prison if they present themselves as Muslims or if they perform the call to prayer in the traditional Islamic manner.

derogatory remarks against Muslim holy figures became an offense punishable by imprisonment. In 1982 a clause was added to make desecration of the Qur'an punishable by life imprisonment, and in 1986 a further clause was added to make blasphemy against Muhammad punishable by death (a position argued for, as mentioned above, by Ibn Taymiyya in the thirteenth century).

Approximately half of those prosecuted under the blasphemy laws have been non-Muslims (for the most part Christians). Many human-rights activists—besides criticizing the very concept of these laws—have expressed concern over the rigor of the judicial process in such cases, which take place in Islamic courts. Most troubling, however, has been the vigilantism surrounding these laws. In 1993, Manzur Masih was killed on the way out of a Lahore courthouse where he had been acquitted of the crime of blasphemy. The Muslim judge who heard his case was killed four years later. The sentencing to death of a young, poor Christian named Ayub Masih for

blasphemy led a Catholic bishop named John Joseph to shoot himself in 1998, in front of the courthouse in Sahiwal where Masih had been sentenced. This shocking act of protest, however, did not lead to any change in these laws or the vigilantism surrounding them.

In November 2010 a Christian mother of five, Asia Bibi, was sentenced to death for insulting Muhammad and was only acquitted in 2018 (in 2019 she fled to Canada in fear for her life from vigilantes). On January 4, 2011, Salmaan Taseer, a Muslim governor and critic of the laws, was assassinated. On March 2, 2011, Shahbaz Bhatti, a Christian government minister who had fought for the release of Bibi, was likewise killed. The Pakistani government publicly condemned these latest murders, but they have also publicly declared that the laws of blasphemy will not be changed. On April 30, 2011, a Muslim mob attacked Christian shops and homes in the city of Gujranwala after discovering a burnt Qur'an.

The rise of the Taliban, who rose to power in Afghanistan in the mid-1990s, and returned to power with the US withdrawal from the country in 2021, is best understood in light of this longer history of movements and trends within South Asian Islam. During the time of Zia ul-Haqq, certain Deobandi madrasas in Pakistan became centers of training for jihadis (only some of whom were Pakistani) preparing to enter into Afghanistan to resist the Soviet-sponsored government there. From the midst of these madrasas emerged the movement known as the Taliban (meaning "the Students") in 1994. The movement was not simply tolerated but actively supported and armed by the Pakistani government. The Taliban seized control of the country in 1996 and maintained close relations with other radical Sunni movements, including al-Qaeda. This particular connection led to their downfall. The Taliban refused to turn over the leadership of al-Qaeda, including Usama bin Laden, after the attacks of September 11, 2001. The US invaded the country, and the Taliban retreated to Pakistan. In Pakistan, however, they found a major source of new fighters, funds, and networks that allowed them to purchase arms. They led a major campaign in 2021 through Afghanistan as the United States retreated from the country, and entered the country's capital, Kabul, with no resistance on August 15.

Scholars are divided over the sources or political and military support for the Taliban, but there is no question regarding the source of the Taliban's religious ideology. The Taliban are fully shaped by the ideas of Islamic "reform" from Deobandi school.

Their teachings against women's education, music, recreation, religious and intellectual freedom, and their implementation of traditional Islamic penalties for crimes, are all justified with fatwas (juridical opinions) that have their origin in Deoband. This notion of "reform" shows just how powerful narratives of Islam's emergence are in debates over Islam today. The "Taliban," like their Deobandi predecessors, desire to recapture the original purity of Islam, convinced that this will lead to a society that is faithful to religious law and pleasing to God.

The Hidden Imam, the Ayatollah Khomeini, and the "Guardianship of the Jurisprudent"

Just across the western border of Afghanistan is Iran, where the institutions of the government have been in the hands of Muslim clerics since the Islamic revolution of 1979. The story of political Islam's rise in Iran, however, has very little in common with the story of the Taliban in Afghanistan.

The success of the Islamic revolution in Iran is especially remarkable for two reasons. First, it took place in a country that had been ruled for most of the twentieth century by a secular-minded monarchy. This monarchy pursued a policy of social reform meant to substitute "modern" values for the traditional religious values of the Iranian people. To this end, the emperor Reza Shah (r. 1925–41; d. 1944) instituted a movement in 1936 known as the "Women's Awakening," a movement that involved not only laws to increase female education and equity between the sexes in

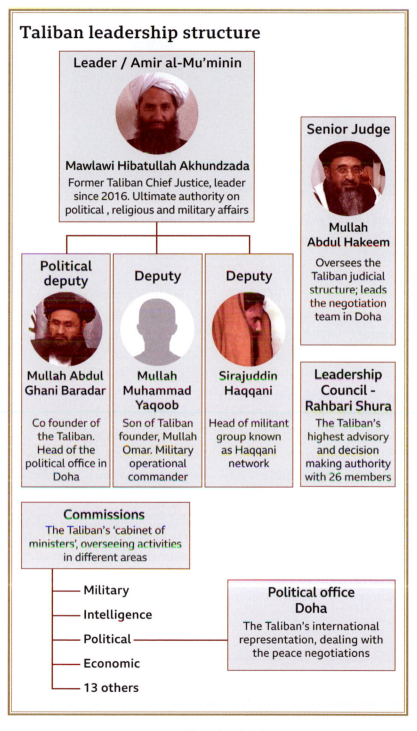

FIGURE 8.3. *Taliban leadership structure.*

FIGURE 8.4. *An official gathering in 1936 of Iranian military officers and their families to commemorate the abolition of the veil.*

the workplace but also a series of restrictions meant to encourage women to remove the Islamic headscarf. Veiled women were banned from schools, cinemas, and public transportation.

Much of the rural population of Iran resisted this movement, but many urban Iranians who had already embraced Western values and habits supported it. Indeed, a visitor to Tehran in the mid-twentieth century might have found it to be a city with a remarkably European flavor. In her work *The Good Daughter*, the Iranian-American author Jasmin Darznik tells the story of her mother's life in Iran during this time. In one passage, she notes the European tendencies of her family.

> The women of his family had not worn veils for many years, and the men had long since abandoned their tunics and turbans in favor of European-style jackets, ties and hats. The Khorrami family was headed by Kazem's

maternal grandmother, whom they all called Ma Mère—this despite the fact that none of them spoke more than ten words of French, including Ma Mère herself. (J. Darznik *The Good Daughter*, 41–42)

Tehran in 2022 has quite a different flavor. Men are encouraged not to wear ties (which are understood to be symbolic of Western habits), and women are obliged to wear headscarves. Religious police patrol the streets to make sure that they do so properly. Alcohol is forbidden. Movies and literature are carefully censored. Many Internet sites and telephone apps are blocked.

Second, the Islamic revolution in Iran is remarkable because it was a Shiʿite revolution. Before the revolution, Shiʿite scholars had long taught that their faithful should *not* aspire to the creation of an Islamic state. The logic of their teaching is based on the Shiʿite narrative of Islam's emergence (introduced in chapter 3 of the present work).

BOX 8.2 ❖ DEMOGRAPHICS IN EGYPT, IRAN, AFGHANISTAN, AND PAKISTAN

Country	Total Population	Principal Languages	Religious Demographics	Population Growth Rate
Egypt	106.4 million	Arabic	Sunni Muslims 90%, Christian 10%	2.17%
Iran	85.9 million	Farsi, Turkic dialects, Kurdish	Shi'ite Muslim 95%, Sunni Muslim 4.7%, Other 0.3%	1.03%
Afghanistan	37.4 million	Afghani Persian (Dari), Pashtu, Uzbeck	Sunni Muslims 85%, Shi'ite Muslims 15%	2.34%
Pakistan	238.2 million	Urdu, Punjabi, Sindhi, Pashtu	Sunni Muslim 87%. Shi'ite Muslim 9%, Other (Christians and Hindus) 4%	1.99%

From CIA World Factbook updated September 2021.

According to Shiʿites, the rightly guided caliphs—with the exception of ʿAli—were not rightly guided. After the death of Muhammad, God intended the Muslim community to be ruled by the Imams, twelve (according to the largest Shiʿite community, "Twelver" Shiʿites) successors to Muhammad who came from his own family, and not by caliphs at all. The first of these Imams was ʿAli, the cousin and son-in-law of the Prophet, and the second was Hasan, the son of ʿAli and grandson of Muhammad through his mother Fatima. The last of these Imams was (and is) Muhammad al-Mahdi, who never died but rather entered into a state of invisibility soon after his birth (c. 869; he is accordingly known as the "Hidden" Imam). Yet Sunni rulers prevented all of these Imams from establishing their leadership as God had intended. This was the case even for ʿAli, who was unable to establish fully his leadership during the years of his caliphate due to the constant opposition of figures such as ʿAʾisha, daughter of Abu Bakr and widow of the Prophet.

Nevertheless, the conspiracies of Sunni Muslims against the Imams in no way affected their position as representatives of God on earth and as the source of infallible religious teaching. Indeed, God himself decreed that between the death of the Prophet and the end of the world an Imam would always be present on earth. The Imam of the current age is still Muhammad al-Mahdi, the "Hidden" Imam. At some unknown moment, he will emerge from his hiding (or "occultation") to establish an Islamic state according to the true sharia.

According to traditional teaching, Shiʿites should *not* seek to establish an Islamic state before that moment. Only God knows when the right time to establish an Islamic state will be, and He will send forth the Hidden Imam at that time. Shiʿites might long for the Imam's emergence (in fact, pious Shiʿites often add the phrase "may God hasten his emergence!" whenever they mention the Hidden Imam), but otherwise they are to accept the rules of the state they live in. They might even, when faced with Sunni persecution, deny their Shiʿite beliefs outwardly while holding on to them in their hearts, in deference to a principle known as *taqiyya*, or "dissimulation."

The idea of *taqiyya*, however, was to be challenged by a charismatic figure named Ruhollah Khomeini (d. 1989), known to the world as the Ayatollah ("Sign of God"), a technical title bestowed on Shiʿite clerics respected for their mastery of law and theology. Khomeini was not the only ayatollah of his day; by all counts, a number of other Iranian clerics were considered to be superior religious authorities. However, he set himself apart by his magnetic personality and by his unique teaching, known as *wilayat al-faqih*, or "The Guardianship of the Jurisprudent."

We can detect the foundation for this teaching already in a speech delivered on April 10, 1964, to clerics and religion students in Qom, Iran, in which Khomeini (who had just been released from prison) expressed his conviction that Muslim leaders must be involved with politics.

> Gentlemen, do your utmost to raise the flag of Islam in the universities, to promote religion, to build mosques, to perform prayers in congregation and to let the act of prayer be seen by others. Religious unity is of the essence. It is religious unity that makes this society so great and cohesive; if you would like Iran to be independent then be united in religion. . . . I am not one of those mullahs who merely sits with rosary beads in hand. I am not the Pope to perform certain ceremonies on Sundays only, spending the rest of my time imagining that I'm a sultan and not concerning myself with any other affairs. This is where the key to Islamic independence lies. (Ayatollah Khomeini, Speech to Religious Leaders in Qom [Iran], April 10, 1964)

During his later exile in the holy Shiʿte city of Najaf, Iraq, Khomeini began to elaborate his politically activist theology, arguing that the notion of *taqiyya* should not prevent

FIGURE 8.5. *The Ayatollah Ruhollah Khomeini (d. 1459) at prayer.*

Shiʿite clerics from working to develop an Islamic state.

The purpose of *taqiyya* is the preservation of Islam and the Shiʿite school; if people had not resorted to it, our school of thought would have been destroyed. *Taqiyya* relates to the branches of religion; for example—performing ablution in different ways. But when the chief principles of Islam and its welfare are endangered, there can be no question of silence or *taqiyya*. . . .

The Muslims will be able to live in security and tranquility and preserve their faith and morals only when they enjoy the protection of a government based on justice and law, a government whose form, administrative system, and laws have been laid down by Islam. It is our duty now to implement and put into practice the plan of a government established by Islam. I hope that by presenting the system of government and the political and social principles of Islam to broad segments of humanity, we will create a strong new current of thought and a powerful and popular movement that will result in the establishment of an Islamic government. O God, foreshorten the arms of the oppressors that are stretched out against the lands of the Muslims and root out all traitors to Islam and the Islamic countries! (Ayatollah Khomeini, *Governance of the Jurist*, 93–94)

Khomeini's argument that Muslim clerics—in their capacity as interpreters of Islamic law—should assume authority in the absence of the Imam represents a radical departure from traditional Shiʿite thought. It was, one might say, the ideological revolution necessary for the political revolution of 1979.

Khomeini's ideological revolution was in part a reaction to the particular context of twentieth-century Iran. It is one thing for Shiʿites to tolerate the rule of Sunni Muslims who, despite their opposition to the Imams, still sought to run a society according to Islamic law; it was quite another to tolerate the rule of the Iranian Shah Muhammad Reza Pahlavi (d. 1980; r. 1941–79).

Like his father Reza Shah, Muhammad Reza Pahlavi held a secular vision of Iran. He celebrated Iran's pre-Islamic imperial past, supported various social reforms that conflicted with traditional Islamic ideas, and firmly opposed religious clerics who objected to his policies. In 1963 he went to the religious heart of Iran, the ancient city of Qom, where he delivered a fierce condemnation of clerics, whom he accused of backwardness. In foreign affairs, moreover, Muhammad Reza Pahlavi had a distinctively pro-Western policy. Under his rule, Iran was the first majority-Muslim state to recognize Israel, and Iran continued to maintain close ties with the Jewish state

even after the six-day war of 1967, which saw Israel occupy the old city of Jerusalem with its Islamic holy sites.

For Khomeini, opposition to the shah was also a personal matter. In the early 1960s, Muhammad Reza Pahlavi grew particularly disdainful—and fearful—of Khomeini. In 1964, he sent Khomeini into exile. Fifteen years later, Khomeini would return to Iran in triumph.

On January 16, 1979, in the wake of months of mass protests, Muhammad Reza Pahlavi fled Iran, leaving a caretaker prime minister in his stead. On February 1, Khomeini, who had managed to establish his leadership of the protest movement from abroad, arrived in Iran from France to a welcoming crowd of several million people. He immediately denounced the prime minister the shah had left in place and moved to establish his own government.

In the subsequent months, Khomeini crafted a government run by Shiʿite clerics but firmly within his personal control. Khomeini, whose public personage was that of a gentle and pensive sage, now orchestrated a systematic and merciless campaign to eliminate his rivals within the protest movement (which included both secular Communist parties and religious parties hostile to the idea of *wilayat al-faqih*). He displayed sharp political instincts during the hostage crisis at the American embassy in Tehran (when Iranian students held fifty-two Americans in captivity from November 4, 1979, to January 20, 1981). Khomeini, who was not aware of the plan to besiege the embassy beforehand, astutely

Personalities in Islam 8.2
KHOMEINI

The name Khomeini comes from the village Khomein in central Iran, where the future leader of the Islamic revolution, whose first name was Ruhollah ("spirit of God"), grew up. His family claimed descent from the Prophet Muhammad through the seventh of the Shi'ite imams. The men in the family thus had the right to wear a black (as opposed to a white) turban. The people looked upon them with a special respect, and they were expected to be especially religious.

When he was still a young boy, Ruhollah Khomeni's father, Mostafa, was killed, leaving him an orphan. At the age of seventeen, his relatives sent him to the holy city of Qom, south of Tehran, to pursue a religious education. Ruhollah soon gained a reputation as a pious and industrious student. He lived in a simple room and woke up before dawn to begin his studies and perform the morning prayer. Khomeini's reputation for simplicity would remain with him throughout his life. Even after assuming power as the supreme cleric of Islamic Iran, he was still known to eat simple meals, seated on the floor in cleric's garb. Yet he also gained a reputation for ambition. He was eager to win the respect and, eventually, the obedience of his fellow clerics. Khomeini had no greed for material possessions, but he did have a desire for power.

In his student days, Khomeini was also a witness to the manner in which Reza Shah lorded his power over the clergy. When, on March 21, 1928, a cleric in Qom named Bafqi condemned the shah, Reza Shah personally rode to Qom, entered the holy shrine there with his troops, and had Bafqi publicly flogged. We can only presume that Khomeini dreamed of retribution from that day forward. He must have felt great satisfaction when, many years later, in 1979, he successfully overthrew the son of Reza Shah. Yet his campaign against the enemies of Islam did not end with the Revolution. He continued it by purging Iran of those who had been sympathetic to the shah, and of members of secular socialist parties (who had once resisted the shah alongside Khomeini). Yet Khomeini's principal enemy was America, the "great Satan." As Satan whispers temptations in the ears of Muslims to distract them from their prayers, so the United States, Khomeini argued, promotes false ideologies to Muslim rulers to keep them from applying Islamic law in their countries. Khomeini supported the takeover of the American embassy in Tehran, instituted an anti-American curriculum in Iranian schools (including the chant "death to America!" at the beginning of the school day), and sponsored a protest of America during the annual pilgrimage in Mecca (which contributed to a bloody conflict in 1987 with Saudi authorities).

For its part the United States, which had long supported the shah (and became the home of Muhammad Reza Pahlavi's son), sought persistently to isolate Khomeini and lessen his influence. Iran and the United States have not gone to war, but the two countries did meet in a soccer match in the 2002 World Cup. Iran won 2–1. They met again in the 2022 World Cup.

realized afterward that the crisis would further rally Iranians to support the Islamic revolution, and he began personally to dictate strategy to the hostage takers.

On March 29 and 30, 1979, a national referendum was held in which, according to the official results, 98.2 percent of participants voted for an "Islamic Republic." In November of that same year, Khomeini became the "Supreme Leader of the Revolution," a position that effectively gave him final authority in all questions of government (not unlike the authority the shah had once possessed), and a position he would hold until his death in 1989 (and that has been held since by ʿAli Khamenei). For his part, Muhammad Reza Pahlavi, the former shah who had exiled Khomeini, died in exile in Cairo on July 27, 1980.

Thus the state that Khomeini had envisioned in his speeches, the "Guardianship of the Jurisprudent," came into being. The Iranian constitution of 1983 insists in its second article that the Islamic Republic of Iran is to be based on the principle that God alone possesses "the right to legislate," while the people are bound by "the necessity of submission to His commands." Later in that same article, the constitution insists that divine laws are to be established by "Muslim jurisprudents possessing necessary qualifications, exercised on the basis of the Qurʾan and the Sunnah of the Infallible imams, upon all of whom be peace."

The rise of an Islamic state in Iran was an extraordinary event. Khomeini had to fight against both the traditional doctrine of Shiʿite Islam that would make such a state impossible (before the emergence of the Hidden Imam) and against the effects of the shah's campaign to secularize the nation. That Khomeini prevailed is no doubt a tribute to his charismatic personality and his political talent. But the success of the Islamic revolution in Iran also says something about the enduring attractiveness of the notion of the sharia to Muslims. Khomeini was able to appeal to the general Muslim conviction that God revealed to Muhammad much more than spiritual wisdom, that he revealed instructions on all aspects of life, and that the state that Muhammad established in Medina should be the model for Islamic states of later times. Thus the story of Islam's emergence in seventh-century Arabia held enormous importance to Muslims of the twentieth century, from Egypt to Pakistan to Iran. It holds no less importance to Muslims today.

Islam and Modernity and Islam in the West

The cases of Egypt, Pakistan, Afghanistan, and Iran introduced above testify to the power of the story of Islam's emergence to shape the world we live in today. At the same time, the world we live in today has also shaped the way that Muslims tell the story of Islam's emergence.

In the modern period, Muslims have been confronted with challenges to their faith in an unprecedented fashion. Before the period of colonialism and mass communication, Muslims were generally isolated from criticism of their religion. There were many non-Muslims in Islamic states, of course (whether Christians in the Arab world or Hindus in India), but they were generally prohibited from criticizing Islam by the dictates of Islamic law. In Europe, Christians had long attacked Islam (the Italian poet Dante, for example, placed Muhammad and ʿAli in the lowest level of hell in his work the *Inferno*). However, their attacks were published in European languages and remained largely unknown in the Islamic world.

The Qurʾan and Scientific Miracles

By the nineteenth century, however, European countries had established colonies in the Islamic world. The colonists brought their religion with them, while Catholic and Protestant organizations alike organized missions. Among the missionaries was Samuel Zwemer (d. 1952), a Protestant native of Michigan who served in the Arabian Peninsula from 1891 to 1905 and then in Cairo from 1913 to 1929.

Zwemer, known to evangelical Christians still today as "the Apostle to Islam," is the author of numerous works critical of Islam, including *Islam: A Challenge to Faith*, a guide for prospective missionaries originally published by the Student Volunteer Movement for Student Missions in 1907. In that work, Zwemer describes the Qurʾan, as regards form, as a haphazard and poorly organized work: "The book has no chronological order, logical sequence, or rhetorical climax. Its jumbled verses throw together, piecemeal, fact and fancy, laws, legends, prayers and imprecations. It is unintelligible without a commentary, even for a Muslim" (Zwemer, 90).

On the following page, he adds that, as regards content, the Qurʾan is hardly more impressive: "The defects of its teaching are many: (a) It is full of historical errors; (b) it contains monstrous fables; (c) it teaches a false cosmogony; (d) it is full of superstitions; (e) it perpetuates slavery, polygamy, divorce, religious intolerance, the seclusion and degradation of women, and it petrifies social life" (Zwemer, 91).

Zwemer and other missionaries began to publish works, and publish journals, in Arabic (and other Islamic languages) with material meant to convert Muslims to Christianity with these sorts of arguments. As Muslim intellectuals became increasingly aware of the activity of Christian missionaries and their arguments, a movement arose among them to counter them. Among these intellectuals was Rashid Rida (d. 1935), a Lebanese Sunni

Muslim who settled in Cairo in 1897 (and who would later influence Sayyid Qutb). In his 1905 work *Christian Criticisms, Islamic Proofs* (an Arabic collection of articles originally published in the journal founded by Rida and his mentor, Muhammad Abduh, *al-Manar*), Rida responds to the arguments against Islam presented by Christian missionaries in Arabic-language missionary journals in Egypt. Rida presents the Bible as a confusing and contradictory collection of documents written to replace the true Islamic revelations given to Moses and Jesus, and the Qur'an as a work of logic and wisdom. After quoting several passages in which the Qur'an invites its audience to reflect on God's signs, Rida comments,

> Those short verses demonstrate that Islam is the religion of reason, that it is a science, and that certainty is sought through it. They demonstrate that supposition does not suffice for faith in its fundamental principles. These include God Almighty's oneness, knowledge, omnipotence, sending of prophets, and the mission of the seal of the prophets, prayer and peace be upon him and upon them. Verily, the verb "to reason" occurs approximately fifty times in the Qur'an. . . . The word "intellects" occurs in ten to twenty verses. Thus, knowledge of the universe is the way of faith and Islam. (Rida, 170)

As the allusion to "knowledge of the universe" suggests, to Rida the Qur'an is a book of modern science. In this way his writing anticipates a dramatic development of Islamic thought in the twentieth century, namely the rise of the belief that the Qur'an actually contains scientific miracles, that is, scientific information unknown to humanity at the time of the Prophet Muhammad, and which has since been verified by the tools of modern science.

This idea is fundamentally the stuff of religious apology. Muslim advocates for scientific miracles do not use the Qur'an as a resource in their biological experiments or mathematical equations. Rather, they use it to compare passages of the Qur'an with the results of others' scientific research in order to argue that the Qur'an is a miraculous text, that Muhammad was truly a prophet, and that Islam is the true religion. As Ahmad Dallal notes, this idea is a purely modern creation: "Classical commentators on the Qur'an never even hinted that the miracle of the Qur'an lies in its prediction of scientific discoveries that were made centuries after the coming of the revelation" (Dallal, "Science and the Qur'an," *Encyclopaedia of the Qur'an*, 4:552).

Perhaps the most famous work on the scientific miracles of the Qur'an is that of a French medical doctor named Maurice Bucaille; that Bucaille comes from a Christian background (whether he ever converted to Islam is an ongoing controversy) adds to the attraction of the work, since he appears to be an objective observer. Bucaille's work, *The Bible, the Qur'an, and Science* (originally published in 1976 in French, but since translated into several languages) is distributed today throughout the world by Islamic organizations and is available on numerous Islamic websites.

Bucaille (after criticizing the Bible from an Islamic perspective) argues that the Qurʾan contains accurate scientific information on creation, astronomy, and biological sciences. He explains the Qurʾan's proclamation, "We created man from a drop of mixed liquid" (Q 76:2, my translation), as an astounding reference to the "spermatic liquid" which is produced by secretions from "the testicles," "the seminal vesicles," "the prostate gland," and "the glands annexed to the urinary tract" (Bucaille, 215). He also provides explanations for those qurʾanic passages that would seem to be inaccurate on scientific matters: the Qurʾan's references to the creation of the earth in six days (e.g., Q 54:7) are by his reading allusions to six "periods" of creation recently discovered by astrophysicists (but he concludes that the biblical description of creation in six days is an error; 148); the Qurʾan's description of the sun moving like the moon in an orbit around the earth (see Q 21:33 and 36:36) is a "verbal nuance" that refers only to the revolution of the sun on its axis (168). As for the Qurʾan's reference to God casting the stars at demons (e.g., Q 67:5), Bucaille writes, "At the present stage however, it would seem that scientific data are unable to cast any light on a subject that goes beyond human understanding" (165). Ultimately Bucaille concludes,

> The Qurʾan follows on from the two Revelations [to Moses and Jesus] that preceded it and is not only free from contradictions in its narrations, the sign of the various human manipulations to be found in the Gospels, but provides a quality all of its own

for those who examine it objectively and in the light of science i.e. its complete agreement with modern scientific data. (Bucaille, *The Bible, the Qurʾan, and Science*, 268)

Bucaille's work is only one example of a genre that is today widespread. The Internet is filled with claims (and fancy videos to back them up) about scientific miracles in the Qurʾan.

The website www.quranandscience.com (which prominently displays the link "Convert To Islam") explains on its introductory page,

> At the age of revealing the holy Quran Arabs were excelled in poetry and prose, so the holy Quran challenged them by its eloquence. Nowadays miracles of the holy Quran appeared in the scientific signs mentioned in a lot of verses, these verses indicate to scientific facts which have been discovered since only few decades, This is an absolute proof that the holy Quran is the word of God.

The topic of scientific miracles is today a fundamental element of the Muslim missionary enterprise (often referred to with the Arabic term daʿwa). The Muslim World League, an international organization supported by the Saudi Arabian government and dedicated to the propagation of Islam, established a "Committee on the Scientific Miracles of the Qurʾan" in the 1980s, and has subsequently held numerous conferences and sponsored the publication of materials in a variety of languages. In an interview with the London-based Arabic newspaper *al-Sharq al-Awsat* on September 5, 2003, the head of this

FIGURE 8.6. *Webpage on scientific miracles and the Qur'an.*

committee at the time, Zaghloul El-Naggar, explained that the scientific miracles of the Qur'an "astound the contemporary scientists and thinkers of the world" (quoted by Dallal, 541).

Muhammad and Morality

The idea of scientific miracles in the Qur'an thus appears to be a response to the modern world, and in particular to the increasing awareness among Muslims of Western critiques of the Qur'an. By insisting that the Qur'an is perfect even in its scientific information, Muslims found an appropriately modern answer to these critiques.

A similar development in Islamic thought has taken place in the modern era in regard to Muhammad. Christians have long accused Muhammad of being a false prophet who used his claims of revelation to justify his multiple marriages and military adventures. In modern times Western Christians began to attribute the social and cultural problems they found in the Islamic world to Muhammad's moral deficiency. By the nineteenth century, the Islamic world appeared to many Westerners to have fallen into a state of backwardness. Islamic societies seemed to them inferior to Western countries in political, social, and economic matters. To many Westerners they also seemed to be behind in moral matters. In the holy cities of Mecca and Medina, for example, slavery and concubinage were still widespread through the mid-twentieth century.

In much of the Islamic world, girls were generally restricted to their homes, deprived of an education, and forced to marry against their will, sometimes as second wives. To Westerners with a moralizing tendency like Samuel Zwemer, the one responsible for this human suffering was Muhammad himself, who offered Muslims a poor model and left them with an oppressive social system.

A stream cannot rise higher than its source; a tower cannot be broader than its foundation. The measure of the moral stature of

---

BOX 8.3 ❖ SIR RICHARD BURTON'S PILGRIMAGE TO MECCA

In 1853 the flamboyant English explorer Sir Richard Burton set out in disguise (as an Afghan mystic) from Egypt to join the Muslim faithful in their pilgrimage to Mecca (a city into which non-Muslims are not allowed). In his memoirs (written in 1855) of the pilgrimage, he remembers passing through a slave market in Mecca on a donkey. There he dreamed of putting an end to the slave trade: "Again remounting, we proceeded at a leisurely pace homewards, and on the way passed through the principal slave-market. It is a large street roofed with matting, and full of coffee-houses. The merchandise sat in rows, parallel with the walls. The prettiest girls occupied the highest benches, below were the plainer sort, and lowest of all the boys. They were all gaily dressed in pink and other light-coloured muslins, with transparent veils over their heads. . . . And here I matured a resolve to strike, if favoured by fortune, a death-blow at a trade which is eating into the vitals of industry in Eastern Africa. The reflection was pleasant—the idea that the humble Haji [pilgrim], contemplating the scene from his donkey, might become the instrument of the total abolition of this pernicious traffic" (Burton, *A Pilgrimage to Al-Madinah and Mecca*, 3rd ed., 2:252).

Mohammed is the source and foundation of all moral ideals in Islam. His conduct is the standard of character. We need not be surprised, therefore, that the ethical standard is so low. Raymund Lull, the first missionary to Moslems, used to show in his bold preaching that Mohammed had none of the seven cardinal virtues and was guilty of the seven deadly sins; he doubtless went too far. But it would not be difficult to show that pride, lust, envy and anger were prominent traits in the Prophet's character. (Zwemer, 123)

These sorts of critiques were not left without a response. Just as Rida argued that the Qur'an is a book of modern science, Muhammad Husayn Haykal (d. 1956)—the Egyptian author of the most famous twentieth-century Muslim biography of Muhammad—argued that Muhammad was a man of modern morals. In fact, the tactics of the two authors are similar. Rida criticizes the Bible while defending the Qur'an, while Haykal opens his biography of Muhammad with a critique of Western Christian morals.

> Christianity—with its call for asceticism, other-worldliness, forgiveness, and the high personalist values—does not accord with the nature of western man whose religious life had for thousands of years been determined by polytheism and whose geographic position had imposed upon him the struggle against the extreme cold and inclement nature. When historical circumstances brought about his Christianization, it was necessary for him to interpret it as a religion of struggle and to alter its tolerant and gentle nature. Thereby western man spoiled the spiritual sequence, completed by Islam, in which Christianity stood as a link in the chain. (Haykal, Preface to the First Edition, xxxix)

By invoking a "spiritual sequence," Haykal means to present Christianity as religion that prepared the way for Islam. According to this notion, Judaism is a strict, legalistic religion (an idea suggested by passages [e.g., Q 4:160] where the Qur'an reports that God forbade the Jews things that were otherwise permitted due to their sins), whereas Christianity was something of a reaction to the strictness to Judaism (in Q 3:50, Jesus announces that he has made some things permitted that were once forbidden), for which reason it is (overly) tolerant and gentle. Islam is a perfect balance of the two (in 2:143, the divine voice of the Qur'an declares: "We have made you a community of the middle"). In line with this notion, Haykal presents Muhammad as the perfect model for all human societies. Indeed, to Haykal, Muhammad points the way to human happiness.

> It therefore behooves any scholar applying himself to such a study to address his work not only to the Muslims but to mankind as a whole. The final purpose of such work is not, as some of them think, purely religious. Rather, it is, following the example of Muhammad, that all mankind may better learn the way to perfection. Fulfillment of this purpose is not possible without the guidance of reason and heart, and the conviction and

certainty they bring when founded on true perception and knowledge. (Haykal, Preface to the Second Edition, lxxxiv)

In his 1959 novel, *The Children of Gebelawi* (or *The Children of the Alley*), the Egyptian Nobel laureate Naguib Mahfouz (d. 2006) similarly presents Muhammad as a figure of perfect balance between Moses and Jesus. Mahfouz tells the story of a neighborhood in Cairo that through the years is visited by various figures meant to represent the prophets. The Moses figure (Gabal or "mountain," a reference to Mount Sinai) is at once righteous and brutal. He deals with gangsters in the neighborhood by having them trapped in a pit where they are drowned by water and pelted by stones cast down by residents from their windows. The Jesus figure, Rifaa, who works in his father's carpentry shop, is excessively passive. Rifaa arouses the anger of religious fanatics in the neighborhood when he decides to marry a woman accused of adultery. After teaching his followers that it is better to be killed than to kill, Rifaa is murdered. Finally, the Muhammad figure, Qasim, is a leader of perfect reason and great courage, who combines the best of the previous two leaders: "We shall raise our cudgels as Gebel did, but for the sake of the mercy that Rifaa called for. Then we'll use the estate for the common good" (Mahfouz, 262–63).

Mahfouz's presentation of Qasim matches the manner in which Haykal justifies Muhammad's raids. In response to Western criticisms of the Prophet, Haykal insists that Muhammad only fought for righteous causes.

It is here that the Orientalists and the missionaries raise their eyebrows and voices, shouting: "Do you see? Here is Muhammad agreeing that his religion actually calls to war, to *jihad* in the cause of God, that is, to compel man by the sword to enter into Islam. Isn't this precisely what is meant by fanaticism? Now contrast this with Christianity, which denies fighting and condemns war, which calls for peace and advocates tolerance, which binds men in bonds of brotherhood in God and in Christ." In arguing this point I do not wish to mention the statement of the New Testament, "I have not come to send peace but a sword. . . ." Rather I want to begin by refuting the claim that Muhammad's religion calls for fighting and coercion of men into Islam.

[Jihad's] definite meaning is to fight those who sway the Muslim away from his religion and prevent him from walking in the path of God. This fight is waged solely for the freedom to call men unto God and unto His religion. To use a modern expression consonant with the usage of the present age, we may say that war in Islam is permitted—nay, it is rather a duty—when undertaken in defense of freedom of thought and opinion. (Haykal, 205)

Thus in Haykal's telling, Muhammad's raids, far from a moral problem, show him to be a moral exemplar who appreciated modern moral values such as freedom of thought and opinion. In the conclusion of part 2 of the present work, I noted William Montgomery Watt's opinion that Muhammad might be considered a good man according to the standards of his historical context, but not by the standards of Europe in 1950. Haykal would no doubt respond that Muhammad would be considered a good man in any place, and in any year.

Haykal writes in the preface to the second edition that Muhammad offers the modern world a solution to its fundamental problems.

> I had hoped that this and similar studies would clear for science a number of psychic and spiritual problems and establish facts which would guide mankind to the new civilization for which it is groping. There is no doubt that deepening of analysis and extending the scope of the investigation would unlock many secrets which many people have thought for a long time to lie beyond scientific explanation. The clearer the understanding mankind achieves of the psychological and spiritual secrets of the world, the stronger man's relation to the world will become and, hence, the greater his happiness. Man will then be better able to rehabilitate himself in the world when he knows its secrets, just as he became better able to enjoy it when he understood the latent forces of electricity and radio. (Haykal, Preface to the Second Edition, lxxxiv)

Whereas Bucaille holds that scientists today are astounded to discover information in the Qur'an that was unknown to the world in the seventh century, Haykal insists that the biography of Muhammad is similarly astounding. In seventh-century Arabia, the Prophet of Islam demonstrated moral, spiritual, and psychological qualities that offer humanity the secret of happiness today.

Islam in the New World

In this chapter we've followed the rise of Islamism from Egypt to Pakistan. Without a doubt the late twentieth and early twenty-first centuries have seen political Islam assert itself in different contexts: from Nigeria in West Africa to Indonesia in Southeast Asia. Perhaps the most shocking manifestation of political Islam was the rise of ISIS in Iraq and Syria, and the return of slavery, in the mid-2010s. On the other side of the world, however, new and very different trends have arisen in recent years among Muslims.

Islam, as it has in many other contexts, has risen significantly in the United States. The Pew Research Center estimates that the American Muslim population rose from 2.35 million in 2007 to 3.45 million in 2017, a remarkable increase of 68% in only ten years. By 2040, Pew estimates, Muslims will outnumber Jews as the second-largest religious group in America, and by 2050 Muslims will be 8.1 million, well over twice their population in 2017.

Yet perhaps what is most remarkable in Pew's data of the American Muslim population is not the mere change in number but the change in attitudes. On a wide range of questions American Muslims increasingly depart from traditional teachings of Islam. For example in 2007 only 27 percent of American Muslims agreed that "homosexuality should be accepted by society." By 2017 that number had risen to 52 percent. These

Like Americans overall, Muslims now more accepting of homosexuality

% who say homosexuality should be accepted by society

	2007	2011	2017	Change '07-'17
	%	%	%	
U.S. Muslims	27	39	52	**+25**
Men	22	36	42	**+20**
Women	32	42	63	**+31**
Millennial	33	45	60	**+27**
Generation X	27	40	45	**+18**
Baby Boomer or older	24	29	42	**+18**
Some college or less	25	37	48	**+23**
College graduate	31	46	63	**+32**
U.S. born	30	41	57	**+27**
Foreign born	26	38	49	**+23**
Religion very important	19	32	47	**+28**
Religion less important	47	54	62	**+15**

FIGURE 8.7. *Data from the 2017 Pew Research Center survey of American Muslims.*

numbers might be compared to a 2013 survey in Indonesia which indicated that 93 percent of Indonesians held that society should *not* accept homosexuality. A more recent, 2018, survey of Indonesians by Saiful Mujani Research & Consulting indicates that those numbers have effectively remained the same.

There are other indicators which show that American Islam has seen the growth of a progressive movement that distinguishes it from Islam in Muslim-majority countries. In 2015 amina wadud became one of the first women to lead a mixed male–female congregation in Islamic prayer in the United States. Since then a number of mosques in American cities, such as Rabia al-Basri mosque in Chicago, now feature mixed congregations. Mixing female and male worshippers in a mosque is generally not seen in Muslim-majority countries. Instead a separate space is often assigned to women, often in the back of mosques. Indeed, this, or something similar, is the rule too for most mosques in the United States. My local mosque puts women in the side of prayer hall, but in a section blocked off from the men and the imam (whom they can only see on a television screen) by a wooden barrier.

FIGURE 8.8. *Laleh Bakhtiar.*

The presence of progressive Islam in America is a significant development, and it involves a different vision of Islam's origins. Those passages of the Qurʾan or hadith that seem to encourage patriarchal attitudes are often freely reinterpreted by progressive American Muslims. In her translation of the Qurʾan Laleh Bakhtiar interprets a passage in the Qurʾan (Q 4:34) that seems to give men permission to hit (Arabic *daraba*) their wives when they misbehave, such that it gives them permission only to leave their wives. While Bakhtiar's translation was criticized by some Muslim scholars, it still is a sign of the dynamic, contested nature of Islam in America, where progressive Islamic views increasingly challenge traditional views.

As Omid Safi has explained, progressive Muslims often privilege the Qurʾan over the hadith and traditional legal opinions (*fatwa*s) on questions of practice and doctrine (*Progressive Muslims*, 1–22). In addition, progressive Muslims often question whether the medieval Muslim scholars who interpret the Qurʾan were faithful stewards of its meaning. If these scholars were themselves the products of a patriarchal society, perhaps their interpretations are necessarily patriarchal.

Some Muslims, although not many, go still further and question whether every verse of the Qur'an can still be seen as authoritative in the twenty-first century, an idea discussed by Ayesha Hidayatullah in the 2014 book *Feminist Edges of the Qur'an.*

What has allowed for this rise of a new progressive movement with its distinct view of the emergence of Islam? Part of the answer is certainly related to larger trends in American society, where the public has generally become more progressive on a number of issues. Still this question cannot be fully answered without attention to the structures of authority and traditional education that allow religious movements in the Islamic world to shape (and limit) attitudes to Islam. These structures allow for widespread censorship in many countries, the inculcating of traditional Islamic ideas through state educational curricula, and even criminal prosecution of those accused of blasphemy. In 2021 the Algerian journalist Said Djabelkhir was sentenced to three years in prison for questioning certain traditional ideas about the Qur'an, such as the historicity of Noah's flood.

Thus questions surrounding the Qur'an, the life of Muhammad, and Islam's emergence generally have important implications in the world today. Contemporary Islam is incredibly diverse. From the return of the Taliban in Afghanistan, to the rise of progressive Islam in the United States, a wide range of trends are simultaneously on the rise in the Islamic world. Meanwhile, and not surprisingly, intense debate unfolds every day between these trends in the media and on social media from Twitter to Instagram. The key question in these debates over what Islam will look like in the future is what Islam looked like in the beginning.

STUDY QUESTIONS

1   What is the sharia? According to thinkers such as Ibn Taymiyya and Sayyid Qutb, what sorts of issues does the sharia address?

2   What is the difference between the vision for Pakistan held by Jinnah and that held by Mawdudi?

3   How did Khomeini's teaching on the "Guardianship of the Jurisprudent" alter traditional Shiʿite ideas?

4   Describe the Islamic idea of the "scientific miracles" of the Qur'an. How is it related to the Islamic encounter with the West and modernity?

5   How do Haykal and Mahfouz present Muhammad as a "moral exemplar"? How is this presentation related to the Islamic encounter with the West and modernity?

6   Looking back at this book, what key elements of Islam's emergence inform debates over Islam today?

CONCLUSION

In the course of this book it has become apparent that the question of Islam's emergence is far from settled. Earlier generations of critical scholars, following medieval Islamic historical sources, generally thought of Islam as a tradition that emerged in reaction to a sort of vulgar Arab paganism. Today, however, an increasing number of scholars, following the Qur'an, think of Islam as a tradition that emerged in conversation with the earlier monotheistic religious traditions of the Middle East, and in particular with Christianity. Indeed, it now seems that the story of Islam's emergence involves Christianity to a surprising degree.

This development reflects in part the growth of a scholarly conviction that the medieval Islamic historical sources are dependent on the Qur'an. These sources, which were written considerably later than the Qur'an, appear to have been written in large part to explain the Qur'an. Moreover, non-Islamic sources from the time of Muhammad's life do not speak of him or his city. The writings of non-Arabic cultures (Greek, Syriac, Ethiopic, Persian, and so on) of the pre-Islamic Middle East mention neither the pagan Arabs of Mecca (who were supposed to have been international traders) nor the Jews of Medina. They do not mention the great events of Muhammad's life, even those events that involve the surrounding region (such as the emigration of Muslims to Ethiopia, or the sending of emissaries to the leaders of the empires). Thus there is reason to doubt the traditional Islamic biography of Muhammad.

In light of these questions, it now appears that the Qur'an itself is the most important historical document for the rise of Islam. And while the Qur'an is not a book that shares much explicit information (indeed, it rarely gives even the names of the people and places of its day), its religious message allows us to develop a general idea, at least, of the context in which Islam emerged.

The Qur'an's great concern with a transcendent God, and in particular its refutation of the Christian teaching of the incarnation, suggests that Islam was first preached in a context where Christian debates over theology and Christology were a topic of general interest. The Qur'an's presentation of Abraham as the model of its own Prophet and its emphasis on the Arabic language suggest that the emergence of Islam was connected with a conviction that the Arabs are the descendants of Abraham no less than the Jews.

Of course, from the perspective of most Muslims there is no reason to doubt the traditional biography of the Prophet. While both Sunni and Shi'ite Muslims concede that some of the traditions in the medieval works on Muhammad's life are inauthentic, they also insist that these works contain a core of authentic traditions (although Sunnis and Shi'ites disagree over exactly which traditions) that were passed down by a rigorous process of oral transmission.

Moreover, those traditions with precise reports on the words or deeds of the Prophet—that is, the *hadith*—are to most Muslims more than an important source of historical information. They are also a source of revelation. By the ninth century, a conviction emerged among Muslim scholars (in part through the influence of the Muslim scholar Shafi'i) that Muhammad was both impeccable and infallible, and therefore that authentic reports of his words or deeds have a religious authority no less than the Qur'an itself. This conviction would fundamentally shape the further development of Islam. Indeed, the rulings of sharia are based more often on the *hadith* than the Qur'an (a book with few practical instructions).

As we saw in part 3 of this book, the sharia is at the center of the ideology of Sunni Islamist movements such as the Muslim Brotherhood and the *Jamaat-e Islami*. These movements, inspired in part by the teaching of medieval Muslim scholars such as Ibn Taymiyya, insist that Muhammad and the early caliphs successfully established an Islamic state faithful to the sharia, and they argue that this state should be the model for Islamic states today. Through the influence of Ayatollah Khomeini and his idea of *wilayat al-faqih*, many Shi'ite Muslims in Iran and elsewhere have come to accept a similar idea (even if they do not accept the legitimacy of the first three caliphs). In general the concern with sharia in the Islamic world is today widespread. The remarkable multiplication of online fatwas seems to testify to this concern.

Some Muslims today are dismayed by the sharia-minded nature of recent trends in Islam. Nasr Hamid Abu Zayd (d. 2010), a liberal Egyptian intellectual (condemned as

FROM A CLASSIC TEXT ❖ CONCL.I

A Vision of Ethics Based on Virtues

In the excerpt below (taken from an interview with Michiel Leezenberg published in a European journal on Islam), the Iranian Shiuite philosopher Abdolkarim Soroush (b. 1945) discusses the common notion that Western ethics, based on rights, are fundamentally in conflict with Islamic ethics, based on obligations (established by Muslim scholars in their explanations of the sharia). He cites the controversy surrounding the publication of cartoons lampooning the Prophet Muhammad, first published in Denmark on September 30, 2005, as a case where both ethical systems were found wanting.

ML: You argue that the classical Islamic notion of justice (*'adala*) as a hierarchical order imposed by a ruler in order to avoid social chaos overlaps with modern liberal rights-based conceptions of justice. Does that imply that modern Islamists and liberals are divided by a common language of rights? Would you suggest that you can speak of a common modernity shared between Islamists and secular liberals, or are there bigger differences between them?

AS: There are big differences, no doubt about it. In my own characterization, modern culture is a rights-based culture, whereas pre-modern or religious culture was duty- or obligation-based. It does not mean that these two are totally at loggerheads, but the emphasis is different. Modern man is seen as freed from the bondage of religion, and as having exiled God to the remote heavens; but he is very close to a morally deterring kind of egoism. In the religious atmosphere, you are supposed to be more humble and conscious of your obligations.

Now can duty- and rights-based views be reconciled? Both have their shortcomings. What we need is neither to combine nor to eliminate the two, but perhaps a third paradigm. Perhaps we should revalue the concept of virtue, which may do justice to both obligations and rights. During the ugly episode of the publication of cartoons of the prophet Muhammad, the people in favour of publication emphasized the publisher's right to free speech. Although this argument is based on the language of rights, I find it very weak. Rights always give you a number of choices. You will not be prosecuted because you have published it, fine; but you had the right to publish or not to publish. The language of rights is not satisfactory in explaining what one has to do. The language of obligations has no such shortcoming: its explanatory power is much bigger than that of the language of rights. In order to have both rights, which is a beautiful thing, and the more powerful explanation of obligations, we need a third paradigm; perhaps one of love, perhaps one of virtue. (*ISIM* [Institute for the Study of Islam in the Modern World] *Review* 20 [Autumn 2007]: 37) an apostate by an Egyptian religious court in 1995), laments that for many contemporary Muslims Islam *is* sharia: "In the modern Muslim world, where theology, philosophy and mysticism have been marginalized for centuries, the sharia paradigm has become the only representative of Islam. Thus two different terms, sharia and Islam, have become synonymous" (Abu Zayd, 77). Meanwhile, a number of philosophically minded Iranian scholars—notably Abdolkarim Soroush (b. 1945), once an activist who supported the Islamic Revolution—argue that Muslims should build an ethical system based on the virtues that are central to Islam's fundamental religious message.

While Muslims like Soroush are interested in bringing western and Islamic ideas into a conversation, other Muslims today are concerned with preaching Islam to non-Muslims. This dedication to proselytism, or *da'wa*, is evident in the appearance of Islamic works (and increasingly, websites and social media accounts), which maintain that modern scientific discoveries prove the Qur'an to be the word of God, and others that insist that Muhammad's superior ethical conduct proves him to be a prophet. These sorts of arguments appear to have been provoked by Islam's encounter with the West in the modern period; they are in part a response to conflicts with Western power, Christian missionaries, and Western ideas of science and human rights. The diffusion of these ideas has also been helped in recent years by the significant funding (primarily from Saudi Arabia) offered to mosques, educational institutions, and publishing houses dedicated to *da'wa*.

Those committed to *da'wa* might find the approach of the present work inimicable to that enterprise. Yet in the present work I have done my best not to avoid difficult questions about Islam. For example, I have asked the following: (1) What can we actually know of Islam's emergence in history? and (2) How do faithful Muslims understand Islam's emergence? My principal concern has been the first question. Indeed, I have suggested that both traditional Muslim scholars and earlier generations of Western scholars have largely failed to understand the Qur'an's intimate relationship with its religious context. Yet if this work also leads to a greater appreciation for the manner in which Muslims themselves understand the emergence of their faith, then so much the better.

Abu Bakr: According to the traditional biography, the first adult male to convert to Islam. Abu Bakr is said to have traveled along with Muhammad on his migration from Mecca to Medina. Upon the death of the Prophet, Abu Bakr became the first caliph and pursued an aggressive military campaign (known as the "Wars of Apostasy") to suppress those Arab tribes that did not acknowledge his authority over them.

ahl al-kitab: "People of the Book" (see, e.g., Q 2:105, 109; 3:64, 65). In the Qur'an, a term used for those people (such as Jews and Christians) who have already received revelation (from the heavenly "Book"). In later Islamic tradition, *ahl al-kitab* becomes a technical term for Jews and Christians in particular; it is often (incorrectly) assumed that Jews and Christians are properly called "People of the Book" because they have a scripture (the Bible).

ʿA'isha: The daughter of Abu Bakr, and Muhammad's preferred wife, in whose arms he passed away. ʿA'isha is said to have opposed the election of ʿAli to the caliphate and indeed to have helped raise an armed force of rebels against him (eventually defeated at the Battle of the Camel).

ʿAli: The paternal cousin of Muhammad and husband of the latter's daughter Fatima. According to Shiʿites, ʿAli was appointed by God (and designated by Muhammad) to be the first Imam upon the death of the Prophet; Abu Bakr, however, was (wrongly) acclaimed as the first caliph in his place. ʿAli became the fourth caliph upon the death of ʿUthman in 656 but was assassinated by an aggrieved former follower in 661.

ansar: "Allies." Those Arabs of Medina who, according to the traditional biography, invited Muhammad to migrate to Medina from Mecca and later supported him there in his struggles against the pagan Meccans.

apostasy: The renunciation of a religion. According to traditional Islamic law, apostates are to be executed if they refuse to return to Islam. A precedent for this ruling is sometimes found in the wars conducted by Abu Bakr against those Arab tribes that refused to recognize his authority after the death of Muhammad.

apostle, messenger, prophet: "Apostle" and "messenger" are commonly used to translate the Arabic word *rasul*. The Qur'an uses *rasul* to describe (in addition to angels) those humans who receive a message from God and who are sent to preach that message to a people. "Prophet" is commonly used to translate the Arabic word *nabi*. In the Qur'an, *nabi* seems to be used interchangeably with *rasul*, but later Muslims often maintain that a *rasul* is a particular sort of prophet (*nabi*), namely, one who has a written revelation.

bidʿa: "Innovation." A term often invoked by certain Muslims—Salafis in particular—to condemn doctrines or practices alleged to have a non-Islamic origin.

caliph: Arabic *khalifa*, meaning "representative" or "successor." The Qur'an (2:30) describes Adam as a *khalifa*. Historically, Muslims used this term for political leaders, the "successors" to the Prophet Muhammad.

daʿwa: Literally, "call," a term used by contemporary Muslims (even in English) to refer to Islamic apologetics. Of central concern to Muslim apologists are the arguments for scientific miracles in the Qur'an and for the superior moral ethics of the Prophet Muhammad.

fatwa: A juridical opinion offered by a Muslim authority, or mufti, upon receipt of a question. Fatwas are meant to represent the position of the eternal divine law, or sharia, which is knowable above all through the Qur'an and the *hadith*.

fitna: "Discord," or "persecution," described by the Qur'an as "worse than killing" (2:191, 217). Medieval Muslim authors describe the political rivalries that led to military clashes between Muslims in the first two Islamic centuries as *fitnas*.

hadith: A term that usually indicates a report of Muhammad's words or deeds, generally attributed to an eyewitness from among his companions or wives and often accompanied with a chain of transmission (*isnad*) to support its claim to authenticity. Because Muhammad was generally understood to be protected by God from sin or error, the *hadith* are largely considered a source of revelation second only to the Qur'an. Shiʿites give the status of revelation also to *hadith* attributed to one of the Imams.

Hajj: The annual Islamic pilgrimage commemorating the actions of Abraham, Hagar, and Ishmael in Mecca. All able Muslims are required to perform the Hajj once in their life.

hijra: The Arabic term for the migration of Muhammad from Mecca to Medina (which, according to the traditional date, took place in 622 CE). The *hijra* was later chosen to mark the beginning of the Islamic calendar.

Imam: A term meaning "the man in front." To Sunnis, it refers to the prayer leader in mosques. To Shiʿites, the term also refers to one of twelve descendants of Muhammad, beginning with ʿAli (and ending with the *mahdi*), who were designated by God to be his representatives on earth until the end of time.

Injil: The term (from Greek *euangelion*, "gospel") used by the Qur'an to refer to a revelation given to Jesus. According to Islamic tradition, this revelation was lost, or destroyed intentionally, and the Christian New Testament written in its place.

Ishmael: The son of Abraham by Hagar and the ancestor of Muhammad. According to Islamic tradition, Ishmael traveled with Abraham and Hagar to the site where Mecca would later be built.

isnad: The list, or "chain," of authorities that precedes traditional reports, including *hadith* attributed to Muhammad. In Islamic tradition, the authenticity of *hadith* is generally judged by the quality of its *isnad*.

jahiliyya: The "state" or "era" "of ignorance" (see Q 3:154; 5:50; 33:33; 48:26). In later Islamic literature, the term is used in particular for the pagan culture of pre-Islamic Arabia, although some Islamists such as Sayyid Qutb use this term for modern societies that do not implement Islamic law.

jizya: A term that appears once in the Qurʾan (9:29) and was later used as the name of a special tax to be paid by non-Muslims who had submitted to Islamic political authority.

Kaʿba: The square building in Mecca around which Muslim pilgrims process, and the direction toward which all Muslims pray. According to Islamic tradition, the Kaʿba was originally built by Abraham and Ishmael (or by Adam, and only rebuilt by Abraham and Ishmael) for the worship of God. In Muhammad's day, the Kaʿba had become a site of pagan worship. The Prophet destroyed the idols inside upon his conquest of Mecca.

Khadija: According to traditional sources, Khadija was a wealthy merchant in Mecca who hired Muhammad when she had been told that he was favored by God. She and Muhammad were later married, and she gave birth to his daughter Fatima. Muhammad never married another woman as long as Khadija lived.

mahdi: A title (not found in the Qurʾan) related to the Arabic root associated with guidance (*h.d.y.*). To Shiʿites, the *mahdi* is the twelfth Imam who was put into a state of invisibility soon after his birth (c. 869) and who will emerge from that state in the end times to establish Islamic rule. To Sunnis, the term *mahdi* is reserved for a (Sunni) ruler who will establish a just Islamic reign, after the descent of Jesus from heaven, in the final era of human history before the Day of Judgment.

messenger, see: "apostle, messenger, prophet"

muhajirun: "Emigrants." The Muslim Meccans who joined Muhammad in Medina.

prophet, see: "apostle, messenger, prophet"

qibla: The direction of Islamic ritual prayer, namely, Mecca (or more specifically the Kaʿba). According to the traditional biography, however, the *qibla* was Jerusalem for a period of time toward the beginning of Muhammad's stay in Medina.

Quraysh: According to the traditional biography, the principal tribe of Mecca, to which Muhammad himself belonged. The Quraysh are reviled in this biography for their stubborn opposition to the Prophet. However, those Quraysh who became Muslims were later considered to have a certain merit because of their genealogical proximity to him.

Salafism: A movement within Sunni Islam dedicated to reforming Islamic doctrine and practice according to the example of the first three generation of Muslims, or the "pious forbearers" (*al-salaf al-salih*). While the majority of Salafis work through proselytism and politics, a minority—known as Salafi-Jihadis—embrace violent opposition to their enemies.

sharia: The Islamic law established by God, covering all aspects of religious, social, political, and personal life. According to standard Islamic teaching, Muhammad implemented the sharia perfectly in the state he established in Medina, and Muslims are called to follow sharia by implementing rules, policies, and laws based on the Qurʾan, the *hadith*, reasoning by analogy, and consensus.

shirk: A term based in the frequent qurʾanic condemnations of those who attribute power or authority to anything or anyone other than God. Muslim scholars frequently accuse Christians of *shirk* (since from an Islamic perspective God did not become man in Christ, Christians made a man into a God).

Sufism: A mystical movement within both Sunni and Shiʿite Islam shaped around the individual's spiritual path toward God. Sufis often rely on the guidance of a spiritual master (or shaykh) and interpret passages of the Qurʾan allegorically to search out a hidden aspect of spiritual guidance.

Tawrah: The term (from Hebrew *torah*) used by the Qurʾan to refer to a revelation given to Moses. According to later Islamic tradition, this revelation was lost, or destroyed intentionally, and the Hebrew Bible/Old Testament was written in its place.

ʿUmar: According to the traditional Islamic sources, ʿUmar was initially an opponent of Muhammad in Mecca. He converted to Islam and was chosen as the second caliph upon the death of Abu Bakr. During his caliphate, ʿUmar aggressively led the Islamic holy war. His armies conquered much of the Middle East and North Africa. ʿUmar is said to have personally entered into Jerusalem, where he received the submission of the city from the Christian patriarch Sophronius.

ʿUthman: According to the traditional Islamic sources, ʿUthman converted to Islam during the life of the Prophet and later became the third caliph when he was chosen over ʿAli by a committee of six people appointed by ʿUmar. He is remembered especially for collecting the authoritative version of the Qurʾan (and destroying all other versions). ʿUthman, who was accused of impiety and partiality during his reign as caliph, was eventually assassinated by a group of Muslim rebels from Egypt.

Zamzam: A well of holy water next to the Kaʿba in Mecca. The well, according to Islamic tradition, was originally dug by Abraham's son Ishmael (or by the angel Gabriel).

English Translations of the Qur᾿an

Abdel Haleem, M. A. S. *The Qur᾿an*. Oxford: Oxford University Press, 2004.

> A translation of the Qur᾿an based on the views of medieval Muslim interpreters and marked by the frequent use of paraphrases.

Arberry, A. J. *The Koran Interpreted*. London: George Allen & Unwin, 1955.

> A translation distinguished by its elevated literary style and consistent use of vocabulary. Note, however, that Arberry uses an old system of verse numbering.

Asad, Muhammad. *The Message of the Qur᾿ān*. Gibraltar: Dar al-Andalus, 1984.

> The rationalist translation of an Austrian convert to Islam with extensive commentary on medieval Muslim interpretation of the Qur᾿an.

Droge, Arthur. *The Qur'an: A New Annotated Translation*: Sheffield: Equinox, 2013.

> A clear translation of the Qur᾿an with a unique, useful set of footnotes that include cross-references, biblical parallels, and academic analysis.

Fakhry, Majid. *An Interpretation of the Qur᾿an: English Translation of the Meanings; a Bilingual Edition*. New York: New York University Press, 2004.

> A translation by a scholar of Islamic philosophy presented along with the Arabic text of the Qur᾿an.

Khalidi, Tarif. *The Qur᾿an: A New Translation* London: Viking, 2008.

> A translation in a clear, consistent, and contemporary English style; Khalidi puts text passages with a dramatic or poetic flavor in vertical formatting.

The Message: A Pure and Literal Translation of the Qur᾿an. N.p.: The Monotheist Group, 2008.

> A translation by an anonymous group of Muslims ("the Monotheist Group") from the qur᾿anist movement, who seek to present the Qur᾿an free from the influence of *hadith* or medieval Islamic traditions.

Pickthall, Marmaduke William. *The Meaning of the Glorious Qur'an*. London: George Allen & Unwin, 1930.

> A translation by a British convert to Islam; Pickthall writes with an English style close to that of the King James Bible, and translates controversial passages in a manner meant to make the text appealing to a Western audience.

The Qur'an and the Bible. New Haven: Yale University Press, 2018.

> This volume brings together a revised translation of the Qur'an by Ali Quli Qarai with parallel biblical texts selected and analyzed by Gabriel Said Reynolds. Readers are able to see immediately the relationship between particular qur'anic passages and their biblical subtext.

Yousef Ali. *The Holy Quran*. Lahore: Muhammad Ashraf, 1938.

> The translation of an Indian Shiʿite who lived much of his life in England. Yousef Ali adds extensive commentary to his translation, including citations of English poetry and his own poetic reflections. His translation was republished by the Saudi government, after having been purged of ʿAli's "heterodoxy."

Primary Islamic Sources

ʿAbd al-Jabbār (d. 1025). *The Critique of Christian Origins*. Edited by S. K. Samir. Translated by G. S. Reynolds. Provo, UT: Brigham Young University Press, 2010.

> The first work to present an Islamic vision of the composition of the Bible and the development of Christian faith, written by a rationalist Muslim theologian.

Abu Zayd, Nasr Hamid (d. 2010). "Towards Understanding the Qur'an's Worldview: An Autobiographical Reflection." In *New Reflections on the Qur'an*, edited by Gabriel Said Reynolds, 47–87. London: Routledge, 2010.

> The reflections of a modern liberal intellectual on the history of Muslim interpretation of the Qur'an.

al-Baladhuri (d. 892). *The Origins of the Islamic State*. Translated by Philip Hitti. New York: Columbia University Press, 1916.

> A standard history of the earliest period of the Islamic state, focusing on the battles of the Prophet Muhammad and the Islamic conquests.

al-Bazzar, Abu Hafs (d. 1349). *The Lofty Virtues of Ibn Taymiyya*. http://www.kalamullah.com/Books/TheLoftyVirtuesOfIbnTaymiyyah.pdf.

> A brief biography of Ibn Taymiyya (d. 1328) by one of his disciples.

Bucaille, Maurice (d. 1998). *The Bible, the Qur'an, and Science*. Translated by Maurice Bucaille and Alastair Pannell. New York: TTQ, 2000.

> An apologetic work dedicated to showing the errors of the Bible and proving the miraculous nature of the Qur'an (above all by arguing that it contains scientific miracles).

al-Bukhārī, Muḥammad (d. 870). *Ṣaḥīḥ al-Bukhārī. The Translation of the Meanings of Ṣaḥīḥ al-Bukhārī.* Translated by Muhammad Muhsin Khan. Medina: Dār al-ʿArabīyah, 1981.

> The Arabic text and English translation (presented in parallel columns) of the most important Sunni collection of prophetic *hadith*.

Haykal, Muhammad Husayn (d. 1956). *The Life of the Prophet.* Translated by I. Faruqi. N.p., 2005 (first published in Arabic 1933).

> An influential twentieth-century biography of Muhammad. Haykal both defends the Prophet from Western criticisms and rejects traditional narratives about the Prophet that might present him in an unfavorable light in the modern context.

Ibn Ishaq, Muhammad (d. ca. 767). *The Life of Muḥammad.* Translated by Alfred Guillaume. London: Oxford University Press, 1955.

> The earliest biography of Muhammad, still largely regarded as the most authoritative source on his life.

Ibn Kathir (d. 1373). *Tafsīr Ibn Kathir.* Translated by Sayf al-Rahman Mubarakuri et al. Riyadh: Darussalam, 2000.

> An abridged Arabic edition and translation of the Qurʾan commentary of Ibn Kathir, a scholar known for his dependence on *hadith* as well as for his polemics against non-Muslims and deviant (in Ibn Kathir's view) Muslims.

Ibn Saʿd (d. 845). *Ibn Saʿd's Kitab al-Tabaqat al-Kabir.* Translated by Moinul Haq and H. K. Ghazanfar. Karachi: Pakistan Historical Society, 1967–72.

> An extensive early Islamic history covering the life of the Prophet and the first generations of Muslims. Demonstrates the increasing importance of prophetic *hadith* in the transmission of religious knowledge.

Khomeini, Ruhollah (d. 1989). *Governance of the Jurist.* Translated by Hamid Algar. Tehran: Institute for Publication of Khomeini's Work, 1971.

> The translation of an Arabic work based on thirteen speeches given by Khomeini in Najaf, Iraq (between January 21 and February 8, 1970) on his vision for an Islamic government.

al-Mahalli, Jalal al-Din (d. 1459) and Jalal al-Din al-Suyuti (d. 1505). *Tafsir al-Jalalayn.* Translated by Feras Hamza. Louisville: Fons Vitae, 2008.

> A later Sunni commentary of the Qurʾan with brief explanations of qurʾanic verses. (*Tafsir al-Jalalayn* has been described as "a translation of the Qurʾan into Arabic.") The Arabic text is presented here along with an English translation.

Mahfouz, Naguib (d. 2006). *Children of Gebelawi.* Translated by Philip Stewart. London: Heinemann, 1981.

> An allegorical tale that represents Moses, Jesus, and Muhammad in a modern setting, told from a modernist Muslim perspective.

al-Mawdudi, Abu al-ʿAla (d. 1979). "Twenty-Nine Years of the *Jamaat-e Islami*." *The Criterion* 5 (1970): 28–623.

> An extensive reflection by Mawdudi on the activities and mission of *Jamaat-e Islami*, the movement he founded. The article commemorates the first twenty-nine years of the *Jamaat-e Islami*, a period that matches that of the "rightly guided" caliphs.

Nahjul Balagha: Peak of Eloquence. Attributed to ʿAlī b. Abī Talib (d. 661); likely compiled by al-Radi (d. 1015). Translated by Sayed ʿAli Reza. New York: TTQ, 1996.

> A collection of pious sermons attributed to ʿAli, the cousin and son-in-law of Muhammad, and a work of enormous spiritual importance to Shiʿite Muslims.

Al-Qaradawi, Yusuf. *The Lawful and Prohibited in Islam*. Translated by K. El-Helbawy et al. (Houston, TX: ElFarouq Foundation, 1423/2003).

> A collection of fatwas or juridical opinions on principals and practical matters of daily life by the influential Sunni Muslim Egyptian cleric.

Qutb, Sayyid (d. 1956). "The America I Have Seen." Translated by T. Masoud and A. Fakeeh. In *America in an Arab Mirror*, edited by K. Abdel-Malek, 9–27. New York: Palgrave Macmillan, 2000.

> Sayyid Qutb's brief memoir of his sojourn in America between 1948 and 1950.

———. *Milestones.* Translated by M. Siddiqui. N.p.: CreateSpace, 2005.

> A work, written in prison, in which Sayyid Qutb condemns secular Egyptian society and lays out his vision of Islam as a complete religious, social, and political program.

Rida, Rashid (d. 1935). *Christian Criticisms, Islamic Proofs.* Translated by Simon A. Wood. Oxford: Oxford University Press, 2008.

> A collection of articles written by a Sunni Muslim apologist in response to Christian missionary critique of Islam.

al-Shafiʿi, Muḥammad b. Idris (d. 820). *Treatise on the Foundations of Islamic Jurisprudence.* Translated by Majid Khadduri. Cambridge: Islamic Texts Society, 1987.

> An important early work of Islamic jurisprudence; Shafiʿi argues that the Qurʾan itself points to the authoritative role of *hadith* and insists that authentic *hadith* from Muhammad are, like the Qurʾan, a source of revelation.

al-Shaykh al-Mufid (d. 1022), *Kitab al-Irshad: The Book of Guidance into the Lives of the Twelve Imams.* Translated by I. K. A. Howard. New York: TTQ, 1981.

> A Shiʿite work celebrating the lives of the twelve imams who, according to al-Shaykh al-Mufid, were protected from error and sin no less than Muhammad himself.

al-Tabari, Abu Jaʿfar (d. 923). *The Commentary on the Qurʾan.* Translated by Wilfred Madelung. Oxford: Oxford University Press, 1987.

> A translation of the first part of Tabari's extensive commentary on the Qurʾan (through most of the second sura), a commentary generally recognized as the cardinal work of medieval Islamic exegesis.

al-Ṭabarī, Abu Jaʿfar (d. 923). *The History of al-Tabari*. Albany, NY: SUNY Press, 1985–2007.

> A forty-volume complete translation (by various translators) of Ṭabarī's extensive history of Islam, from the creation of the world through 915 CE.

Primary Non-Islamic Sources

John of Damascus (d. 753), *On Heresies* (Islam). In Daniel J. Sahas. *John of Damascus on Islam*, 133–41. Leiden: Brill, 1972.

> The 101st chapter of John of Damascus's catalog of Christian heresies, dedicated to the "heresy of the Ishmaelites." The section therein on "Ishmaelite" scripture represents one of the earliest descriptions of the Qurʾan.

Norris Jr., Richard A., ed. and trans. *The Christological Controversy*. Philadelphia: Fortress Press, 1980.

> A collection of passages from the writings of the church fathers on Christ through the Council of Chalcedon (451).

The Protoevangelium of James. Translated by Cullmann, Oscar, in *New Testament Apocrypha*, edited by R. Wilson, 426–37. Louisville: Westminster John Knox, 1991.

> An early Greek Christian work (likely composed toward the end of the second century) describing the events preceding the birth of Christ, including the birth and childhood of Mary.

Sebeos (d. late 7th c.). *The Armenian History Attributed to Sebeos*. Translated by R. W. Thomson and James Howard-Johnston. Liverpool: Liverpool University Press, 1999.

> A Christian historical work shaped by a biblical perspective. Sebeos describes the Islamic conquests according to his vision of the Arabs as descendants of Abraham through Ishmael.

Sozomen (d. ca. 450). *The Ecclesiastical History*. Translated by Chester D. Hartranft. In vol. 2 of *The Nicene and Post-Nicene Fathers*, Series 2. Edited by Philip Schaff. 239–427. Grand Rapids: Eerdmans, 2007 (originally published Buffalo: Christian Literature Co., 1886–90).

> A history of the church in Greek by a Byzantine scholar. Sozomen refers to the conversion of Arabs to Christianity and to the diffusion of the idea that the Arabs are descendants of Abraham.

Theodosius. *The Pilgrimage of Theodosius*. Translated by J. H. Bernard. London: Palestine Pilgrims Text Society, 1893.

> The account of a Christian pilgrim who visited the Holy Land around the year 530. In his description of Ephesus, Theodosius mentions the legend of the Seven Sleepers.

Zwemer, S. (d. 1952). *Islam: A Challenge to Faith*. New York: Student Volunteer Movement for Foreign Missions, 1909.

> An introduction to Islam by a prominent American Protestant missionary.

General Reference Works

The Encyclopaedia of Islam. 2nd edition, ed. Bosworth et al. Leiden: Brill, 1954–2006; 3rd edition, edited by Nawas et al. 2002–present.

> The standard reference work in Islamic Studies; entries in the second edition are listed under Arabic names (e.g., "Jesus" is under "'Isa"). The third edition is in progress and regularly updated online.

Meri, Josef W., ed. *Medieval Islamic Civilization: An Encyclopedia*. London: Routledge, 2005.

> A one-volume general reference work focused on the society, culture, and major religious figures of the medieval Islamic world.

Rippin, Andrew, ed. *The Islamic World*. London: Routledge, 2008.

> A one-volume reference work covering major religious topics and religious figures of the early and medieval Islamic period.

Islamic Origins/Pre-Islamic Arabia

Al-Jallad, Ahmad. "The Linguistic Landscape of Pre-Islamic Arabia: Context for the Qur'an." In *Oxford Handbook of Qur'anic Studies*, edited by Mustafa Shah and Muhammad Abdel Haleem. Oxford: Oxford University Press, 2020, 111–27.

> A meticulous study of the Arabic dialects and non-Arabic languages (along with their scripts) in the Arabian Peninsula at the rise of Islam.

———. "The Pre-Islamic *Basmala*: Reflections on Its First Epigraphic Attestation and Its Original Significance." *Jerusalem Studies in Arabic and Islam*, forthcoming.

> An analysis of a pre-Islamic inscription found in Yemen and first published in 2018 that uses a formula close to the qur'anic invocation "In the Name of God, the Merciful, the Benevolent."

Al-Jallad, Ahmad and Hythem Sidky, "A Paleo-Arabic Inscription on a Route North of Taaif," Arabian Archaeology and Epigraphy (2021), 1–14.

> An important new analysis of an early Arabic inscription, probably monotheistic, not far from Mecca.

Berg, Herbert, ed. *Method and Theory in the Study of Islamic Origins*. Leiden: Brill, 2003.

> A collection of technical academic articles on recent debates surrounding the origins of Islam.

Donner, Fred McGraw. *Muhammad and the Believers*. Cambridge, MA: Harvard University Press, 2010.

> A work in which Donner argues, with reference to qur'anic passages in which belief in one God is emphasized without sectarian polemic, that Islam was originally a religious movement of monotheists of various religions.

Griffith, Sidney H. *Church in the Shadow of the Mosque*. Princeton: Princeton University Press, 2008.

> A detailed presentation of the history of Christianity and Christian theology under Islamic rule, focused on the Arab world in the early medieval period.

Hoyland, Robert G. *Arabia and the Arabs: From the Bronze Age to the Coming of Islam*. London: Routledge, 2001.

> An informative study on the history of Arabic-speaking peoples before the rise of Islam, including information on archeological remains and the presentation of "Arabs" in non-Arabic sources.

———. *In God's Path: The Arab Conquests and the Creation of the Islamic Empire*. Oxford: Oxford University Press, 2015.

> A well-written narrative of the early Arab conquests. Hoyland describes in detail the causes of the conquests, the reasons for their astounding successes, and the consequences for the conquered peoples.

Peters, F. E. *Muhammad and the Origins of Islam*. Albany, NY: SUNY Press, 1994.

> A work that begins with a critical discussion of Islam's origins but continues with a traditional retelling of Muhammad's biography.

Shahid, Irfan. *Byzantium and the Arabs in the Fourth Century*. Washington, DC: Dumbarton Oaks, 1984.
———. *Byzantium and the Arabs in the Fifth Century*. Washington, DC: Dumbarton Oaks, 1989.
———. *Byzantium and the Arabs in the Sixth Century*. Washington, DC: Dumbarton Oaks, 1995, 2009.

> A series of detailed works on the relationship of the Byzantine Empire with Arab tribes in the centuries preceding Islam. Shahid pays particular attention to the spread of Christianity among the Arabs.

Qur'an

Griffith, Sidney H. "Christian Lore and the Arabic Qur'ān: The 'Companions of the Cave' in *Sūrat al-Kahf* and in Syriac Christian Tradition." In *The Qur'ān in Its Historical Context*, edited by Gabriel Said Reynolds, 109–37. London: Routledge, 2008.

> A clear scholarly description of the relationship between the Christian legend of the *Seven Sleepers of Ephesus* and the qur'anic passage on the "Companions of the Cave" (Q 18).

Jeffery, Arthur. *The Foreign Vocabulary of the Qur'ān*. Leiden: Brill, 2007 (first published 1938).

> A technical discussion of the relationship of select qur'anic vocabulary (proper names and otherwise) with related vocabulary used before the Qur'an in non-Arabic languages (a knowledge of the various scripts [e.g., Greek, Syriac, Ethiopic, etc.] is often necessary in order to follow Jeffery's discussion).

McAuliffe, Jane Dammen, ed. *The Cambridge Companion to the Qur'ān*. Cambridge: Cambridge University Press, 2006.

> A brief one-volume work covering the contents and form of the Qur'an, the history of qur'anic exegesis, and recent scholarly debates in the field of qur'anic studies.

————. *The Encyclopaedia of the Qurʾān*. Leiden: Brill, 2001–6.

> The standard reference work in qurʾanic studies; its entries are listed under English names. Many articles address Islamic interpretation of the Qurʾan more than the Qurʾan itself. Currently being updated and expanded in a digital version.

Nasser, Shady, *The Transmission of the Variant Readings of the Qurʾan*. Leiden: Brill, 2013.

> A technical and thoroughly documented study of the different readings of the Qurʾan transmitted in early Islamic literature.

Reynolds, Gabriel Said. *Allah: God in the Qurʾan*. New Haven: Yale University Press, 2020.

> A clear introduction to the character and features of the qurʾanic God with comparative reflections on God in the Bible.

Sinai, Nicolai. *The Qurʾan: A Historical-Critical Introduction*. Edinburgh: Edinburgh University Press, 2017.

> A detailed introduction to the main features of the qurʾanic text, including its principal literary features, the dating of suras to the Meccan or Medinan periods, and the context of its proclamation.

Wansbrough, John. *Qurʾānic Studies*. Amherst, NY: Prometheus, 2004 (first published 1977).

> A learned discussion of the Qurʾan's literary qualities, the canonization of the Qurʾan, the historical development of Islamic exegesis, and the development of the Arabic language.

Watt, W. Montgomery, and Richard Bell. *Introduction to the Qurʾan*. Edinburgh: Edinburgh University Press, 1977 (first published 1970).

> Watt's presentation of the ideas and notes of his teacher (Richard Bell) on the content of the Qurʾan and the manner in which the text was collected. Watt tends to moderate those theories of Bell that depart substantially from Islamic tradition.

Muhammad

Andrae, Tor. *Mohammad: The Man and His Faith*. Translated by Theophil Menzel. Mineola, NY: Dover, 2000 (translation first published 1936; original German first published 1932).

> A classic Western biography of Muhammad focusing on his religious vision.

Anthony, Sean, *Muhammad and the Empires of Faith: The Making of the Prophet of Islam*. Oakland: University of California Press, 2020.

> In this study of early sources for the life of Muhammad, Anthony integrates evidence from the earliest non-Muslim sources with evidence from a critical reading of Islamic sources. He argues that key information on the Prophet's life can be achieved thereby.

Haykal, Muhammad Husayn. *The Life of Muḥammad*. Translated by Ismael Raji al-Faruqi. Plainfield, IN: American Trust Publications, 1976 (original Arabic first published 1933).

> The translation of the biography of Muhammad by a prominent twentieth-century Egyptian Muslim intellectual. Haykal presents the Muslim Prophet as an exemplary model for modern man in regard to morals and rationalism. In so doing, he accuses both traditionalist Muslims and Western scholars of distorting Muhammad's image.

Khalidi, Tarif. *Images of Muhammad*. New York: Doubleday, 2009.
> A presentation of Islamic traditions in praise of the Prophet, illustrating the diverse ways in which Muhammad's image developed in Islamic tradition.

Peters, F. E. *Jesus and Muhammad: Parallel Tracks, Parallel Lives*. Oxford: Oxford University Press, 2011.
> A study of Jesus and Muhammad meant to be based exclusively on historical evidence.

Rodinson, Maxime. *Muḥammad*. Translated by Anne Carter. New York: Penguin, 1980.
> A biography of Muhammad in which Mecca is presented as a city suffering from the greed of the merchant tribe of the Quraysh. Muhammad, by Rodinson's telling, was above all a social reformer concerned with the fate of the oppressed.

Watt, William Montgomery. *Muhammad at Mecca*. Oxford: Oxford University Press, 1953.
———. *Muhammad at Medina*. Oxford: Oxford University Press, 1981.
> A biography of Muhammad based on Watt's search for authentic anecdotes in medieval Islamic literature. Watt generally discards material that appears to him to be apologetical or superstitious but otherwise accepts most of the traditional material.

On *Hadith*

Burton, John. *An Introduction to the Hadith*. Edinburgh: Edinburgh University Press, 1994.
> A presentation of the historical development of the *hadith* and their place in Islamic religious thought.

Goldziher, Ignaz. *Muslim Studies*. Edited by S. M. Stern. Translated by C. R. Barber and S. M. Stern. New Brunswick, NJ: Transaction 2006 (translation first published 1967, 1991; original German first published 1889, 1890).
> A collection of studies on Islamic religious tradition, literature, and culture. In the second volume, Goldziher focuses on the *hadith* and demonstrates the manner in which medieval Muslims fabricated *hadith* to defend a political or religious cause.

On the Rise of the Islamic State

Donner, Fred McGraw. *The Early Islamic Conquests*. Princeton: Princeton University Press, 1981.
> The standard scholarly work on the Islamic conquests under the first caliphs. Donner works carefully through the mass of reports in Islamic literature in order to reconstruct a likely historical scenario by which the conquests took place. In order to explain their success, he emphasizes the role of Islam as a uniting force.

Madelung, Wilfred. *The Succession to Muhammad: A Study of the Early Caliphate*. Cambridge: Cambridge University Press, 1997.
> A study of the transition of leadership from Muhammad to Abu Bakr, ʿUmar, ʿUthman, and ʿAli. Madelung shows sympathy for the claims of Shiʿites that the first caliphs assumed power by ignoring the rights of ʿAli.

On Modern Islam

Kuiper, Matthew. *Daʿwa and Other Religions: Indian Muslims and the Modern Resurgence of Global Islamic Activism*. London: Routledge Press, 2018.

> A careful study of the history and ideology of the call (*daʿwa*) to Islam from its origins in the Qurʾan to the present day, with a focus on modern India in the second half of the book.

The Princeton Encyclopedia of Islamic Political Thought, ed . G. Böwering, P. Crone, and M. Mirza. Princeton: Princeton University Press, 2013.

> A thorough research work on classical contemporary Islamic political philosophies, theories, and movements.

Progressive Islam on Justice, Gender, and Pluralism. Edited by O. Safi. London: OneWorld, 2003.

> A collected volume exploring the teachings of progressive Muslims, and their theological foundations, on a number of political and social issues.

Tareen, SherAli. *Defending Muhammad in Modernity*. Notre Dame, IN: University of Notre Dame Press, 2020.

> Tareen's work addresses the various intellectual currents in modern South Asia and in particular debates over Muhammad's spiritual status, as well as the veneration of Muhammad through traditional practices.

Online Resources for the Study of Islam's Emergence

A number of websites exist with significant academic value for the study of Islam's emergence. Among these is the Quranic Arabic Corpus (http://corpus.quran.com/), which offers a word-by-word analysis of the grammar, syntax, and meaning of the Qurʾan, along with several Qurʾan translations, a detailed dictionary of the Qurʾan, and audio files of Qurʾan recitation. A wide number of sites offer various English translations of the Qurʾan. One of the easiest to use is Quran Browser (http://qb.gomen.org/QuranBrowser/), which allows readers to compare ten different translations (classified by "Orthodox Muslim," "Non-Orthodox Muslim," and "Non-Muslim") in an interlinear fashion; tanzil.net offers, in addition to the Arabic text, translations of the Qurʾan into multiple languages and Qurʾan recitation.

There are many websites, YouTube channels, and social media accounts that are concerned with Islamic apologetics (or *daʿwa*) and religious debate, including www.islamweb.net/en/. Readers may also profit from the YouTube channel "Reasons for Our Hope," which offers three-minute videos with a basic introduction to Muslim and Christian teaching. The YouTube channel "Exploring the Qurʾan and the Bible" offers interviews with leading scholars of the Bible and the Qurʾan.

Both primary and secondary sources on Islam are increasingly available online. For original Islamic sources, the website www.altafsir.com offers a number of Islamic commentaries of the Qur'an in English translation, along with a database of variant readings of the Qur'an and Qur'an translations in various languages (see http://www.altafsir.com/tafasir.asp?languageid=2). A number of *hadith* collections (including Bukhari and Muslim, the two most important Sunni collections) are available in translation at sunnah.com. On the religious Shi'ite website Al-Islam.org, a wide number of Shi'ite sources can be found in English translation (http://www.al-islam.org/alpha.php), along with a great deal of contemporary religious discussion. Important excerpts from primary sources (in English translation) and scholarly studies on Islamic history are available at the Internet Islamic History Sourcebook (see http://www.fordham.edu/halsall/islam/islamsbook.html).

Those interested in contemporary Islamic jurisprudence might profit from the English-language fatwas at http://islamqa.info/en, run by the conservative Palestinian mufti Muhammad al-Munajjid, or in the "living *Shari'a*" section of the website directed by the prominent Egyptian Sunni scholar Yusuf al-Qaradawi, https://islamonline.net/en/home; or from the website of the prominent Shi'ite scholar 'Alī Sistani at https://alulbayt.com/questions/.

The Internet also offers intriguing visual presentations relevant to early Islam. A wide range of Islamic Arabic manuscripts can be viewed through the website of Princeton University (see https://dpul.princeton.edu/islamicmss), and the Met Museum website includes a section on Islamic art (https://www.metmuseum.org/about-the-met/collection-areas/islamic-art). A virtual experience of the Islamic pilgrimage to Mecca can be found at https://discoverhajj.com/.